Las Vegas

Las Vegas

by
Dirk Vanderwilt

TOURIST TOWN GUIDES™

Las Vegas, 2nd Edition (*Tourist Town Guides*™ series)
© 2007 by Dirk Vanderwilt

Published by:
Channel Lake, Inc., P.O. Box 1771, New York, NY 10156-1771
http://www.channellake.com

Author: Dirk Vanderwilt
Editor: Emily Wang
Cover Design: Julianna Lee
Photos (Cover): iStockphoto, Dirk Vanderwilt
Photos (Interior): Dirk Vanderwilt

Published in October, 2007

All rights reserved. Published in the United States of America. No part of this book may be reproduced or transmitted in any form or by any means, electronic or mechanical, including photocopying, recording, or by any information storage and retrieval system, without permission in writing from publisher. *Tourist Town Guides*™ is a trademark of Channel Lake, Inc. All other trademarks and service marks are the properties of their respective owners.

ISBN-13: 978-0-9792043-5-7
Library of Congress Control Number: 2007905279

Disclaimer: The information in this book has been checked for accuracy. However, neither the publisher nor the author may be held liable for errors or omissions. *Use this book at your own risk.* To obtain the latest information, we recommend that you contact the vendors directly. If you do find an error, let us know at corrections@channellake.com.

Channel Lake, Inc. is not affiliated with the vendors mentioned in this book, and the vendors have not authorized, approved or endorsed the information contained herein. This book contains the opinions of the author, and your experience may vary.

For more information, visit http://www.touristtown.com

Help Our Environment!

Even when on vacation, your responsibility to protect the environment does not end. Here are some ways you can help our planet without spoiling your fun:

- ✓ Ask your hotel staff not to clean your towels and bed linens each day. This reduces water waste and detergent pollution.

- ✓ Turn off the lights, heater, and/or air conditioner when you leave your hotel room, and keep that thermostat low!

- ✓ Use public transportation when available. Tourist trolleys are very popular, and they are usually cheaper and easier than a car.

- ✓ Recycle everything you can, and properly dispose of rubbish in labeled receptacles.

Tourist towns consume a lot of energy. Have fun, but don't be wasteful. Please do your part to ensure that these attractions are around for future generations to visit and enjoy.

For my parents

COVER IMAGES

Front cover: the Bellagio fountain show, dice[1], a glittery sign[1]; *Back cover*: the Las Vegas sign[1].

[1]Photo courtesy of **iStockphoto**

Channel Lake, Inc.
P.O. Box 1771
New York, NY 10156

Dear Readers,

Tourist towns are a fundamental part of many vacations. Year after year, visitors arrive in droves to enjoy unique attractions. Yet these same visitors are inundated with billboards and promotional flyers that can make even a well-planned trip confusing.

This is the purpose of the *Tourist Town Guides*™ series – to keep you informed with honest, independent advice about national and regional tourist hotspots. Use these guides to look beyond all that self-serving promotion.

Many travel books fail to give tourist towns the coverage they need. *Tourist Town Guides*™ helps make sure you have the necessary information, without unnecessary clutter. Thoughtfully researched and intuitively organized, the books in this series are your comprehensive guides to all things tourist.

I am confident that you will find these guides both informative and useful, and that you will refer to them again and again. Enjoy your vacation!

Sincerely,

Dirk Vanderwilt
Executive Editor
Channel Lake, Inc.

www.touristtown.com

A Word About Age Restrictions

You must be at least 21 years old to enter a Nevada casino. Additionally, there may be age restrictions on other attractions as well. If you are traveling with somebody under 21, keep in mind that not every attraction mentioned in this book will be available to your group.

Table of Contents

Introduction	**19**
How to Use this Book	20
Las Vegas History	**25**
The Birth of Las Vegas	26
The Business Tycoons	30
The Entertainers	35
Area Orientation	**41**
Seasons and Temperatures	41
Getting Information	43
Packing for your Trip	45
Getting to Las Vegas	46
Getting Around Las Vegas	48
What to Do	51
Where to Stay	53
Where to Eat	55
The Las Vegas Resorts	**59**
Casino Comparison	59
Resort Sections	61
What to Look For	63
Resorts: South Strip	**67**
Mandalay Bay	68
Luxor	72
Excalibur	76
Tropicana	78
MGM Grand	80
New York - New York	85
Monte Carlo	88
Aladdin / Planet Hollywood	90
Bellagio	93

Paris Las Vegas	96
Bally's	99

Resorts: Mid-Strip **105**

Barbary Coast	105
Caesars Palace	107
Flamingo	110
Imperial Palace	113
Harrah's Las Vegas	115
The Mirage	117
The Venetian	121
Treasure Island	126

Resorts: North Strip **131**

Wynn Las Vegas	131
New Frontier	135
The Riviera	137
Circus Circus	139
Sahara	142
Stratosphere	144

Resorts: Downtown Las Vegas **149**

The Fremont Street Experience	150
Downtown vs. The Strip	151
El Cortez Hotel	152
Fitzgeralds Las Vegas	154
The Fremont	155
Four Queens	156
Binion's Gambling Hall	157
Golden Nugget	159
The Vegas Club	161
Golden Gate Hotel	162
Plaza Las Vegas	163
Main Street Station	164
California Hotel	166

Resorts: Off-Strip **169**

Palace Station	169
Las Vegas Hilton	170
Gold Coast	173
Rio	175
Palms	176
The Orleans	178
Terrible's	180
Hard Rock Hotel	181
Hooters Casino	183
Boulder Station	184
Sam's Town	185
Texas Station	186
Greek Isles Hotel & Casino	188

Select Live Shows **195**

The Celebrity Show	196
Exotic Shows	197
Cirque du Soleil	200
Magic Shows	201
Impersonation Shows	203
Broadway Shows	204
Other Shows	206

Select Restaurants **211**

Gourmet	211
Buffets	216
Theme Restaurants	220
Steakhouses	223

Select Night Clubs **227**

Bars and Clubs	227
Strip Clubs	231

Area Attractions 235

    Museums   235

    Shopping   239

    Golf Courses   242

    Lake Mead   244

    Nearby Cities   246

    Lake Las Vegas   247

    Other Adventures   250

The Grand Canyon 253

    About the Grand Canyon   253

    Getting to the Grand Canyon   255

    Navigating the Grand Canyon   257

    Viewing the Grand Canyon   259

    Accommodations   261

    Canyon Rim Accommodations   261

    Off-Rim Accommodations   263

    Other Accommodations   264

    Restaurants   265

    Select Attractions   266

Recommendations 271

    Travel Scenarios   271

    The "Best"   274

    Internet Resources   275

Index 279

Southern Nevada Map
Las Vegas - California - Arizona - Utah - Death Valley
Nevada Test Site - Grand Canyon - Mojave Desert

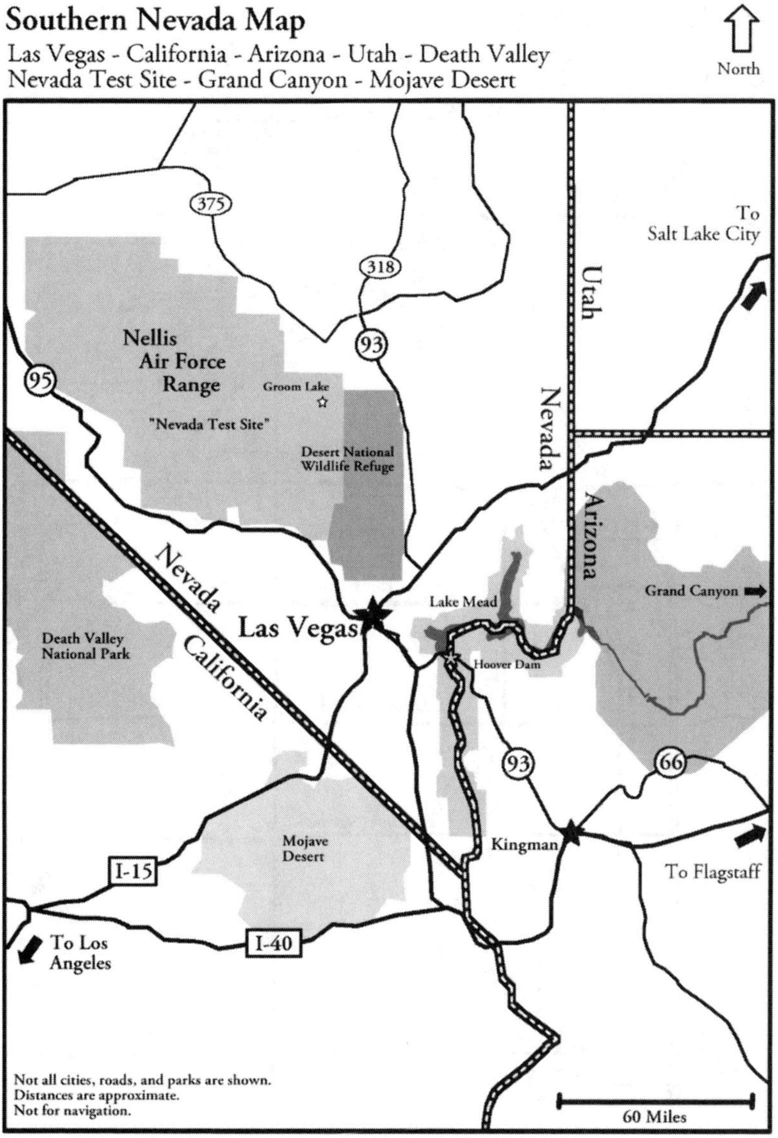

North

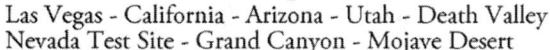

Las Vegas Area Map
Las Vegas Boulevard ("The Strip") - Downtown Las Vegas
McCarran Airport - I-15 / I-515

North

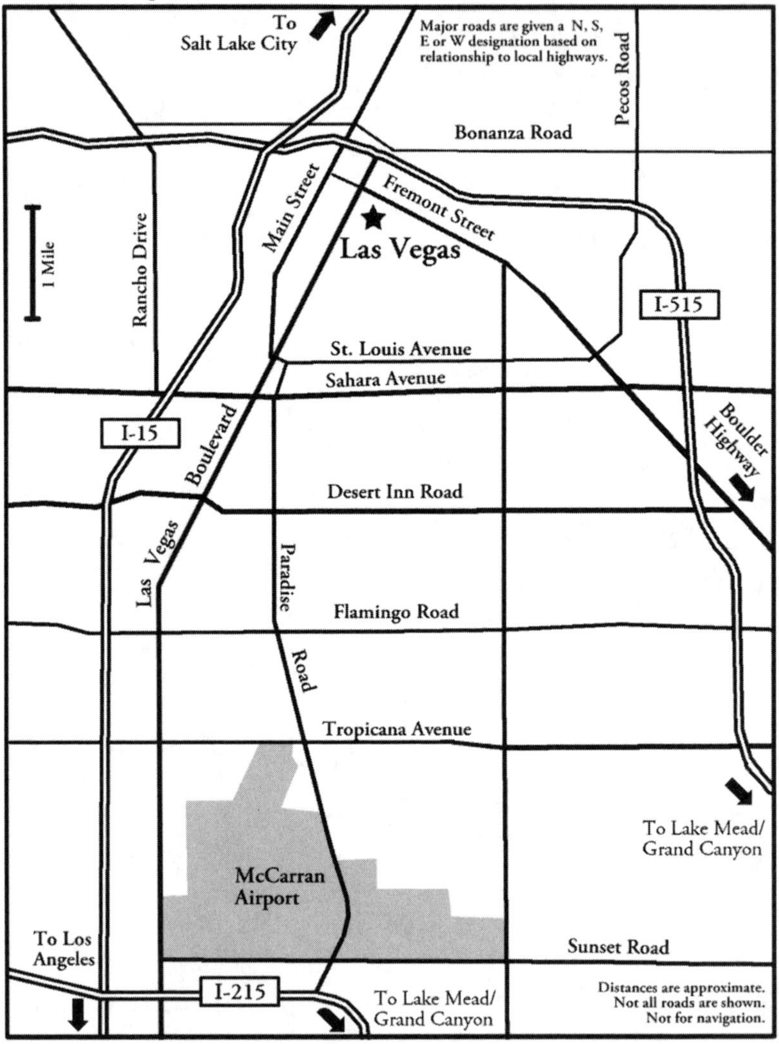

Las Vegas Strip Map

South Strip - Mid-Strip - North Strip

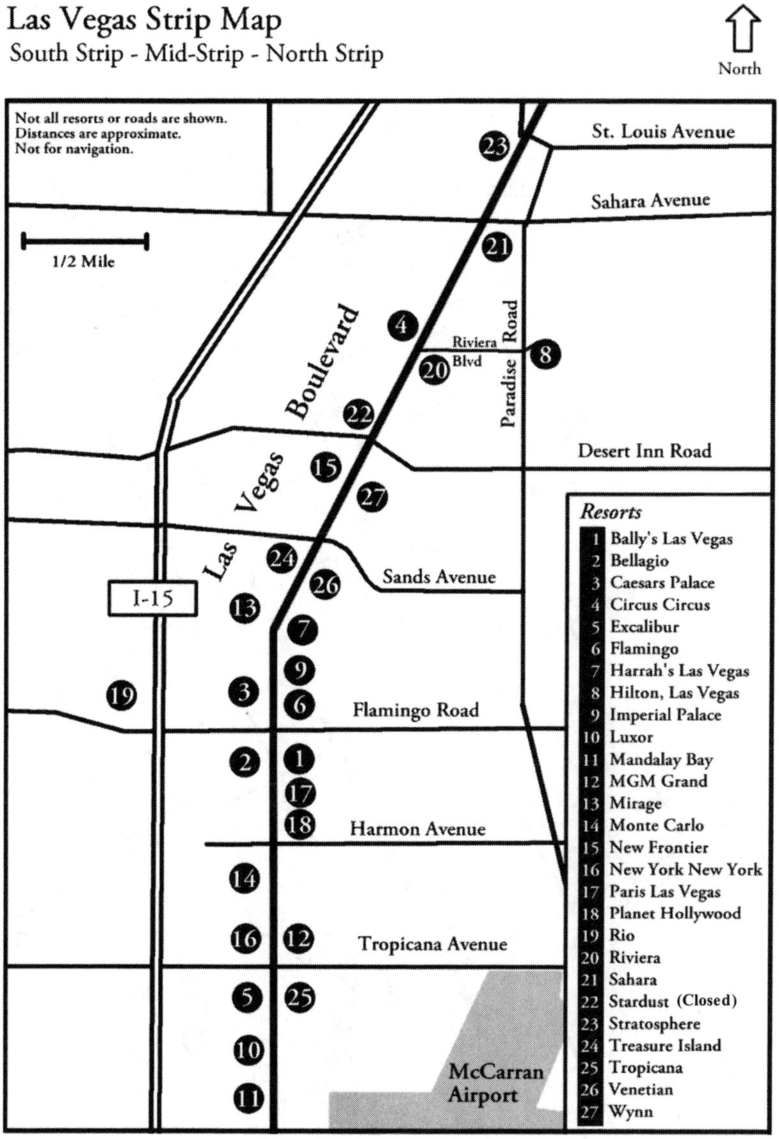
North
Not all resorts or roads are shown.
Distances are approximate.
Not for navigation.
1/2 Mile
St. Louis Avenue
Sahara Avenue
Las Vegas Boulevard
Riviera Blvd
Paradise Road
Desert Inn Road
Sands Avenue
I-15
Flamingo Road
Harmon Avenue
Tropicana Avenue
McCarran Airport
Resorts
1 Bally's Las Vegas
2 Bellagio
3 Caesars Palace
4 Circus Circus
5 Excalibur
6 Flamingo
7 Harrah's Las Vegas
8 Hilton, Las Vegas
9 Imperial Palace
10 Luxor
11 Mandalay Bay
12 MGM Grand
13 Mirage
14 Monte Carlo
15 New Frontier
16 New York New York
17 Paris Las Vegas
18 Planet Hollywood
19 Rio
20 Riviera
21 Sahara
22 Stardust (Closed)
23 Stratosphere
24 Treasure Island
25 Tropicana
26 Venetian
27 Wynn

Downtown Las Vegas Map
Fremont Street ("The Fremont Street Experience")

North

Distances are approximate.
Not all roads or attractions are shown.
Not for navigation.

I-515

1,000 Feet

"The Fremont Street Experience"

Stewart Ave.
Ogden Avenue
Fremont Street
Carson Avenue
Bridger Avenue

Main Street
1st Street
Casino Center Blvd
3th Street
4th Street
Las Vegas Boulevard
Bonneville Avenue

To "The Strip"

Resorts

1	Binions	7	Golden Gate Hotel
2	California	8	Goden Nugget
3	El Cortez	9	Lady Luck
4	Fitzgeralds	10	Main Street Station
5	Four Queens	11	Plaza Las Vegas
6	Fremont	12	Vegas Club

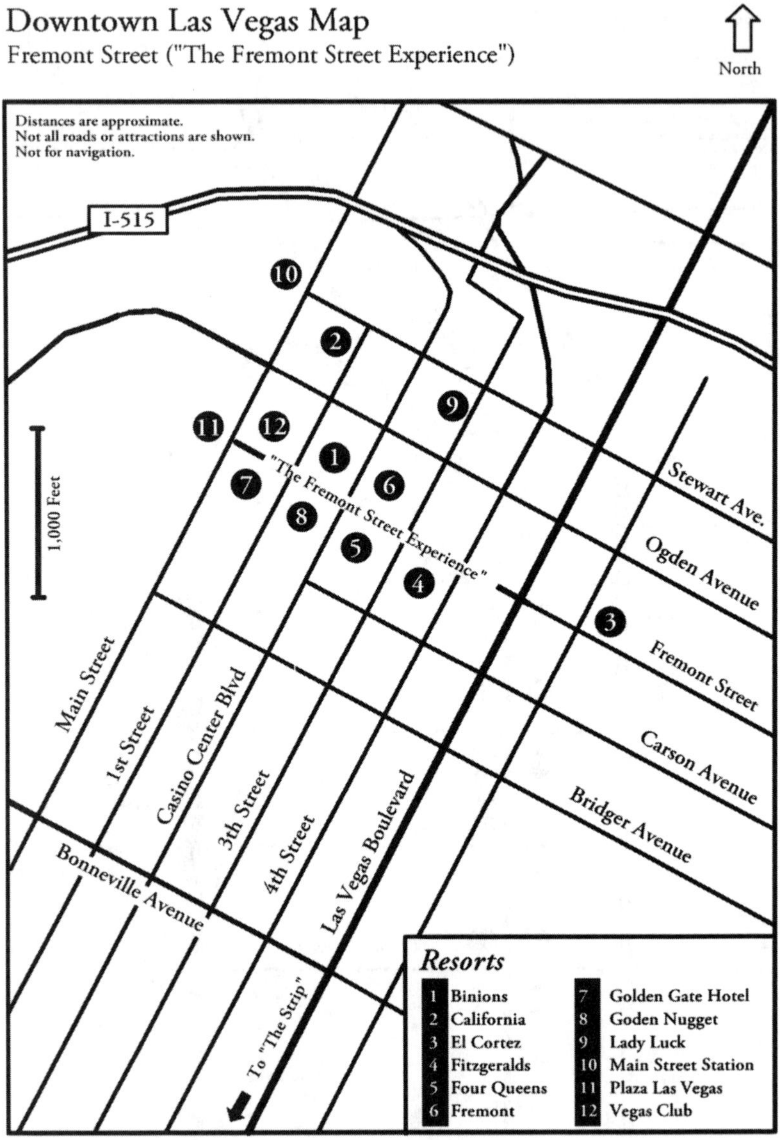

Introduction

There is no way to properly introduce Las Vegas. It is everything you've read about, and nothing you'd expect. It is a corporate centerpiece pressed from countless molds, and yet so vastly unique and independent that no reasonable amount of financial backing could duplicate it. There is no adjective to describe this otherwise random section of the American desert except that... it is Las Vegas.

Even if you despise everything Las Vegas stands for, you have to admire its design. It has been said that "in Las Vegas, if they could make the lights any brighter, and the veneer any thinner, they would have already done it."

There was no gradual increase in population, no resource to attract industry, no port and no natural wonders. It was literally a decision to put a resort town *here*, in the middle of the desert. Like Atlantic City had been about a century earlier, Las Vegas was predetermined to be a resort town long before it even really became a town at all.

Las Vegas is all about resorts. This is the most important part. *Las Vegas is all about resorts.* If you venture to Vegas with the desire to stay in a quaint motel with personal service and an intimate setting, you will be disappointed. Here it is always loud, noisy, swarming with people, and aglow with light even at midnight. Sure, there are nooks and crannies for romantic or peaceful moments, but they are almost always huge nooks or gargantuan crannies smashed in the middle of an even more gargantuan resort complex.

Welcome to Las Vegas. It is a daunting topic for a travel guide for many reasons. For one thing, there is so much to do, so many things to see and places to eat that any hearty person would be hard-pressed to research or visit in a month, or even a year. Not only that, but the attractions keep *changing* so much that to accurately document them all would require not a book, not even a magazine, but perhaps daily or weekly newsletter highlighting the latest crazes. Everything in Vegas changes, from the restaurants to the shows to the performers to even the resorts themselves. In fact, considering the influx of mega-resorts in the past decade alone, the only thing constant about Vegas is its willingness to change.

However, along with the wide range of entertainment, dining, and attraction options comes an air of consistency. Each resort has its share of casino games, upscale dining, shows, and entertainment options. In this respect much of Las Vegas is simple repetition based on a resort formula that has proved successful over the years. Instead, what really makes a resort stand out is the *differences*. It is odd to find a 2000-room hotel without a buffet, just as a special headlining stage show can attract audiences.

With that in mind, a Las Vegas travel guide need not be all encompassing. It need not list every restaurant in every resort or part of town. Instead, it should focus on the special places; the unique attractions that separate any given resort or establishment from the standard boilerplate.

This section answers a few of the common questions about the choices the author made with regard to the attractions, recommendations, and more.

HOW TO USE THIS BOOK

Items are listed within subject groups. Based on information availability, the attraction may have an address, website (🖰), and/or telephone number (☎). Some items have other items within them (for example, a restaurant within a casino). In this case, the contact information may be with the inline text, or there may be no contact information. If there is no contact information, please see the attraction or section heading.

Must-See Attractions: Headlining must-see attractions, or those that are otherwise iconic or defining, are designated with the 🈲 symbol. The author and/or editor made these and all other qualitative value judgments.

Coverage: This book is not all-inclusive. It is comprehensive, with many different options for entertainment, dining, eating, shopping, etc., but there are many establishments not listed here. Since this is an independent guide, the decision of what to include was made entirely by the author and/or editor.

Attraction Pricing: When applicable, at the end of each attraction listing is a general pricing reference, indicated by dollar signs, relative to other attractions in the region. The scale is from "$" (least expensive) to "$$$$" (most expensive). Contact the attraction directly for specific pricing information. **Please note that** if the attraction is free, of if no pricing information is available at the time of publication, or if a price indication is otherwise irrelevant, then the dollar sign scale is omitted from the listing.

"Family Friendly" Designations: This book mentions attractions that may have a "family friendly" attitude. *However,* this does *not* guarantee that the attraction meets any kind of standards for you or your family. It is merely an opinion that the attraction tends to be acceptable to some families as being appropriate for children. You are urged to contact all establishments directly to avoid possibly exposing your children to something inappropriate.

Nevada's casinos generate over **9 billion dollars** *in gambling revenue each year.*

Las Vegas History

Las Vegas history is unusually well documented, considering its young age. In 2005 the city turned a baby 100, and had a population of less than 600,000. What is it then, about Las Vegas, that makes it such a well-researched historical city despite its infancy?

Quite simply, Las Vegas is the embodiment of the American ideal of "dream big, build bigger." How big can you build? How well can you advertise? How loud and gaudy can you be? How can you make the lights as bright as possible and the veneer as thin as possible? How can you waste what little power and water are available, and make as much money as possible as you create something useless? The apparent answer: build a resort in Vegas.

The result might seem like the American cynic's worst nightmare. And yet in its complicated ugliness and tackiness comes a striking simplicity – a beauty that exists nowhere else in the world. If money had absolute power, it would be Las Vegas. And there is a peace in such a place, a peace which resides in the facts that (1) a place such as a Las Vegas exists, and (2) there is only one place in America like Las Vegas.

Today Las Vegas is a melting pot of corporate power. At the beginning, however, then the city was nothing more than a sleepy town, it took several key individuals with dreams and vision, to turn the city into what it has become today. It was these visionaries who built Las Vegas and deserve much of the credit for this city.

What follows is a thumbnail sketch of the History of Las Vegas, and about some of the key people that mad the city what it is today. Of course, much more comprehensive information can be found in the vast amount of literature on the subject, but what follows is the basic run-down:

THE BIRTH OF LAS VEGAS

Hundreds of thousands of years ago, the Las Vegas Valley was alive with lakes, rivers, plants and animals. It was a marshy landscape filled with all kinds of creatures. Through time, however, the water sank underground, popping up only occasionally as tributaries to the Colorado River. As a result, while the surrounding landscape was largely harsh and arid, the valley was a green and fertile area.

EARLY INHABITANTS
For years, the indigenous Southern Paiute lived within the fertile valley of Las Vegas. In the 1700s, while Spanish explorers were busy looking for an easy route to Los Angeles, the Paiute were largely isolated due to outsider fears that the large valley was an uninhabitable, unforgiving wasteland.

However, Rafael Rivera, the first European to see the valley, told his fellows that it was in fact a lush landscape, with water and wildlife unseen in the surrounding desert. As such, the explorers named it "Las Vegas", which means "fertile valley". With this discovery, the explorers' trip to Los Angeles was cut short and the livelihoods of the Paiutes, who had lived there for generations, would forever be threatened.

FREMONT'S FIRST ACCOUNT
In 1844, when the area was still part of Mexico, a group from the Army Corps of Engineers came across the land, led by Captain John C. Frémont. Fremont wrote about the fertile Las Vegas valley in 1852, and thus the first published Western account of Las Vegas came to be:

"After a day's journey of 18 miles, in a northeasterly direction, we encamped in the midst of another very large basin, at a camping ground called *las Vegas* – a term which the Spaniards use to signify fertile or marshy plains, in contradistinction to *llanos*, which they apply to dry and sterile plains. Two narrow streams of clear water, four or five feet deep, gush suddenly, with a quick current, from two singularly large springs; these, and other waters of the basin, pass out in a gap to the eastward. The taste of the water is good, but rather too warm to be agreeable; the temperature being 71° in the one, and 73° in the other. They, however, afford a delightful bathing-place."

WESTERN EXPANSION
When the Treaty of Guadalupe Hidalgo was signed in 1848 giving United States control over the southwest, it was open season for Americans to mold the countryside to their liking. In 1855, under the direction of Mormon leader Brigham Young, 30 Mormon missionaries were sent to the valley to convert the Paiutes that inhabited the region. A fort was built in what would later be Downtown Las Vegas, but the Mormons largely abandoned it only two years later, leaving only a few behind. By the late 1860s, the Las Vegas area was largely irrigated for growing grapes for wine, as well other foods, and it was a favored stop on the Mormon Pioneer Trail.

In 1885, the State Land Act brought many farmers to the fertile valley of Las Vegas. As a result, for the next two decades, Las Vegas' farming industry boomed. With so much irrigation and water availability, Las Vegas became an industrial and travel stop at the start of the twentieth century for many trails from Los Angeles and neighboring towns and cities.

THE CITY IS OFFICIAL
By 1905, there were successful industries for mining as well as agriculture within the Las Vegas area. That, coupled with a completed railroad between Los Angeles and Salt Lake City (of which Las Vegas was a prime stop), helped the town's finances

look promising, and commerce began to take off. On May 15 of that same year, with the sale of the downtown area to various interested parties, Las Vegas was founded. Six years later, in 1911, Las Vegas was incorporated into Clark County, Nevada.

On March 19, 1911, Nevada legalized gambling, marking the introduction of one of the most prosperous industries in the state. Less than one month later, six gambling licenses were issued in the City of Las Vegas to various qualified establishments.

LINKING LAS VEGAS
At the turn of the 20th century, Las Vegas was a railroad town. When the city was incorporated, the railway industry boomed as the city linked Los Angeles to Salt Lake City and others. However, in 1917, the primary rail company went broke. Although Union Pacific attempted to re-establish the route, the 1922 rail strike left people without an economical way to get to Las Vegas.

Four years later, in 1926, the blossoming United States Highway system finally completed a road connecting the country to Las Vegas, thus ending a four-year period of the city's commercial inaccessibility. The Las Vegas stretch of this road, U.S. Highway 91, connecting Utah, California, Arizona and other area states, would eventually become Las Vegas Boulevard. Even with the road and legal gambling, however, the country was in the midst of the Great Depression, and Las Vegas still needed a real boost to bring in the industry and the economy.

THE HOOVER DAM
In 1922, plans were shown to then Secretary of Commerce Herbert Hoover of a dam along the Colorado River about 30 miles southeast of Las Vegas. In addition to saving certain farming communities from the occasional flooding, the dam would provide much-needed water for Las Vegas and surrounding communities, as far west as Los Angeles. After much planning, con-

struction of the "Boulder Dam" began in 1931, and the population of the town swelled to well over five times the size of the previous year (25,000 people). In fact, during the dam's construction, a separate town, Boulder City, was erected specifically to house workers of the project. Nevertheless, nearby Las Vegas was the primary benefactor of this major influx of people.

The dam's construction was completed in 1936, and ultimately re-named the Hoover Dam to honor Herbert Hoover's influence in its creation. As an anticipated result of the dam, water behind it began to back up, creating Lake Mead, the largest man-made lake in the United States. Unfortunately, the lake forced several area communities to permanently evacuate, including St. Thomas, Nevada (abandoned in 1938), the remains of which can be seen when the lake's water level is low.

LEGALIZED GAMBLING
During the Dam's construction, in 1931, Las Vegas officially "legalized" gambling. Now, as opposed to it being a thrown-together collection of gambling locations, it was to be regulated, controlled, and monitored by the local government. The first license was issued that year to the Northern Club, with several more to follow in the downtown area. By 1941, hotels and gambling establishments were beginning to spring up not only in the downtown area, but also onto U.S. Highway 91 (later known as "the strip").

CASINO RESORTS
With gambling having such tremendous profit potential, several of the nation's organized crime syndicates began investing their money into hotels and resorts in both the downtown and strip areas. During the forties and fifties, several crime-funded resorts made their debuts. The Flamingo was the first, spearheaded by

Benjamin "Bugsy" Siegel; others on the list include the Sands, the Sahara, and the Tropicana.

With the incredible successes of these flagship casino resorts, others entered the hospitality and gambling industry within Las Vegas. The sixties and seventies saw an impressive boom in resorts along the Las Vegas strip. By the eighties, established gaming companies had bought out or opened chains of their resorts throughout the city. In the 1990s, the new mega-resorts had thousands of guest rooms.

THE BUSINESS TYCOONS

Though Las Vegas is a corporate paradise, it is a city shaped by individual people with strong visions. This section details a few of the more prominent movers and shakers that made Las Vegas what it is today. These are the influential people that bought, operated, controlled or created casino resorts or otherwise molded the city.

BENJAMIN SIEGEL
Though he hated the name, Benjamin Siegel was often called "Bugsy". He is considered by many to be the unofficial father of the Las Vegas strip, and – to a lesser extent – of the entire "resort" concept. Born in New York City in 1906, Siegel quickly affiliated himself with members of American organized crime, and rose through the ranks as a gambling profiteer.

When gambling was legalized in Las Vegas in 1931, he saw potential for moving gamblers away from the downtown area, which at the time attracted mainly those working on the nearby Boulder Dam project. His vision called for a major destination that included amenities beyond gambling, including entertainment, dining, and other more "all-encompassing" resort options. It would be located on a largely uninhabited stretch of road seven miles from downtown. "Flamingo" came from the nickname of his girlfriend, Virginia Hill.

When the resort first opened in 1946, it had just over 100 rooms and was billed as being the most luxurious in the world. However, it cost six times the estimated $1 million price tag and failed to make money during its first few months of operation. As a result, in 1947 Siegel was shot in the eye, killing him almost instantly. To this day, Benjamin Siegel's influence on Las Vegas resort designs is widespread, and a plaque in the courtyard of the current Flamingo Resort, near where the original once stood, is dedicated to him.

HOWARD HUGHES

A name synonymous with many endeavors, Howard Hughes was a quintessential entrepreneur, and at the same time famous for his brash behavior, his eccentricities, and eventually his psychological disorders. On one of his early quests, one to become the best filmmaker, he spent large fortunes inherited from his father's company producing and directing a few successful films in the late 1920s and 1930s.

Hughes' early major successes came from aviation projects. Though he never earned a college degree, he designed and built aircraft throughout the 1940s, and even broke world records of speed and flight times. He contributed many technologies to the world of aviation and airplane design, such as pressurized passenger cabins and retractable landing gear.

However, in 1946, during a test flight of one of his experimental aircrafts, Hughes had a near-fatal crash that scarred and damaged him, both physically and mentally, for the rest of his life. Many suspect this accident triggered his later reclusiveness, drug addiction, and pronounced obsessive-compulsive disorder. It is during these later years where Hughes' major foray into Las Vegas begins.

Deciding that Las Vegas resorts should be his next endeavor, in 1966 Hughes rented a floor in the Desert Inn on the Las Vegas Strip, where he locked himself away in recluse. When the hotel threatened to kick him out despite being paid up for the rooms less than a month later, he bought the Desert Inn and moved his entire headquarters to the eighth and ninth floors of the hotel. Within the next two years, he had bought several other resorts in Las Vegas, including the Sands and the New Frontier. By the time Hughes left Las Vegas a few years later, through his various resort buyouts, he had effectively freed Las Vegas from organized crime connections.

WILLIAM HARRAH

William Harrah was born in 1911 in South Pasadena, California. His early interests involved mechanical engineering, particularly cars. However, his father's organized bingo games (illegal in California) were interesting ventures. He eventually bought the business from his father and moved it to Reno, where gambling laws allowed such a game to take place.

In 1937 he opened his first legit bingo parlor in Reno, effectively starting Harrah's Entertainment. His first permanent venture, a bingo parlor in Reno, was very successful. In 1946, Harrah's Club opened in downtown Reno. About a decade later, Harrah began to acquire property in nearby Lake Tahoe, which would become his first major resort, Harrah's Lake Tahoe.

Harrah's company continued to grow and expand his Lake Tahoe and Reno properties. In 1971, Harrah's became a publicly traded company, and in 1973 became the first gaming and casino company listed on the New York Stock Exchange.

In 1978, at the age of 66, Harrah died, but his company continues to grow. It wasn't until after his death that any Harrah's casino existed in Las Vegas. In early 2004, Harrah's Entertainment acquired Caesars Entertainment, making Harrah's Entertainment the largest casino resort company in the world.

KIRK KERKORIAN

Kirk Kerkorian's interest in Las Vegas was largely founded by investment as opposed to passion. Born in 1917, one of his earliest ambitions was airplanes, and in 1948 he took ownership of a small airline company, and began to fly passengers to and around the west coast, including Las Vegas. Through his airline and personal enjoyment, he spent much time in Las Vegas starting in the 1940s. However, it wasn't until 1962 when he began to make investments in the growing region.

That year, he bought a large plot of land on the strip and shortly thereafter rented the land to Jay Sarno, who spearheaded the creation of Caesars Palace on that spot. The resort opened in 1966, and Kerkorian sold the property to Sarno for a hefty profit. Kerkorian subsequently bought and sold several other resorts as investments in Las Vegas, including The Flamingo.

His major Vegas endeavor, however, was not until 1967, when he purchased a financially struggling Metro-Goldwyn-Mayor (MGM) for its valuable real estate and movie memorabilia. In 1973, he opened up the MGM Grand Hotel and Casino, which was the largest hotel in the world at the time. He sold off much of the studio and eventually declared that it was primarily a hotel company. However, he has sold and bought assets to the company several times since.

In 2000, MGM's hotel business ultimately combined with Steve Wynn's Mirage Resorts. It now exists as a separate company, MGM Mirage, but Kerkorian maintains majority ownership. As a financial inspiration and a brilliant investor, Kirk Kerkorian is considered by many to be the father of the mega-resort.

STEVE WYNN

Perhaps the most famous of the modern-day Las Vegas visionaries is Steve Wynn. His likeness has become synonymous with the Las Vegas resort tycoon. Wynn and his enterprises embody the Las Vegas success story.

Wynn was born in 1942. Trained in business, he moved to Las Vegas when he was 25 and bought interest into the New Frontier Hotel. After a few successful years, in 1972 he purchased enough interest in the Golden Nugget on Fremont Street to acquire control of it. At the time it was an old, run-down casino, but Wynn revamped it, upgraded it, and ultimately turned it into the best resort in Downtown Las Vegas. For almost two decades, Golden Nugget was an incredible success. Wynn duplicated his Golden Nugget resort namesake in Atlantic City a few years later, but ultimately abandoned the Atlantic City resort concept altogether.

In 1987, Wynn acquired the Castaways Resort from Howard Hughes. On the property he proceeded to build what was at the time the most lavish and upscale casino resort in the world. In 1989, The Mirage, his crowning achievement at the time, first opened.

Using The Mirage as an example, Wynn's Company, Mirage Resorts, would later become the model for mega-resort creation. Among others, he re-built Las Vegas with the likes of Treasure Island, Monte Carlo, and his ultimate creation, the Bellagio, in 1998.

However, in 2000 Wynn sold his coveted Mirage Resorts, and for a brief moment Las Vegas was without a Steve Wynn-run resort. But all was not lost. In 2002 he purchased and imploded the Desert Inn and Golf Course to make way for a new independent venture, the most expensive hotel ever built, Wynn Las Vegas. The new resort opened in 2005.

The Entertainers

With the advent of national tourism due to legal gambling, Las Vegas eventually became known as one of America's major entertainment venues. From as early as the 1940s, when Benjamin Siegel hired performers for his Flamingo resort, the stage was set for some of the world's biggest names in entertainment to grace Las Vegas' many stages. Following are some examples of entertainers that made a name for themselves in Las Vegas.

THE RAT PACK
Frank Sinatra, Peter Lawford, Joey Bishop, Sammy Davis, Jr., and Dean Martin performed at sold-out venues throughout Las Vegas during the 1950s and 1960s. Purportedly named (perhaps by Humphrey Bogart) for being "rascals", these five entertainers provided great influence and marketability to Las Vegas at a time when such an influx of tourism and population began to make the city one of America's go-to places for entertainment.

Though they were never officially billed or known as the "Rat Pack", and the group was in reality only a loose collection that sometimes shifted from the five best-known members, the name ultimately stuck. Their show, which featured a lively collection of music, comedy skits, and other predominantly upbeat sketches, was for a long time the most popular in Las Vegas. Sometimes they would all perform together, sometimes separately, but due to the ad-libbed nature of the acts, it was uncommon to see all Rat Pack members appear at one show.

However, Sinatra, being a tourist draw in his own right, owned a portion of the Sands resort. In 1960 at the Sands, the group officially performed together for the first time. The engagement lasted about three weeks, and made Sands the most famous hotel on the blossoming Las Vegas strip.

The group contributed tremendously positive ideals to Las Vegas, including removal of segregation laws (they would not perform at any venue where such laws existed). The group's popularity waned by the 1970s and, although they were each famous individually, after then the Rat Pack was no more.

ELVIS PRESLEY
Though it is Graceland in Memphis that Elvis Presley called home, Las Vegas was one of his favorite performance venues. Selling out concert after concert, Presley's flashy shows and cutting-edge popular culture status made him the perfect match for the fast-growing Las Vegas of the time.

Elvis was born in 1935 in East Tulepo, Mississippi. When he was 13, his family moved to Memphis, which he would call home for the rest of his life. Though he had always been a performer, he began achieving fame as a Rock and Roll icon in the late 1950s.

In 1956, Elvis made his Las Vegas performance debut at the Hotel Last Frontier. However, the performance was far from a hit, as his musical style did not fit into a town where Frank Sinatra reigned supreme. Elvis would not return to Las Vegas for many years, until well after his music and film careers (including MGM's 1964 release of *Viva Las Vegas*) were well-established, and after returning from the military. As a result, Las Vegas saw Elvis primarily in his later years.

In 1967, Elvis married Priscilla at the Aladdin Resort & Casino. Two years later, in 1969, his real Las Vegas legacy would begin when he signed a contract with Kirk Kerkorian's International Hotel (renamed in 1971 to the Las Vegas Hilton). It was there, for the next eight years, that Elvis would perform over 830 shows, regularly selling out and breaking attendance and performance records despite his drug problems. In 1976, he left Las

Vegas and went on tour for the next year, before his death in 1977.

Today, Elvis' existence in Las Vegas is that of homage and tradition. Elvis-impersonators and even an Elvis-themed wedding chapel are nostalgic tributes to the King of Rock and Roll and his near decade-long presence in one of his favorite cities.

LIBERACE

His name brings to mind extraordinary showmanship, flamboyance, and extravagant costumes. He was a television and movie actor, an author, and a concert performer. However, Liberace's claim to fame all began with the piano. And on this piano sat a candelabrum, his trademark stage prop.

Born in Wisconsin in 1919, Wladziu Liberace was a classically trained pianist, but as he primarily performed popular tunes early on in his career, he was able to bring himself into the pop culture arena. In the 1940s he achieved mild fame performing in various small-scale clubs across America.

However, in 1952 he starred in "The Liberace Show" on television, where he gained national notoriety as a master pianist. His fame eventually grew as he played to packed houses in Carnegie Hall, Hollywood Bowl, and even Madison Square Garden. His television and movie career blossomed, and he eventually opened at the Riviera in Las Vegas as the highest-paid entertainer in Las Vegas at the time.

He went on to perform on a rotating basis throughout many venues in the United States and abroad. At one point, he was considered to be the world's fastest piano player by playing 6,000 notes in 2 minutes. Much of his profits would go to funding for the arts, and in 1979 he opened The Liberace Museum in Las Vegas, filled with artifacts from his personal collection. Proceeds benefited his Liberace Foundation for the Performing and Creative Arts.

Liberace performed up until the very end of his life, and in 1987, at age 67, he died of complications from AIDS. His life was always filled with controversy, perhaps to his ultimate benefit. After all, he was a master showman, a brilliant pianist, and an expert at bridging popular culture with classical concert performance.

SIEGFRIED & ROY

Siegfried Fischbacher and Roy Horn headlined one of Las Vegas' most famous and iconic shows for several decades. A mix of magic, grand showmanship, and their famous exotic white tigers, the Siegfried & Roy show became a staple of Las Vegas entertainment and of the mega-production.

Both born in Germany (in 1939 and 1944, respectively), the two met in the late 1950s, and began their professional relationship shortly thereafter. Siegfried's experience as a magician coupled well with Roy's experience with exotic animals. After performing at various European venues, they debuted at the Tropicana in 1967, and in 1972 their performance in Las Vegas won them an award.

Their performances attracted worldwide attention to the preservation of exotic animals, and they began conservation efforts to protect these animals, particularly the white tigers. The duo continued to perform at various Las Vegas venues and elsewhere, until 1990 when they landed residency at the Mirage by signing a long-term contract with Steve Wynn.

However, in 2003, a highly publicized tragedy took place that would forever change the face of the Mirage. During a performance in early October of that year, Horn was attacked onstage, in full view of the audience; by one of the trained white tigers he'd spent years working with. The attack left him in critical condition, with various injuries and partial paralysis. As a result, after over 5,000 shows, the Siegfried & Roy show closed its doors indefinitely at the Mirage.

Area Orientation

The dry and desolate desert of the American Southwest, flanked by mountains and the mighty Colorado River, is the last place anyone would expect to find one of the top vacation destinations in the United States. Yet it is here that the fertile Las Vegas valley lies. Not too long ago it was a peaceful oasis seen only by adventurous travelers and intrepid settlers, but today it is a sprawling urban landscape and tourist haven.

At over six hundred square miles, bordered by mountains, a river, and a man-made lake, the Las Vegas metropolitan area is home to the largest concentration of people in the otherwise wide-open state of Nevada. Tourism here is big business. Since the early 1900s, people have flocked to Las Vegas for one reason: gambling.

Today there are many more reasons to visit Las Vegas. In addition to the allure of legal gambling, Las Vegas has earned the reputation as an entire city synonymous with entertainment and fun. Everywhere you look sparkling hotels and casinos vie for your attention and patronage. Huge animated signs and glittering billboards advertise outrageous over-the-top attractions and shows. World-renowned chefs show off their culinary feats in huge, visually-stunning venues. Monolithic themed shopping complexes litter the strip. Every conceivable form of entertainment is available, although not necessarily for cheap. Las Vegas is truly a city of light and life.

SEASONS AND TEMPERATURES

Las Vegas is a year-round vacation destination. The vast majority of attractions are open in all weather and all seasons, and the strip is always swarming with activity. Though there are a few bargain months, good deals can always be found even in the busy season. However, there are some important seasonal differences that visitors should be aware of before planning a trip. *Average temperatures are approximate, and are in Fahrenheit.*

SPRING

(Average High: 70° F; *Average Low:* 45° F) Springtime is one of Las Vegas' busiest seasons, when the weather is not to warm and many of the outdoor activities (such as swimming pools) are up and running in full swing. Hotel room prices are expensive, even for mid-week travel.

SUMMER

(Average High: 101° F; *Average Low:* 72° F) Las Vegas is in the desert, and summertime excursion during the year's hottest months means battling dry desert heat all day and all night. On the other hand, summertime is more of an off-season, and offers some great hotel bargains. Plus, when you're in a resort all day, it is easy to stay out of the hot summer sun.

FALL

(Average High: 75° F; *Average Low:* 50° F) The other busy season is the fall (particularly later fall), when the weather has cooled down but the outdoor attractions are still open. Thanksgiving weekend is one of the busiest times of the year.

WINTER

(Average High: 62° F; *Average Low:* 45° F) Winter in the Las Vegas valley is very mild and overall pleasant. Outdoor pools, restaurants and other activities may be closed or have limited service. Room rates and specials may be abundant. Christmas and New Year's, however, are among the busiest days of the year, and should be avoided if you want to beat the crowds.

BUSIEST TIMES

Weekends (Thursday, Friday, Saturday, and Sunday) are much busier than the mid-week (Monday, Tuesday, and Wednesday), so prices climb and availability sinks. For holidays, the city sees peak tourist influx during the major U.S. holidays, including the week around Christmas and New Year's, Independence Day, and Memorial Day. The city is also crowded (and prices climb) during Valentine's Day and around major sporting events.

GETTING INFORMATION

The more you know about Las Vegas before you go, the more you can do, and the more fun you'll have. Whenever possible, take care to learn about the area's history, culture, and any specific landmarks and attractions that pique your interest. Not only will you better appreciate your time there, the anticipation of seeing the sights will be that much greater.

LAS VEGAS CONVENTION & VISITOR'S AUTHORITY *(3150 Paradise Rd ☎ 702.892.0711 ⌁ lvcva.com)* For cities with particularly large amounts of commerce generated by tourism, cities like Las Vegas, a separate division of the Chamber of Commerce will exist. Called the "Convention & Visitor's Bureau" or "Visitor's Authority" or some other such name, this special branch of the Chamber of Commerce is dedicated to promoting tourism. If it exists, this can be the best resource for finding out about what a city has to offer tourists.

Promotional booklets and fliers containing area information are funded by the businesses themselves and the Bureau. Therefore, information obtained via these sources is biased, but it still offers up enough information to give visitors a thorough idea of the area's offerings.

INDEPENDENTLY PRINTED TRAVEL GUIDES

With few exceptions, printed travel guides tend to offer a lot more information than the vacationer needs, which may result in overcomplicated vacation planning. Certain high profile destinations, such as Las Vegas and Orlando, have many books devoted to that specific location. Just visit your local bookstore and head towards the travel section – there is bound to be plenty of Las Vegas travel guides.

TRAVEL AGENTS

Commercial travel agents make planning vacations to Las Vegas a breeze. They can search for the best deals, book flights and hotels, make restaurant reservations, and even make special requests on your behalf. Their most important asset, however, is their personal knowledge of the destination. They can recommend places to stay and things to see and do like no book or website ever could.

However, their service comes with its own price tag, which can be avoided by simply doing your own research – travel agents have no real greater power than a well-informed customer; they just have access to the right information.

THE INTERNET

Las Vegas information constantly changes, and the Internet is a great way to keep up. Unfortunately, because of the largely level playing field of web sites, it is hard to know which sites to trust and which sites to examine with a bit more skepticism.

A definitive Internet source cannot be offered here; the best advice in learning about your destination of choice would be to (1) check multiple internet sources, including promotional sites, online travel agencies, and sites with user comments, and (2) check the "official" site, if any – official, meaning the site owned by the attraction or city you are interested in.

LOCAL PUBLICATIONS

Las Vegas offers several local publications that feature information about the area, and newsworthy events. The Las Vegas Sun (✆ lasvegassun.com) and the **Las Vegas Review-Journal** (✆ reviewjournal.com) both have sections devoted to tourism with the region. Additionally, the **Las Vegas Weekly** (✆ lasvegasweekly.com) is an alternative weekly newspaper with lots of information about local goings-on.

PACKING FOR YOUR TRIP

A good suitcase isn't only filled with things you know you'll use, but also what you *might* use. This section provides some tips on packing the right items for your vacation. But don't worry; if you do end up forgetting something, chances are you can buy a cheap one at one of Las Vegas' many gift shops.

CLOTHES

For most of Las Vegas, there is no real dress code. Chances are you will be welcome regardless of whether you're wearing a suit or short sleeves. Keeping in mind that the city is a warmer destination (check local weather prior to packing), and you are basically free to dress however you feel comfortable (unless you plan on going out to a fine restaurant or a live show). Keep in mind that the average Las Vegas rainfall is *less than 1 inch per month*, so pack accordingly.

Many resorts offer laundry-cleaning services. If you are planning a vacation for more than a few days, consider using the resort's on-premises.

TOILETRIES

Toiletry kits are the easiest way to store and manage these basic items. On the upside, basic toiletries are cheap and small and widely accessible, so even if you do forget something, in many cases they might be cheap to replace, or even free – many hotels offer free toiletry items (razors, toothbrushes, etc.) to guests upon request.

MEDICATIONS

Make sure you have all necessary medications with you before leaving home. It is highly recommended that you pack medications the night before you leave, and double/triple check to ensure you have the right medications and enough to cover your trip, plus at least one day to be on the safe side. Also, keep medications close to you at all times (carry onto airplanes, keep nearby in the car, etc.)

ADDITIONAL ITEMS

Don't forget sunscreen, camera, film and batteries, bathing suit, sunglasses, contact lenses, warm coat, waist pack, purse, long socks, a nice set of clothes (for a nice dinner), packed food for munching, driver's license or photo identification (or passport if you are a non-U.S. citizen), and whatever else your trip to Las Vegas may call for.

GETTING TO LAS VEGAS

Despite its relatively remote location (depending on who you talk to), Las Vegas' immense tourist draw makes it one of the most accessible locations in the United States. Over 34 million people trek to Las Vegas each year, and they can arrive in one of several ways.

BY PLANE

One of the busiest airports in America is located only a few short minutes from the Las Vegas strip – **McCarran International Airport** (Airport Code: LAS, www.mccarran.com). In fact, the southern Las Vegas Strip is clearly visible from the tarmac and airport. Nearly all flights in and out of Las Vegas come through McCarran, a small but extremely crowded transit hub.

Additionally, since most visitors to Las Vegas come from McCarran, many popular resorts even have check-in windows within the airport (call the hotel in advance to check availability). Taxis and shuttles to area hotels are abundant. South strip resorts are almost across the street. North strip and Downtown resorts are a few miles away. However, don't be fooled by the apparent proximity of the strip. A taxi ride to the mid-strip may cost up to $20, after taking into account complicated roads and traffic. North strip and Downtown resorts will be even more. Shuttle buses and vans, on the other hand, usually charge between $5-$10 per person regardless of destination, but you may be required to reserve ahead.

BY CAR

Though Las Vegas itself is not necessarily a "driving" city, its location in the heart of the American desert offers unique scenic vistas, hot weather and bright sun that make a worthy trek for those coming from nearby cities.

The Los Angeles Metropolitan area and its sprawling suburban landscape account for most of the road trips to Las Vegas. The 270-plus mile journey takes about four hours, most of which is along the rural I-15. The fastest route takes passengers through the town of Barstow, one of the hottest cities (temperature-wise) in the United States, and around the perimeter of the Mojave Desert region.

I-15 also connects to Salt Lake City about 420 miles northeast of Las Vegas. San Francisco and Sacramento do not have a direct route; travelers are recommended to go south to Barstow and follow I-15. Driving from Phoenix is under 300 miles, but without a direct interstate highway (unless traveling through Flagstaff); travelers take US Route 93.

BY BUS
Casino bus service, designed especially for gamblers, is available at major cities around Las Vegas. These services provide a drastically reduced round-trip bus fare to a casino, as well as complimentary dining coupons, gaming chips, and more. In order to qualify for this exceptional value, travelers must be over the age of 21.

Several different bus lines, including Greyhound (greyhound.com) offer these junket services through Los Angeles and other cities. Some of them depart very frequently, often many times per day. Check with local bus providers and major transit depots for information on these often unbeatable bargains.

BY TRAIN
Las Vegas does not have a commuter or nationwide railroad station anywhere nearby (ironic given the city's rail-rich history). Instead, visitors traveling by train will have to take **Amtrak** (Amtrak.com) to its nearest stop – generally the distant Needles or Kingston, or even Los Angeles – and endure a four-hour bus ride.

GETTING AROUND LAS VEGAS

Getting around within Las Vegas and vicinity is quite convenient. Visitors can travel to any resort or casino downtown, on the strip, or in out-of-the-way places on several different transit systems, both public and private.

BY CAR
The abundance of free parking at many of the resorts is a relief when it comes to finding that perfect parking space. However, navigating these gargantuan facilities, as well as driving up and down the strip can add many minutes to your commute between resorts. Especially if your destination is nearby, it is recommended that you either walk, take an inexpensive taxi or other public transportation option.

Be warned, however, that the four-mile stretch of the Las Vegas Strip is always congested with cars and people. The pedestrian walkways over the streets help traffic a bit, but there are always street lights, traffic bubbles, and other unavoidable delays in automotive commuting.

BY TAXICAB
Taxis through Las Vegas are abundant and among the easiest ways to get to your nearby resort destination. However, unlike other cities, these for-hire vehicles are not allowed to pick up pedestrians on the street (no cab-hailing in Vegas). Instead, they are required to pick up passengers at designated taxi stands. Not to worry, though, these stands are conveniently located and easy to find – each resort has one or more. Expect a cab ride from north strip to south strip to be about $10-$15, although it really depends on traffic.

BY MONORAIL
(*lvmonorail.com*) Though not the cheapest or most convenient way to traverse the Las Vegas Strip, the brand new **Las Vegas Monorail** is certainly one of the coolest and most modern ways, especially for those who are already familiar with Las Vegas.

The monorail runs from the MGM Grand all the way to the Sahara, making several stops on the east side of the strip. (Those staying on the west side will have to cross the street). Some of these stops are within a resort, some are on the street. Getting to a monorail station is almost always a hassle, but the rides are smooth, clean, air-conditioned, and efficient once you're on board.

BY PRIVATE LIMO
The streets of Las Vegas are packed with stretch limos and other such private car services. They are very easy to come by but expensive. Generally, the hotel you are staying at can arrange for private car service.

CITIZEN'S AREA TRANSIT (PUBLIC BUS)
(*☝ rtcsouthernnevada.com* ☎ *800.228.3911)* The **Regional Transportation Commission of Southern Nevada** operates the **Citizens Area Transit** ("CAT"), a commuter bus service operating throughout the Las Vegas area, including points on and off the strip, downtown, and surrounding neighborhoods. Though built for (and primarily used by) locals, this service is very inexpensive (less than $2 a ride) and provides a cheap and easy way to get to out-of-the-way resorts and casinos that may not be normally served by popular tourist transit options.

Please check the maps and schedules and riding information well beforehand before using the CAT services. You should feel comfortable riding local public transportation before deciding to use it. Accessible rides are also available, call for information.

LAS VEGAS STRIP TROLLEY
(*☝ striptrolley.com* ☎ *702.386.7429)* For visitors without a tight schedule, the Las Vegas Tourist Trolley is another way for tour-

ists to see the Las Vegas strip. With stops at many major strip resorts, the trolley has two loops – north and south. It may be cheaper ($2 per trip or $5 for a day pass). The bus keeps a somewhat loose schedule.

WHAT TO DO

There is so, so much to do in Las Vegas. However, even with all the attraction choices, sometimes the best thing is doing nothing at all. The following is a breakdown of a few of the major activities enjoyed by the millions of Las Vegas tourists each year.

GAMBLE

Of course! If you're over 21, gambling is probably one of the main reasons (if not THE reason) why you decided to make a trip to Las Vegas in the first place. No matter what time of day or night, or what season of the year, there will always, always be plenty of places to gamble. Most casino games and casino floors are largely the same – huge cavernous rooms filled with rows upon rows of slot machines and table games. Small differences (and occasionally choices) may vary from location to location.

Most larger casinos in Las Vegas (especially those which are part of resorts), will feature a casino loyalty program to keep visitors coming back to that one particular casino. Themes and décor, minimum bids, clientele and other factors determine the nature of the casino, but the games themselves remain the same.

GO SHOPPING

Shopping in Las Vegas is different than anywhere else! Particularly in the resorts, shopping can be a truly over-the-top experience. Malls – if you can even call them that – are as much entertainment and theme park as they are shopping center. As many resort malls are based on the theme of their home resort, visitors are treated to the canals of Venice, the bazaars of the Middle East, the Forum of ancient Rome, and even a promenade of bygone Hollywood.

The stores themselves are almost always upscale (and expensive), with well-known chains represented. However, the shopping *experience* of Vegas makes all the difference.

DINE OUT

There are so many restaurants in Las Vegas! As one of the restaurant capitals of the world, nearly every possible kind of food option is available. Plus, an abundance of celebrity chefs have outposts here, where they test new food ideas, and even make appearances. Buffets have become a Las Vegas staple, though the days of the *inexpensive* buffet have largely gone away. Everything from fine dining to casual chain restaurants to fast food and food courts are abundant throughout the city.

SEE A SHOW

"The Vegas Show" is a special kind of stage production that is very specific to Las Vegas. It is a glitzy, glamorous, and special-effect-filled event featuring bright lights, lavish sets, and the famous Las Vegas showgirls. Of course, Las Vegas hosts other kind of shows too, in the various venues both on and off resort properties. Unlike most aspects of a Vegas vacation, shows require advanced planning. Some shows are very popular and tickets must be purchased well in advance.

SWIM

Swimming pools and related water activities are a natural extension of a resort. Resort "water play centers" can be as small as a single pool or as large as an entire water park. For many visiting Las Vegas, the quality of their resort's swimming pool can make or break their vacation experience. Visitors can spend their entire vacation swimming, sun-tanning, or lounging around their resort's pool area. And this includes sipping a poolside Pina Colada. Las Vegas has some of the world's best pools.

ENJOY A SPA TREATMENT
On par with resorts' pool facilities is their oftentimes extraordinary spa facilities. Like pools, the facilities vary widely depending on the resort, but often include all kinds of massage and body treatment options, saunas and steams rooms, fitness equipment and more. Spa use is popular with gamblers, and can be expensive for certain treatments.

GET MARRIED
Looking to tie the knot? In Las Vegas, weddings can run the gamut of elaborate festivities in lavish ballrooms to themed weddings (say "I Do" dressed as Scarlet and Rhett!) to last-minute impromptus. Many major resorts have wedding chapels, wedding coordinators, and other such resources to help plan the wedding of your dreams.

This book, however, is not designed to help plan your wedding, and does not list wedding chapels or planning services. It is recommended that you contact your resort about your plans, and to not get information to make such an important decision from this (or any) travel guidebook.

WHERE TO STAY

When visiting Las Vegas, you will probably stay at a casino resort – while there are other choices, they oftentimes don't offer the same vacation experience indicative of the city's tourism. Las Vegas has more hotel guest rooms per square mile than most other tourist centers. Therefore, this book focuses *only* on Las Vegas resort accommodations, as they are indicative of the Las

Vegas experience. If you are interested in other non-resort accommodations, consider using an online travel agency such as **Travelocity** (travelocity.com).

ON THE STRIP
By far, the glamorous Las Vegas Strip is the best and most famous place to stay in Las Vegas. It is here that most of the big resort names, restaurants, and entertainment venues are located. As such, most visitors will opt to stay on the strip. However, the strip is the "tourist" section and can be more expensive. Therefore, many visitors prefer more of a local flavor. In any case, during a trip to Las Vegas, most (if not all) visitors explore at least one strip resort during their stay.

OFF THE STRIP
From a block away to many miles away, Las Vegas area resorts are not just confined to the strip. Oftentimes, those traveling on a budget or those who prefer to vacation away from the hectic strip atmosphere will opt for one of the many off-strip resorts. Many times these resorts cater more to locals, may have additional amenities (such as bowling alleys or movie theaters), and often are more reasonably priced. Plus, in many cases, a short taxi ride is all it takes to get to the attractions of the strip. But by day's end, it is easy to leave to a more relaxing atmosphere.

DOWNTOWN
Las Vegas' Fremont Street area downtown is the quintessential "original" Las Vegas. As such, the resorts in this section are smaller, glitzier, older, and reflect the Las Vegas of yesteryear. With its recent renovation into "the Fremont Street Experience", coupled with the four blocks of pedestrian-only traffic, downtown Las Vegas is finally able to provide visitors with a viable (albeit smaller and less upscale) alternative to the strip.

WHERE TO EAT

For many vacationers, eating is the highlight of their trip. For others, however, it is merely a short break from whatever the real attraction is. There are almost always several different dining choices; sometimes even within the hotel itself.

FAST FOOD
The quickest, cheapest, and generally least healthy way to eat is with fast food. There are so many fast food choices along highways, in cities and towns both small and large. Some of them are drive-through, some are eat-in, but they all offer the same thing: cheap food fast.

BUFFETS
Casino and large resorts commonly have buffet-style restaurants, where all the food is set out in a communal area, and customers are free to just walk up and take whatever they want. These are all-you-can-eat for one price places, with drinks costing extra.

CASUAL DINING
Table service at its most inexpensive and convenient casual dining choices exists in many different shapes and sizes. Appetizer, entrees, snacks and desserts are often offered. Dress is casual, though individual establishments may have their own requirements. Dining at a casual restaurant may take an hour or more.

FINE DINING
Upscale restaurants generally have a finer ambience, more of a dress code, with better food and better service. Enjoying a fine dining restaurant can take several hours, because at these places, the ambience and service is as important as the food.

TIPS AND TIPPING

Restaurant servers, bartenders, and the rest of the staff work largely on tips given by customers. As such, their wage is substantially lower than other occupations.

At a full service restaurant, fifteen to twenty percent (15-20%) of the total bill is a standard tip, which must be divided up between the server, bartender, and bus-person. Tipping of the host or maitre 'd is optional, depending on any special requests made (birthday cakes, special seating, etc.). Tipping at buffets is generally five to ten percent (5-10%), depending on the amount of work that is done by the server.

The first official gambling license in Las Vegas was issued in 1931. Of course, illegal gambling in the city began decades before.

The Las Vegas Resorts

For the tourist, Las Vegas *is* resorts. While other places may have resorts as a means to view the "other" attractions, in Las Vegas, without the resorts, you have nothing but desert. Without these gargantuan complexes taking up dozens and sometimes hundreds of acres, the city would be but a tiny speck of its current self. People don't come for the natural wonders of the desert. They don't come for the theme parks or the historical significance. They come for the casinos, the restaurants, and the shows of the resorts.

Las Vegas is home to 8 out of the 10 biggest hotels in the world, the top 4 of which are located within a half-mile of each other along the strip. The MGM Grand is the largest single-building hotel in the world, with a whopping 5,005 guest rooms. Even the hotels not among the top ten still have thousands of rooms. And what's more impressive is that these hotels are *frequently* booked to capacity.

Such massive tourism naturally calls for an unheard of number of diversions in a very small area. How to entertain the immense traffic? Enter the Las Vegas Resort; a compact facility with accommodations, restaurants, casinos, shows, fitness centers, and more. Most resorts are built with the intention of drawing customers in and keeping them there; in fact, many people enjoy Vegas vacations without ever leaving the resort they are staying in – they are that comprehensive.

CASINO COMPARISON

Of course, the centerpiece for every Las Vegas resort is its casino, and all casinos are almost exactly the same. They are massive stretches of indoor rooms reaching many hundreds of feet in every direction. There is rarely access to daylight, and the rows upon rows of slot machines and table games make these places difficult to navigate. They are smoky, loud, contain flickering masses of impulse entertainment, and are filled with people 24 hours a day, seven days a week. As such, they all have the same basic "look", the same basic games, the same basic amenities, noises, lights and smells. Oftentimes there are bars and restaurants mixed in with the floor. It is a well-studied design concept that has proven immensely successful for the industry. For the most part, if you've seen one casino, you've seen them all. It is a design you either love or you hate. All roads in Las Vegas resorts lead to a casino. In many instances, visitors even have to travel through the casino to reach the hotel's lobby.

Of course, there are little differences between each casino. If you're not a gambler, however, then the differences are moot. Otherwise any given casino's *minimum bid* and *casino loyalty programs* are top reasons for people to choose one resort over another. These two details however are far from minor, because they largely determine the quality of the resort, the clientele, and many times even the price for accommodations.

MINIMUM BID
At table games (and oftentimes on slots), there is a casino-set minimum bid, which means that they will only accept players willing to bet at least a certain amount for each game. The higher the minimum bid, the more expensive the game, and "higher the play". In politically correct casino language, this means the richer the client. So, high minimum bids mean an overall wealthier resort.

So what constitutes a "high" minimum bid? For table games such as **BlackJack** or **Texas Hold'em**, a $3 minimum-bid table is very low; and somewhat unheard of on the strip. Off the strip, however, these tables are common. In more upscale resorts, a $15 or $25 minimum bid is normal. In terms of slots, most resorts have penny slot machines, but the volume of penny (and nickel) slot machines varies depending on the resort.

CASINO LOYALTY PROGRAMS
Often in the guise of a "players club" or "rewards club", loyalty programs track gambling activity and reward patrons with complimentary rooms, food, and other services. This, in turn, keeps the patron coming back to one particular resort. While most loyalty programs are similar, what really sets them apart is their scope. Depending on the corporate ownership of the resort, the rewards earned may be valid at several different resorts.

For example, Harrah's Entertainment and MGM Mirage, two of the largest competing gaming entities, offer players club programs that are valid at all of their resorts, in and out of Nevada. For this benefit, many people may prefer to only stay and play at one of their affiliated resorts.

RESORT SECTIONS

With few exceptions, Las Vegas' resort layout is somewhat linear, with most resorts located on a four-mile stretch of Highway 91, also known as Las Vegas Boulevard. Interestingly, while considered part of "Las Vegas", the strip itself is actually outside the city proper.

Traveling up the strip, from south to north, is very much like taking a trip back in time. With a few notable exceptions, the southernmost resorts are generally the largest, newest, and most modern facilities with contemporary design and more of a luxurious atmosphere. The further north one travels, the resorts become reminiscent of the "classic" Las Vegas, with the flashier lights and glittery symbols made famous in the earlier years of the strip.

Finally, downtown Las Vegas, in an area commonly called Fremont Street, is just a short drive from the strip. This section is the Las Vegas of yesterday. Today it is called the "Fremont Street Experience" which includes a pedestrian-only street covered by a domed roof. It was here that Las Vegas was born.

Not all resorts are on the strip or in downtown, however. Many area locals (and sometimes tourists) venture off the strip to find more inexpensive accommodations, locals casinos, or an intimate, out-of-the-way setting.

SOUTH STRIP

The south strip is along Las Vegas Boulevard, from the tip of the strip to Flamingo Road. This section is where most of the largest hotels in Las Vegas are located. Within a small quarter-mile (or so) are some truly gargantuan properties. In fact, the intersection of Las Vegas Boulevard and Tropicana Avenue is the busiest in America.

MID-STRIP

Between Flamingo Road and Spring Mountain Road is the mid-strip section of town. Mid-strip became the birthplace of the Las Vegas Strip when Bugsy Siegel built the Fabulous Flamingo in the late 1940s. Today, this section of town contains the most compact resorts; they are among the smaller ones on the strip but there are many of them in a small area.

NORTH STRIP

North of Spring Mountain Road all the way to the Stratosphere (north of Sahara), is the north strip area. North strip is the smallest resort area on the strip, but it contains the true "classic" Las Vegas properties from the 1950s. The last remaining hotels of the rat-pack era are here, and the area is a bit more spread out and visibly aging than the other, newer sections of town. Still, it is the best way to enter the Vegas of yesteryear; even Fremont Street has updated itself more than the north strip area.

DOWNTOWN LAS VEGAS / FREMONT STREET

Fremont Street is the quintessential classic Las Vegas, with shimmering light-adorned awnings, cramped smoky gaming quarters, and throngs of onlookers. Everything seems a bit closer here. Fremont Street's attendance has understandably gone downhill since the popularization of strip resorts, but it has been re-invented several times over. Today the 2-block road is closed to automobile traffic, and a sun-blocking canopy (great for hot days) is high above the street.

OFF-STRIP

And then there are the resorts outside of the main area. And with Nevada's liberal casino laws, there are many, all over the place. Drive on a main road, in any direction, and you're sure to come across a large resort complex. Of course, this is not limited to the Las Vegas area; but this book will focus only on nearby off-strip resorts.

WHAT TO LOOK FOR

Make no mistake about it: there are so many resorts in such a small area, that the task of choosing one might seem daunting. With so many resort choices both on the strip and off the strip, how does one choose where to stay? While the resorts vary on some key points, they are largely similar in the amenities they may offer.

PRICE

Most people start to look at accommodations based on their price; which can vary significantly from resort to resort. Cheap resorts can be *really* cheap, but expensive ones can start at hundreds of dollars per night. Keep in mind, however, that you get what you pay for – don't expect five-star service at a three-star resort.

SIZE

Las Vegas is the king of the mega-resort, and this comes down to three basic things: number of guest rooms, casino size, and number of attractions on-site. Any guest room count greater than 3,000 is truly gargantuan, and several area resorts even have thousands more than that.

CASINO

For those interested in gambling, a large casino can be impressive but very daunting. For the most part, larger casino floors don't tend to have different games, but rather more of the same games. Therefore, a 60,000 square foot casino probably has the same kinds of games as a 100,000+ square foot casino, just on a smaller scale.

Casino loyalty programs are also popular reasons to choose a particular resort. If somebody has complimentary bonuses at a particular hotel or hotel chain, they may wish to visit that casino.

FOOD

Las Vegas is known for having many eating choices. A vast majority of on-strip resorts have several (oftentimes dozens of) dining choices, running the gamut from buffet or cafeteria to upscale fine cuisine. Though there are a few restaurants in Las Vegas worthy of resort-hopping, visitors who choose to dine exclusively on-site will likely find quite a vast and fine selection.

POOL / FITNESS

Las Vegas is world-famous for its lavish pool and fitness facilities. Whereas some resorts have small and intimate pools, others have sprawling waterparks, slides, wave pools, lazy rivers, fountains, poolside bars, cabanas for rent, massive fitness and massage centers, and much more. Quality pool and fitness facilities rank as one of the top reasons to choose a particular Las Vegas resort.

SHOWS

The stage shows of Las Vegas are known for their very specific, eclectic style. Most of the major resorts host at least one live show, but a few do not have any. However, it is not necessary, nor popular, to stay at the resort that houses the show you wish to see. Rather, you are free to make that decision after you arrive in Las Vegas (assuming tickets are still available).

ATTRACTIONS

Each resort has something about it that makes it unique. In many cases, the theme of the resort will translate into some kind of attraction; be it an on-property museum, roller coaster, video arcade, or other such specialty.

Resorts: South Strip

In the late 1950s and 1960s, hotels in the south strip area were thought to be "too out of the way" for any real business. However, Las Vegas has expanded southward in leaps and bounds, and the early 1990s saw an incredible boom in south strip resort expansion. The entirety of the strip today stretches about four miles.

The resorts at the southern end of the strip are closest to the airport and are nowadays among the most famous and largest resorts in America. Many of the biggest names are here – Luxor, MGM Grand, and Bellagio - all gracing this section of the "New Las Vegas". This is where many of the newest mega-resorts are located.

Ironically, these resorts, and indeed most of the strip itself, are not even technically in the City of Las Vegas. They are instead located on unincorporated Clark County land under the jurisdiction of "Paradise". Of course, for all intents and purposes, everything in the valley is Las Vegas.

WORLD'S LARGEST HOTELS

The south strip is home to several of the world's largest hotels, including Luxor, Mandalay Bay, and the largest single-building hotel in the world, MGM Grand. Each of these feature well over 4,000 guest rooms each. So it is no surprise that the south strip stands out among the Vegas resort crowd – if you're looking for big, you're in the right place.

AMERICA'S BUSIEST INTERSECTION

On the southern end of the strip was a once-unassuming intersection of Las Vegas Boulevard and Tropicana Avenue. Formerly occupied only by the Tropicana Resort & Casino, today the four corners of the intersection contain four of the biggest hotels in the world: Tropicana, MGM Grand, New York New York, and Excalibur. Tropicana Avenue also happens to be a main thoroughfare connecting the strip to McCarran Airport. With over 12,000 hotel rooms only a few steps away from each other, today this once-barren intersection has become the *busiest intersection in America*.

It is so busy, in fact, that pedestrian traffic is not allowed. Instead, those wishing to cross the street must do so on a series of overpasses connecting the four resorts. Other intersections are following this trend up the strip. The overpasses allow continuous flow of pedestrian traffic; they are generally accessible either directly from the resort, or on street level by an elevator or escalator.

A PARADISE OF POOLS
South Strip resorts are known for their sprawling swimming pool areas. In fact, many of them have graduated beyond a mere pool to complete water playlands with slides, lazy rivers, waterfalls, and even lush shady landscaping – startlingly tropical oases in the otherwise barren desert. For visitors intending to spend much of their Vegas days swimming, sunning, and sipping drinks poolside, a south strip resort is the place to be.

MANDALAY BAY [MUST SEE]

(3950 Las Vegas Blvd ☎ 702.632.7777 ⌂ mandalaybay.com) Mandalay Bay made its debut on the southern end of the Las Vegas Strip in March of 1999. It is currently owned by the MGM Mirage resort group, bought up as a bulk purchase from the Mandalay Bay Resort Group (formerly Circus Circus Enterprises). Prior to opening, the land was no stranger to casino resorts. From 1955 to 1996, it was the home of the Hacienda Resort. In a widely advertised and televised event, the resort was demol-

ished on New Years Eve 1996. A mere three years later, the glistening, towering Mandalay Bay opened its doors.

Mandalay Bay takes its name from a city in Myanmar, in Southeast Asia. As such, the running theme of Mandalay Bay is Southeast Asia. Though some of the restaurants and attractions are derived from other parts of Asia (China, for example), the décor attempts to stick with the Southeast Asian theme. The gleaming gold façade that covers the exterior of the building complex, is however, exclusively Vegas.

ACCOMMODATIONS
Mandalay Bay boasts an impressive 3,300+ rooms, making it one of the largest hotels in Las Vegas. Most of the rooms are in the main hotel, but a good third (over 1,000) were added as recently as 2004 in a new tower called **THEHotel at Mandalay Bay**. More expensive (and more luxurious) than the original hotel, this newer addition is an entirely separate tower from the much larger three-winged main hotel. However, the two are connected in such a way as to allow easier access between them on the lower levels.

CASINO
The casino at Mandalay Bay totals about 135,000 square feet of all the latest table and slot games. Exotic trees, flowing water, and lush interior landscaping distinguish the casino floor amidst the endless rows of games and tables. Of course, all the favorites are represented; craps, poker, slots, baccarat, and sports book betting.

MANDALAY BEACH [MUST SEE]
(☞ *Swimming Pools*) Unofficially the Crown Jewel of Las Vegas pools, the Mandalay Beach environment at Mandalay Bay is regularly voted as the best pool in Las Vegas – a highly distin-

guished honor, as there are many great resort pools along the strip.

Mandalay Beach goes well beyond a simple pool. In fact, the entire 11-acre outdoor complex has three pools, a wave pool complete with sandy beach, three Jacuzzis, and a lazy river. One could easily spend an entire vacation just enjoying this mammoth environment lushly decorated with tropical trees and foliage.

Additionally, the complex features two restaurants, a bar, a beach gear and sundries shop, and rentable cabanas. Plus, an outdoor concert venue features occasional live performances. Also within the complex is **Spa Mandalay**, which includes a fitness and massage center.

RESTAURANTS

Mandalay Bay has a selection of upscale and casual restaurants with many food options. **Aureole** features contemporary American food. **Mix**, a fusion of international cuisine, is located on the top of THEHotel and features great views of Las Vegas. **Fleur de Lys** serves fine French food. The restaurant **rm** serves a variety of seafood. **China Grill** features a mix of Chinese and other Asian-inspired foods. Wolfgang Puck's **Trattoria Del Lupo** specializes in Italian food. **Rumjungle** is a mix of restaurant and club with a tropical island menu. **Burger Bar** offers custom-built hamburgers.

The **Bay Side Buffet** overlooks the Mandalay Beach area and serves breakfast, lunch, and dinner. Also overlooking the pool area is **Raffles Café**, which serves casual food all day and all night.

MANDALAY PLACE

(☞ *Shopping*) The walkway connecting Mandalay Bay to Luxor features over 40 smaller shops and eateries, predominantly popular names including **Urban Outfitters** and **Nike**. It is a relaxing place to stroll and shop, and is an especially attractive way to travel between resorts, out of the desert heat.

SHARK REEF
(☞ *Natural Encounters*) Not only is Mandalay Bay home to Shark Reef, an aquarium in the middle of the desert, it is in fact the largest watery attraction of its kind. Visitors can walk through several different exotic environments, admiring indigenous tropical fish, amphibians, and reptiles. The heart and centerpiece of Shark Reef, however, is the final attraction. After walking through an underwater glass tunnel, visitors will find themselves in the ruined hull of a sunken ship. All around, in about two million gallons of water, different types of sharks, fish and sea turtles swim in the peaceful, mesmerizing environment. An audioguide of all exhibits is included with admission. ($$)

HOUSE OF BLUES
(☞ *Live Shows* ♪ *hob.com*) Mandalay Bay's House of Blues facility is primarily a restaurant and entertainment facility. The venue itself can accommodate about 1,800 audience members and performances vary depending on entertainment schedules. Ticket must be purchased in advance for the shows. Contact the box office or the hotel for more information. As is standard with House of Blues, the on-site **House of Blues Restaurant** features upscale Creole cuisine.

MONORAIL TO NEARBY RESORTS
As several of the neighboring resorts share ownership, access to a few of them north of Mandalay Bay is provided by a complimentary monorail system. Visitors can access the Excalibur and Luxor resorts via this monorail. Transferring may be required, but the entire trip can take about ten minutes, including wait time.

BUSINESS AND CONVENTION SERVICES

One of the largest convention spaces in the world is housed at Mandalay Bay. At about 1.8 million square feet, it is also the largest convention space along the Las Vegas Strip. A part of the center features a 100,000-square-foot ballroom; the largest pillar-free ballroom in the United States. Standard commercial services are also on-site, including a well-equipped business center. Additionally, Internet connections for laptops may be available in some of the rooms.

THE FOUR SEASONS

(☎ 800.819.5053 ↺ fourseasons.com) Cleverly contained within certain floors of the Mandalay Bay resort complex is a AAA Five Star Diamond hotel: **The Four Seasons Hotel Las Vegas**. Though located within the Mandalay Bay tower, the 424-room hotel has its own elevator, its own **spa** and **pool**, its own **dining** and **room service** options, and is basically a separate entity from the rest of the complex. Plus, since it is located on the upper levels, the views of the strip are spectacular. There is no casino within the Four Seasons, though guests have easy access to Mandalay Bay's sprawling casino floor. Reservations for the Four Seasons must be made separately.

LUXOR [MUST SEE]

(3900 Las Vegas Blvd ☎ 702.262.4102 ↺ luxor.com) Almost every resort along the Las Vegas strip is unique and striking in its own way, but few of them ever become truly recognizable staples of the Las Vegas skyline. Mandalay Bay (which is owned, like Luxor, by MGM Mirage), for example, is indeed a unique and noticeable resort, but its boxy hotel tower design does little to distinguish it. On the other hand, the neighboring Luxor is in-

stantly recognizable. By day, the massive sleek black pyramid dominates its surroundings while at night, its famed beam of light shot from the pyramid's apex can be seen from hundreds of miles around.

Luxor opened in October of 1993. It is one of the best-known designs of architect Veldon Simpson, who also designed the MGM Grand and Excalibur resorts. For Luxor, the theme of ancient Egypt is used, but with a number of contemporary twists. The sleek black pyramid is the centerpiece with the Great Sphinx of Giza serving as the entryway. Luxor also serves a place in history as one of the first fully-themed resorts in Las Vegas. Ironically, the town of Luxor (formerly Thebes), in Egypt, from which the hotel got its name, does not contain a single pyramid.

ACCOMMODATIONS

The hotel's rooms are divided into two sections, the pyramid and the tower, both of which contain about half of the 4,400+ rooms on the premises. Unlike the tower rooms, which have a standard hotel layout, the rooms of the pyramid are aligned along the walls of the inside. They are all angled inward to create a great atrium which houses much of the resort's activity.

To transport guests to their pyramid rooms, they ride not an elevator, but an "inclinator", which travels along the inner wall at a 39-degree angle. These rooms, as would be expected, have walls which are slightly angled; however, the angles do not greatly interfere with the room size. A wide array of suites is also available.

CASINO

Luxor's casino is located predominantly within the pyramid. It is about 120,000 square feet and features favorite slot and table games. It is a large, good mid-level casino, with a poker room and medium-sized sports book. Much of its decorative features are of the same ticky-tacky Egyptian style that make up the resort's other areas.

RESTAURANTS
The crown of Luxor's restaurants is the **Luxor Steakhouse**, a fine dining establishment which features intimate wood paneling, and a selection of steaks and wine. **Fusia**, both an upscale restaurant and lounge, has an eclectic mix of foods in an open environment.

More casually, the **Pyramid Café** and **Food Court** offer faster food for quicker eats. The resident buffet is the **Pharaoh's Pheast Buffet**, which serves casual international cuisine for breakfast, lunch and dinner.

POOL AND SPA
(☞ *Swimming Pools*) Vaguely reminiscent of a desert oasis, Luxor features a five-acre outdoor pool area with several different heated pools and Jacuzzis. It is small for a South Strip pool, but very pretty and generally spacious. Food and drinks are available poolside.

Overlooking the pool area is **Oasis Spa**, which features standard services for men and women, including massages and fitness facilities. Plus, it is open 24 hours a day.

SHOPPING
Retail stores at Luxor focus on gift-type items and sundries. The Treasure Chamber, of note, sells antiquities with an Egyptian theme, as well as educational materials. Shoppers have easy access to **Mandalay Place**, with over 40 shops, that connects Luxor to Mandalay Bay via an indoor walkway.

MONORAIL TO NEARBY RESORTS

A local resort monorail located just outside of Luxor can take visitors either south to Mandalay Bay, or north to Excalibur. The monorail is free and is a fairly simple way to navigate between these resorts.

LUXOR'S LIGHT

(☞ *Free Shows*) At night, the Las Vegas skyline lights up with a million twinkles, calling out for tourists to visit the various properties. However, no light – not in Las Vegas, not in the United States, not in the *entire world* – is as bright as the one on the apex of Luxor's pyramid. The beam points directly upwards, and can be seen from the sky as far away as Los Angeles (about 275 miles away). This light, other than to attract people and scores of desert moths, is practically useless. However, it does add to Luxor's status as a brilliant example of postmodern architecture.

KING TUT MUSEUM

(☞ *Museums*) Befitting of a resort inspired by Ancient Egypt is a museum of ancient artifacts. However, the King Tut Museum is much more than that. The exhibit actually features an authentic replica of King Tutankhamun's tomb largely as it looked when discovered in 1922 by Howard Carter. The rooms are replicated in exact scale, and the artifacts were recreated with great care. Visitors can walk through the "tomb" and explore the recreated remains of one of history's most famous rulers.

IMAX EXPERIENCES

(☞ *Rides and Amusements*) Luxor features a complete IMAX movie experience center. Featured on the super big screen is a regular rotation of documentary-style films in the IMAX tradition. There are generally several shows from which visitors may choose on any given day.

Additionally, Luxor features several "motion theater" rides. On these unique attractions, visitors sit in the chairs of the theater while they are jostled around in conjunction with the motions on the screen.

EXCALIBUR

(3850 Las Vegas Blvd ☏ 702.597.7777 ↗ excalibur.com) Excalibur, the magic sword pulled from the stone by Arthur, is a symbol for medieval legend and folklore. On the Las Vegas strip, the sword idea is used as stepping stone into the medieval-themed resort of the same name. The centerpiece of the resort is a castle, complete with flying buttresses and jutting towers. It is a castle based on the mythology, not on the history.

Now part of the vast array of MGM Mirage establishments (formerly part of the Mandalay Bay Group), Excalibur is one of the oldest of the "new" Las Vegas resorts, with an opening in June of 1990. The castle itself is bright and shiny, with lots of color. However, it is relatively hidden and dwarfed by the resort's neighboring hotel towers, which house much of the rooms.

ACCOMMODATIONS
Excalibur has about 4,000 rooms and various levels of suites, making it one of the largest in Las Vegas. It is also known as one of the more affordable major resorts along the south strip area, which makes it particularly popular with families. The rooms are housed in neighboring towers with easy access to the activity within the castle.

CASINO
Excalibur's casino is located directly within the castle's "gates", and totals about 100,000 square feet. The casino features all kinds of popular slot machines, video poker, and table games.

LAS VEGAS

Additionally, the casino at Excalibur has a poker room and a sports book.

RESTAURANTS
The **Steak House at Camelot** is an upscale dining experience featuring fresh beef and seafood. **Sir Galahad's** also specializes in various cuts of meat, within a dining room reminiscent of a medieval banquet hall.

The **Regale Italian Eatery** is suitable for families with moderately-priced Italian cuisine, such as pasta and lasagna. The **Sherwood Forest Café** and **Village Food Court** offer fast food options. The **Round Table Buffet** is relatively inexpensive and features an eclectic mix of food served buffet-style.

CASTLE WALK
(☞ *Shopping*) Most of Excalibur's shops are along Castle Walk. There are over 15 shops in the area, and many of them feature unique medieval-themed merchandise and gifts, holiday decorations, and even children's costumes and accessories.

FANTASY FAIRE MIDWAY
(☞ *Rides and Amusements*) The fairy tale setting of Excalibur is well-suited for one of the larger video arcades in a Las Vegas resort – the Fantasy Faire Midway. Located beneath the main casino floor, the midway is filled with the latest arcade and redemption games, and is suited for families and those too young to gamble. **Merlin's Magic Motion Machine**, a simulator-type ride with several different choices of movie, is also part of the midway. ($)

MONORAIL TO NEARBY RESORTS
As part of the MGM Mirage / Mandalay Bay Resort group, a complimentary monorail is available to connect visitors to the

neighboring Luxor and Mandalay Bay resorts. The total monorail trip, including wait time, is generally around 10 minutes.

POOL AND SPA
(☞ *Swimming Pools*) Excalibur has an outdoor pool section, which features two swimming pools and a Jacuzzi. The decorative rocks and trees are derivative of the fairy tale countryside. It includes waterfalls and some small water activities. A small snack bar serves drinks and light fare.

The area gets the job done on a very basic level – considering it was one of the first resorts in Las Vegas with a major family pool facility. Excalibur also has a spa and fitness facility, the **Royal Treatment Spa**, which overlooks the pool.

TROPICANA

(3801 Las Vegas Blvd ☎ 702.739.2222 ⁂ tropicanalv.com) As the only resort in the south strip area to survive into the modern age, the Tropicana has been a permanent fixture in Las Vegas since its opening in 1957. It is a glitzy, glamorous reminder of the Las Vegas of old. It has kept its classic tropical theme as well as its 1960s architecture and design. It is owned by the Columbia Sussex Corporation, which operates several casino resorts, including the Tropicana resort in Atlantic City, New Jersey. Though it sits on 35 acres of land, the resort has one of the smaller capacities and casino floors of the strip resorts.

But it is still classic Las Vegas; its glamorous past echoed in Hollywood - James Bond himself recommends it: in *Diamonds are Forever*, he says "I hear the hotel Tropicana is quite comfortable."

ACCOMMODATIONS
Tropicana is the smallest major resort in the southern section of the Las Vegas strip. With only about 1,600 rooms, it does not

attract the crowds of some of the newer, larger resorts of the area. However, its old-school atmosphere of glamour and charm would not bode as well in a larger hotel, so Tropicana fits its purpose nicely.

CASINO
The casino floor contains all the standard slots, video, and table games, but it is only about 60,000 square feet – rather small for a Las Vegas casino, particularly for one located in the south strip area. Nonetheless, it has what most gamers would be looking for, including a high-limit area, a race & sports book, and a poker room.

POOL
(☞ *Swimming Pools)* Tropicana's pool complex is surprisingly large compared to the smaller size of the resort itself. It features a large (seasonal) outdoor pool, a portion of which is indoors and opened year-round, and a pool designed for adults only (no shouting, splashing children). Like most Las Vegas pools, it has a tropical theme – only *this* time, the theme fits in well with the rest of the resort.

A unique feature of the complex is a **swim-up blackjack** area and bar, which allows players to play real blackjack, and drink real alcohol, right in the pool area! This feature is only open in the summertime.

For more relaxation and/or fitness, **Spa Tropicana** is available with a full range of fitness equipment, massages for men and women (and couples), and a full range of professional massage services and products.

RESTAURANTS
Tropicana's restaurants are predominantly casual. **Pietro's**, the most upscale restaurant at Tropicana, features a mixture of con-

tinental food choices. **The Savannah Steakhouse** specializes in finer meats, and **Mizuno's** adds a Japanese flair to the grill. The **Tuscany Italian Café** has standard Italian food, such as pasta and pizza.

Calypso's and **Legends Deli** offer lighter food choices. Serving breakfast, lunch, and dinner, the **Island Buffet** also offers views of Tropicana's tropical garden area.

THE COMEDY STOP
What began at the Atlantic City Tropicana sprang up in Las Vegas in 1992. The Comedy Stop is a small venue, which features a regular rotation of up-and-coming comics. Shows rotate depending on available performers. Schedules are available from the box office. ($$)

MGM GRAND [MUST SEE]

(3799 Las Vegas Blvd ☎ 702.891.7777 🖰 mgmgrand.com) Well, this is it; the biggest of the big. Las Vegas is host to 8 out of the 10 largest hotels in the world, and MGM Grand tops the list, in terms of room count, as the *largest single-building hotel in the world*. And what's even more impressive, it is not uncommon for all 5,000+ guest rooms to be completely booked.

MGM Grand's stance on whether or not to bill the resort as a single massive hotel or as several smaller sections has shifted back and forth since its opening in 1993. Regardless, however, this is one gargantuan place that may require more than your basic roadmap to navigate properly and efficiently.

What stands today was not the first incarnation of the MGM Grand. Kirk Kerkorian, already with an established presence on the strip and new owner of Metro-Goldwyn-Mayer, purchased 43 acres of land to build the then largest hotel in the world (with about 2,000 guest rooms); the MGM Grand. The resort opened in 1973 with great success despite the struggling MGM movie studio.

On record as the worst disaster in Las Vegas history, on November 21, 1980, a fire that started in one of the restaurants spread throughout the hotel. It killed 87 people (mostly hotel guests) and injured 784 others; it also damaged much of the building. Although it re-opened only 8 months later, the hotel suffered tremendously. In 1986 they sold the property to Bally's, and the hotel became Bally's Las Vegas. It looked like the end of the MGM Grand legacy.

But all was not lost. In 1990 the Marina Hotel was purchased by Kerkorian about a mile south of the old MGM (now Bally's). The hotel was demolished and in December 1993 the new MGM Grand opened its doors – once again – as the largest hotel in the world. Originally designed to be a Wizard of Oz-themed resort, it was outfitted with Oz memorabilia, and an Emerald City motif. It first opened with the main entryway of a cartoonish lion; visitors walked into the lion's mouth to reach the resort. However, this was re-designed to a lion statue, as some cultures thought the mouth of a lion represented bad luck.

To attract families – the latest Las Vegas trend – the resort even featured the MGM Grand Adventures theme park right in the backyard. The park did little business, however, and it closed in 2000, eventually replaced by a luxury condominium section called "The Residences". Eventually, the entire theme of the resort was re-designed to Art Deco Hollywood.

Today, the MGM Grand has matured to be more a reflection of Hollywood's golden age. The Wizard of Oz is all but eliminated, replaced by a classical Art Deco ambience. It has less of the family attractiveness than was first intended, but it still remains one of the most comprehensive destinations in Las Vegas.

ACCOMMODATIONS

MGM Grand is indeed the largest single-building hotel in the world, and it shows. It houses about 5,030 rooms and suites, most of which are non-smoking. Though the hotel does have several different "towers", they are used mostly for room organization, since they are all interconnected to each other, at least at ground level.

Some of the best guest rooms in Las Vegas are at the MGM Grand; namely, their **Skylofts**. On the top two floors of the building are a series of luxury suites that may just as well be their own hotel. These upscale and pricey quarters are 1-3 bedrooms, which feature contemporary styling and unbeatable views of the Las Vegas skyline. Additionally, the **Residences at MGM Grand** allow true Vegas-lovers to purchase their own condominium on MGM property.

Of course, big resort-hotels inherently have unavoidable flaws. First of all, finding one's room through a network of casino space, entertainment space, and elevators poses an additional challenge. The resort is organized as best it can, but there are limits. Many times it can take as much as 10 minutes to reach your room, and that's if the elevators are waiting for you. Still, with the grand size comes all the greatness of a resort: tons of activity all hours of the day, great attractions and top-notch service.

One nice unique feature of the MGM Grand: **Airport Check-In**. McCarran International Airport has a desk that allows travelers to check-in to their room before they even arrive at the hotel. They were the first hotel to offer this unique service.

CASINO

MGM Grand's casino, measuring a whopping 171,000 square feet, is the largest in Las Vegas and very easy to get lost in. It is not a contiguous casino floor, but rather cleverly divided up into several different sections, probably for easier navigation. All the popular slots and table games are spread out across the floor, including a poker area and race & sports book.

RESTAURANTS

Being the largest hotel in Las Vegas, it is no surprise that MGM Grand has a truly grand amount of dining possibilities, to match many tastes and budgets. The resort also hosts more than its share of celebrity chefs and restaurants.

Fine dining is a specialty here. French chef Joël Robuchon has **Joël Robuchon at the Mansion** and **L'Atelier de Joël Robuchon -** two very upscale French restaurants with the finest foods (the latter is a bit more casual, and features a unique kitchen-centic setup).

Craftsteak, a NYC import, is a fine dining steakhouse with choice meat cuts, and **Nobhill** has food inspired by (and direct from) San Francisco. **Fiamma**, from SoHo in New York, features Italian dishes. **Shibuya** offers fine Japanese dining, and **Pearl** features Chinese-inspired dishes. **Seablue** serves all kinds of seafood dishes, including fish and shellfish served in a variety of ways.

For more casual eating options, Emeril Lagasse heads **Emeril's,** a more casual venue with New Orleans specialties. **Diego** features an array of Mexican food. The **Wolfgang Puck Bar & Grill** has the eclectic Californian-based dishes that have made his style so famous.

For the most casual, MGM Grand has the **Stage Deli** and **Studio Café**. Dine in a rainforest at the **Rainforest Café**. Of course, the large **MGM Grand Buffet** has all the comforts of one Las Vegas' biggest and best buffets.

GRAND POOL
(☞ *Swimming Pools*) A gargantuan hotel deserves a gargantuan pool complex, and although MGM Grand's aquatic activities are basic, there is just so much of it. Within the **Grand Pool Complex**, five swimming pools, three whirlpools, a lazy river, waterfalls, and lots of lounge chairs mean that even on the busiest days there will be room on the patio. During slower times or off-season, some of the pools may be closed, but there will generally always be at least one open. Also, there is a beach store and rental facility, and drinks may be purchased at the nearby bar area. Also available is the **Grand Spa**, with a wide range of massage and spa services, as well as fitness equipment.

LION HABITAT
(☞ *Natural Encounters*) As Metro-Goldwyn-Mayer's logo contains a lion (the logo lion's name is "Leo"), it seems only befitting that one of MGM Grand's most popular attractions is its Lion Habitat. Located just off the casino floor (good luck finding it without a map!), the free-admission habitat is an indoor glass-enclosed environment where a regular rotation of live lions are on display. The habitat is designed naturalistically and visitors can get a close and personal view of the big cats. Zoologists and lion caretakers are frequently on hand to answer questions.

The lions themselves are purportedly well taken care of – they actually live on a ranch about 12 miles outside of town, where they spend most of their time being pampered.

SHOWS AND VENUES
(☞ *Live Shows*) MGM Grand offers two major event centers, the **Grand Garden Arena** and the **Hollywood Theatre**. The Grand Garden Arena is a massive event center that holds all kinds of special events, such as concerts and – most notably – boxing tournaments. It is one of the major venues in Las Vegas,

with many events televised on sporting and other networks. On a smaller scale, the 740-seat Hollywood Theatre shows additional headlining entertainment, such as musical groups and comedians. Contact the hotel for show information.

MGM Grand is also host to the resident Cirque Du Soleil show **KÀ**. The show, suitable for adults and families with older children, features acrobatics, comedy, and other kinds of odd and unique stunts and acts, combined with the unique artistic flair that has made this chain of shows so popular. For adults, direct from Crazy Horse in Paris is **La Femme**. This unique show features nude female dancers in artistic and sensual acts of theater. Children under 18 are not admitted to this show; it is not at all appropriate for young ones.

NEW YORK - NEW YORK

(3790 Las Vegas Blvd ☎ 702.740.6969 ⓗ nynyhotelcasino.com) It is the resort that never sleeps! It's the Big Apple that grows in the middle of the desert!

One of the most brilliantly tacky resorts along the Las Vegas Strip is unquestionably New York – New York. The resort's façade replicates famous buildings of the New York City skyline, albeit scaled down and squished together. Miniature Statue of Liberty and Brooklyn Bridge replicas are nearby, almost like movie props. Yet despite its tack and mess of tinselly eye candy, it has a mess of people, a flurry of activity and noise, and is perfectly indicative of the real Big Apple on the other side of the continent.

The interior of the resort is just as the outside would predict – different parts are labeled after different areas within New York City; Central Park, Greenwich Village, along with many famous landmarks scattered around.

With an opening in January 1997, New York – New York was a joint venture between MGM Grand and Primm Valley Resorts. Eventually, both companies would be absorbed into the vast MGM Mirage roster.

ACCOMMODATIONS
New York – New York, with 2,000 guest rooms, is dwarfed by its bigger brother across the street, the MGM Grand. However, the cluttered design scheme makes this rather difficult to notice. The resort sticks out on the strip like a very tinselly sore thumb, and despite its smaller size, people strolling the strip seem to be naturally drawn to this unique place – unique, even for Vegas. Nonetheless, within the guest rooms are all the comforts of the largest resorts in the world – including standard rooms and suites.

CASINO
The modest (by Vegas standards) 84,000 square-foot casino has a basic Central Park theme, mixed in with other famous city landmarks. The space includes all the standard table games and slot machines, as well as a smaller race & sports book.

RESTAURANTS
Understandably, New York – New York reflects a definitive New York homage in its dining choices. The choices are predominately casual.

Gallagher's Steakhouse is the resident fine dining option, offering choice meats. Other, more casual, choices include **America** (American), **Gonzalez y Gonzalez** (Mexican), **Chin Chin Café** (Chinese), and **Il Fornaio** (Italian). Sports fans will enjoy the greasy foods and televised sports of the **ESPN Zone**.

The resort has several popular bars as well. **Coyote Ugly**, based on the movie and New York City bar of the same name, features female waitstaff dancing on the bar. There is **The Big**

Apple Bar and **Nine Fine Irishmen**, both of which draw large crowds in the evenings.

PARK AVENUE POOLSIDE

(☞ Swimming Pools) Largely surrounded by the Manhattan Express roller coaster, New York-New York's outdoor pool complex, Park Avenue Poolside, is small by Las Vegas standards. There is only one large pool and several smaller Jacuzzis. While the décor and service are vaguely reminiscent of a Park Avenue country club, and there are drink and other personalized services to boot, the space is indeed noticeably small. However, it is landscaped well, with waterfalls and a pleasing New York-meets-tropics layout.

Also available is a **Spa** services center, with fitness equipment, massage center, and other relaxing possibilities.

MANHATTAN EXPRESS

(☞ Rides and Amusements) A popular and highly exposed remnant of a recent Las Vegas attempt to attract more families, Manhattan Express is a 67-mile-per-hour roller coaster. Painted like a New York City taxicab, it twists and turns around the interior and exterior of the resort, and performs all the standard "mega-coaster" moves, like loops and barrel rolls. It even takes a spin outside, so Las Vegas Boulevard passers-by can see (and hear) the coaster in action. Riding the roller coaster is expensive, but there may be an "unlimited" pass available, allowing visitors to ride all day for one price.

Also near the roller coaster loading bay is the **Coney Island** arcade and amusement center, which features popular arcade and redemption games.

MONTE CARLO

(3770 Las Vegas Blvd ☎ 702.730.7777 ⌁ montecarlo.com) In Monaco, along the Mediterranean Sea, is one of Europe's richest and most popular luxury tourist destinations: Monte Carlo. While this area (not an independent city, more of a district within the tiny 2-square-kilometer principality of Monaco) offers many perks for visitors, its most popular attraction is the lavish and luxurious Place du Casino; one of the world's most famous and wealthiest modern gambling complexes.

In Las Vegas, the goal of creating the Monte Carlo was to emulate the opulence of the famous Monaco district, but with less impact on the wallet. In fact, Monte Carlo has been compared to Bellagio as its more affordable but slightly less luxurious neighbor.

As a joint venture between Mirage Resorts and Circus Circus, it opened to the public in June 1996. Eventually it was absorbed into the MGM Mirage series of resorts. While the Monte Carlo theme has more or less evolved into an Old European ambience, it has that classic museum-like feel of the finest houses and resorts in the world. Of course, this is still Vegas, so it is all a beautiful, hollow façade. It has a running theme of classic "top-hat magic" that runs through its gift shops and restaurants, thanks in part to its headlining showman, Lance Burton.

ACCOMMODATIONS

With just over 3,000 rooms, Monte Carlo clocks in as one of the "smallest of the biggest" hotels in the world. Combined with the glamorous European splendor yet more affordable price tag, Monte Carlo is a very popular resort. Its subdued yet classic appeal is a sharp contrast to the most in-your-face showiness of the neighboring New York-New York. Families also choose to stay at

Monte Carlo, in addition to its affordability, because of its more kid-friendly activities.

CASINO
The casino at Monte Carlo is about 90,000 square feet. It is a basic casino floor, without much theme, but the standards are all here; slot and table games, a poker room, and a particularly well-designed midsized race and sports book. It is also an overall relatively clean and affordable casino, on par with the rest of the resort.

RESTAURANTS
Monte Carlo has a small variety of dining choices. **Blackstone's Steakhouse**, named for the magician, features meat and fish in a fine dining environment. The resort is home to one of the several **Andre's** in Las Vegas, a fine French restaurant known for being one of the city's best. **Dragon Noodle** serves moderately-priced Asian food, and **Market City Cafe** features Italian dishes. The resort also has a **Buffet**, serving continental and international foods for all meals of the day.

POOL
(☞ *Swimming Pools*) Monte Carlo's pool is nothing to breeze past; it is full of all kinds of watery wonders perfect for kids, families, and adults alike. In addition to the regular pools, the outdoor area features a kiddie pool, a wave pool (historically the *first one* on the Las Vegas strip) and a lazy river. The tropical country club ambience is accented with tropical trees, waterfalls, and other foliage designed to help visitors forget that they're in the middle of the desert.

Nearby is also a fully-equipped **tennis facility**, which features three outdoor courts, racket and equipment rentals (such as ball machines). The courts are lit for night-time play. Also available is a **spa** and **fitness** facility, with all kinds of massage services and fitness equipment, as well as a **hair salon**.

STREET OF DREAMS
(☞ *Shopping)* Stroll down the Monte Carlo shopping and dining promenade, Street of Dreams, which features a collection of upscale shops and eateries. Of particular note is the **Backstreet Arcade**, which features a nice selection of video and redemption games.

ALADDIN / PLANET HOLLYWOOD

(3667 Las Vegas Blvd ☏ 702.785.5066 ⌘ aladdincasino.com) The Aladdin Resort is changing to become the Planet Hollywood Resort and Casino. Contact the resort for the most current information. As a resort town constantly re-inventing itself, the complex of Aladdin is the perfect example of a casino that can't quite seem to stay afloat. While such favorites as Tropicana, Golden Nugget, and Caesars have been around for years, others need to shift and adjust, try and fail and try again. Aladdin is such a place. As the name suggests, Aladdin's theme is that of Middle Eastern mystique, with more than a hint of "desert oasis" and "Arabian Nights" built in.

The resort's first of several short-lived incarnations was as *Tally-Ho* in 1963. However, the resort was renamed *King's Crown* only a year later. In 1966, it was sold yet again, given major renovations, and re-named *Aladdin*. The "new" resort was made famous by hosting Elvis Presley's wedding to Priscilla. Finally as it stood, the *Aladdin* resort was a success. But in 1998 the resort was destroyed and the land was cleared to make way for a bigger, better *Aladdin*, which opened in 2000. However, the resort still struggled and it was sold to Planet Hollywood and Starwood Resorts in 2003. The transition into **Planet Hollywood Resort & Casino** is slated to be a gradual one.

In the interim between the branding of the resort as Planet Hollywood, major renovations will undoubtedly be underway, and may continue well into the future. During this time, the resort may still function in certain, limited ways. However, *the progress is unpredictable*, though the information contained herein is as accurate as reasonably possible, contact the resort directly for the most up-to-date information.

Will the new Planet Hollywood Resort & Casino be a success? Only time will tell.

ACCOMMODATIONS
As it stands as of this writing, the Aladdin has about 2,600 rooms and suites, with plans to build at least one new tower and a timeshare complex for vacation ownership.

CASINO
The casino is about 100,000 square feet and features all the standard table and slot games. There is also a race & sports book and a poker room on the premises.

POOL
(☞ *Swimming Pools*) The pool area at the Aladdin / Planet Hollywood features two outdoor pools and two Jacuzzis in a desert oasis setting. Drink service may be available poolside, and a nearby bar & grill provides food service.

RESTAURANTS
Top-quality steaks and seafood are available at **Elements**, a fine dining establishment. **Tremezzo** serves classic Italian dishes, while **Bonsai** serves Japanese dishes and features a sushi bar. Quick bites are available at the **Zanzibar Café.** The **Spice Market Buffet** ranks as one of the best in Vegas, serving breakfast, lunch and dinner. Additional dining options are available in

Aladdin's Desert Passage complex. Of note, the Japanese seafood buffet chain, **Todai**, has an outpost here, as does **Max's Café**, which offers unbelievable $3.99 lunch specials and $6.99 dinners. **Cheeseburger Las Vegas** is an offshoot of the popular Hawaiian restaurant, offering their signature burgers.

DESERT PASSAGE
(☞ *Shopping*) A major highlight is the immense, indoor Desert Passage shopping and dining complex, which features over 130 shops in a Middle Eastern marketplace setting. Stores here tend to be more reasonably priced compared to those of neighboring resorts. **BCBG, Eddie Bauer, Victoria's Secret, Urban Outfitters, French connection** and **GAP**, to name only a few, all have stores here. **ABC Stores**, the immensely popular Hawaiian chain, has two locations here, where visitors can stock up on, among other things, bottled water for cheap. In addition to these stores, numerous dining, entertainment and nightlife establishments are all housed within this immense and exciting complex.

THEATRE FOR THE PERFORMING ARTS
(☞ *Live Shows*) Another staple of Aladdin is the Theatre for the Performing Arts. This 7,000-seat venue was the only portion of the resort that survived the demolition in 1998. It was where the first Miss America pageant was held outside of Atlantic City, and it remains one of the largest performance venues in Las Vegas.

BELLAGIO 🔲

(3600 Las Vegas Blvd ☎ 702.693.7111 ⁻❁ bellagio.com) With a location in the near-center of the Las Vegas strip, the Bellagio is famously known to be the most luxurious, most expensive, and most upscale resort in all of Las Vegas. In fact, it is one of the

only properties in Las Vegas that has achieved AAA's most prestigious 5 Star Diamond award. Bellagio takes its Italian flair and likeness from the town of Bellagio on Lake Como in Italy. The tiny town surrounds an inlet of the lake; imitated by Bellagio's own 8-acre lake and surrounding "buildings". Bellagio's lake separates the resort from the rest of the strip. There is nothing understated here; this is a resort that *knows* it is upscale, and does everything it can to make sure everybody else knows it, too.

Bellagio was built by Steve Wynn's Mirage Resorts and opened in October 1998. With a price tag of $1.5 billion, at the time it was the single most expensive hotel ever built. When Wynn sold Mirage Resorts to MGM Grand, the ownership of Bellagio transferred to the newly-created MGM Mirage.

As visitors tour the Bellagio, they will notice that the attractions are entirely upscale. From an art gallery to botanic garden, the Bellagio indeed is the most sophisticated Las Vegas casino-resort. It is also important to note that Bellagio's policy is stricter when it comes to children under age 18, as this is a primarily adult-themed resort.

ACCOMMODATIONS

Bellagio's accommodations and customer service are unsurpassed in the hospitality industry (as proven by the resort's awards). Therefore, guests of this resort will certainly experience ultimate luxury unsurpassed by even the most upscale resorts in Los Angeles or New York. Of course, with all this unsurpassed luxury comes an unsurpassed price tag; on average the Bellagio is also the most expensive casino-resort in Las Vegas.

The rooms at Bellagio run the gamut of regular to super-suites. Views of the strip and the lake are generally the most desirable. The opening of an entirely new tower to Bellagio's already crowded skyline in late 2004 brought the total rooms of the resort to about 3,400. The resort also expanded the spa section and meeting space.

CASINO
Bellagio's beautiful casino floor is as immaculate and expensive as the rest of the resort. It features about 120,000 feet of total casino gaming space featuring popular slot and table games. There is also a poker room, and a large race & sports book.

POOLS & COURTYARDS
Like the rest of the resort, the Bellagio's outdoor pool facility is unsurpassed in terms of design and luxury. With an Italian-Mediterranean feel, the area consists of five different pools surrounded by trees and lush landscaping. Also on the property are spas, cabanas, a pool bar and restaurant, and everything else to make the experience as enjoyable and classy as possible. Plus, the **Pool Café** serves up casual food overlooking the pool area.

There is also a full-service **spa** at Bellagio, with all the latest relaxing massages and treatments available, fitness equipment, a hair salon, and the like.

RESTAURANTS
Dining in Las Vegas doesn't get any classier than this. Food choices at Bellagio are nothing short of exquisite, and with steep price tags to match; some restaurants even offer views of Bellagio's fountain show. Topping the list, direct from New York, is **Le Cirque**, the ultimate in fine French restaurants. Its more casual cousin, **Circo,** featurees the finest Italian food. The famous **Picasso** restaurant allows diners to eat Mediterranean-style food surrounded by actual Pablo Picasso artwork. The **Prime Steakhouse** is consistently named the best steakhouse in Las Vegas by various guides. Chef **Michael Mina**'s restaurant serves primarily seafood dishes. Overlooking the Fountains

of Bellagio, the very romantic **Jasmine** serves the best upscale Chinese food around. **Shintaro** serves Japanese food and features a sushi bar.

Even Bellagio's casual restaurants are really more upscale than casual. **Sensi** features a wide variety of foods and seafood. **Noodles**, **Fix**, and **Olives** are places to relax and dine a bit more casually. **Café Bellagio** overlooks the Conservatory. **The Buffet**, among the most expensive and expansive in Las Vegas, serves a variety of international foods, many cooked to order.

THE FOUNTAINS OF BELLAGIO 🅼🆂

(☞ *Free Shows*) Within the eight acre lake in front of the Bellagio is one of the most wonderful and unique sights in Las Vegas. In fact, the Fountains of Bellagio has become such a staple of the Las Vegas lifestyle that rarely does a recent documentary or narrative film, video or book come out without mentioning it. Yes, this attraction, in many ways, has become indicative of everything Las Vegas stands for: it is an incredible waste, totally useless, yet completely mesmerizing.

The Fountains of Bellagio is an automated water fountain encompassing the breadth of Bellagio's lake that literally dances to the music blasting from seemingly everywhere. The water jets are programmed to spray water in any direction, make water hop around, and move in sync to whatever music (popular or classical) happens to be playing. In the daytime, it is beautiful. At night, however, it is nothing short of spectacular, when the bright lights dance with the water.

The "shows" are each one song long. The performances are regular and frequent; in the evening summertime they can be as little as 5-7 minutes apart. There is always ample viewing space all around the lake.

GALLERY OF FINE ART

(☞ Museums) In keeping with the luxurious nature of this top-quality resort, Bellagio contains within its walls a full-fledged art museum. The Gallery of Fine Art is a complete facility, with rotating exhibits in addition to its permanent collection. The artists that have been showcased within the gallery include Monet, Corot, Van Gogh, Cézanne and Renoir. The hours vary depending upon the season, and a separate fee is required for admission.

BELLAGIO BOTANICAL GARDENS

(☞ Natural Encounters) Within a large glass-roofed atrium near the main entrance to the resort is an indoor garden of sorts, featuring a wide assortment of botany and botanical decorations. There is no admission fee and plenty of opportunities to take photographs of the unique arrangements and artistic creations. All flowers and plants are genuine, and the decorations vary depending on the season. When the lights are dim at night, the flowers are accented by specialized lighting.

More than 100 people work just to maintain this exquisite exhibit. It is open 24 hours a day, seven days a week.

PARIS LAS VEGAS

(3655 Las Vegas Blvd ☏ 702.946.7000 ⏃ parislasvegas.com) As could have easily been expected, the original "City of Lights" has found its way to the *new* City of Lights. It is Paris, Las Vegas style. With the same imitative technique that had made New York-New York a success just a few years prior, Paris' more subdued nature adds a few well-known landmarks to the Las Vegas skyline.

What began as a project by Park Place Entertainment became wholly merged into Caesars Entertainment and, subsequently in 2004, into Harrah's already huge roster of resorts. It was completed in 1999 and features many famous Paris landmarks; namely a 50% scale model of the Eiffel Tower, as well as the Arc De Triomphe and the Montgolfier balloon (the first hot air balloon). But the inside, of course, is strictly Vegas.

ACCOMMODATIONS

Paris' accommodations rival that of many of Las Vegas' larger resorts. With just shy of 3,000 upscale rooms and suites, it is a city in and of itself. The decorations within the rooms tend to be a kind of contemporary French style, with the bright colors indicative of true Vegas delight.

CASINO

Paris Las Vegas' casino floor is about 85,000 square feet; a decent size, and with just enough space to pack in all sorts of the standard table and slot games, including a comprehensive sports book betting center.

The casino here is one of the prettiest in Las Vegas, and deserves particular note. Parts of it are designed to look like the streets of Paris, complete with botany, a sky-painted ceiling and lots of good lighting. One leg of the Eiffel Tower even protrudes through the ceiling of the casino. The edges of the casino look like the facades of Parisian buildings.

POOL AND SPA

(☞ *Swimming Pools)* The three-acre Pool at Paris is on an outdoor rooftop. At the "foot" of the Eiffel Tower (you can actually walk up to it), it features one very large circular pool and several smaller Jacuzzis. There is food and drink service, and sometimes even poolside massages. The pool is not open all year, but it is available *most* of the year. **Du Parc** serves quick and easy food and drinks poolside.

Additionally, the **Spa by Mandara** offers all kinds of expected spa facilities and amenities, included massages, a steam room and fitness center.

RESTAURANTS

Paris Las Vegas's food choices are thoroughly French-inspired; which comes as no surprise. For fine dining: **Mon Ami Gabi** is a traditional fine French experience, and includes an outdoor patio. The **Eiffel Tower Restaurant** offers French food high above the strip. **Ortanique** serves a fusion of French and Caribbean food. **Les Artistes**, serves meat and fish for dinner, prepared numerous ways.

Ah Sin features a unique mix of Asian and Asian-inspired dishes, and has outdoor dining available. Dine in a country setting at **Le Provençal**, featuring South France food. **Le Village Buffet**, in a room styled like a tiny village, prepares buffet-style French and international foods to order. Additionally, the resort is peppered with dessert, bread and pastry shops for instant sweet-tooth gratification and adding considerably to the charming atmosphere.

EIFFEL TOWER EXPERIENCE

(☞ Rides and Amusements) This isn't the real Paris, but this scaled-down replica of the Eiffel Tower sure does its best to simulate the thrilling experience of traveling to the top. The tower is 50 stories high, and the observation deck is located 460 feet above the Las Vegas skyline. Glass elevators take visitors up to the observation deck, where there are many opportunities for Las Vegas photographs. ($)

PARIS CHAPEL

At Paris Las Vegas, a marriage on top of the Eiffel Tower is not only possible, it is much more affordable than its overseas "counterpart"! Paris Las Vegas has several options and packages for wedding ceremonies throughout the resort, including several chapels that can hold anywhere from 30 to 100 guests. The resort staff will assist in planning and carrying out your dream wedding.

LE BOULEVARD

(☞ *Shopping*) The streets of a Paris shopping district, complete with quaint shops and cobblestone streets, are available for your shopping convenience. Of course, in Las Vegas, this means an indoor mall, designed to look outdoors. A sky-painted ceiling, fake store exteriors, realistic "mini-streets" and fake gas lamps all add to the effect of a pleasant Parisian afternoon of shopping. The atmosphere is charming and peaceful, perfect for a break from the bustle of the strip. There are international stores and eateries in the center; dessert shops are particularly popular.

BALLY'S

(3645 Las Vegas Blvd ☎ 702.967.4405 ⌁ ballyslv.com) One would be hard-pressed to find a more well-known resort than Bally's. The Bally's namesake has been stamped on so many things, from video arcades to gaming equipment to fitness clubs. Though the resorts of Bally's are currently owned by Harrah's Corporation, its history in Las Vegas is as diverse as the company itself.

In 1963 the property was host to the *Bonanza Hotel*, and later the *New Bonanza Hotel*. Eventually, the newly-created MGM Grand Corporation acquired the property and re-built the resort. In 1973 the first MGM Grand opened. However, a fire destroyed much of the property in 1980 (killing 87 people), and in

1985 the resort was sold to Bally's Entertainment, when it was re-named *Bally's Grand*, then ultimately *Bally's Las Vegas*.

Bally's was eventually absorbed into Park Place Entertainment, then into Caesars Entertainment, and ultimately into Harrah's. Though the complex is destined to stay on the Las Vegas strip, its future as a Bally's resort brand remains uncertain.

Inside, Bally's is true Las Vegas style all the way, with all that glitter and glamour. Bright lights, neon, wild designs and contemporary flash abound. Basically, the theme of Bally's is modern Las Vegas, in all its tackiness and beauty.

ACCOMMODATIONS

Since the formation of Caesars Entertainment, Bally's resorts have recently become known as the less expensive baby brother of Caesars Palace up the street; rooms are modestly luxurious yet less expensive.

Bally's houses about 2,800 guest rooms and various levels of suites – a decent size even by Las Vegas standards. The original MGM Grand hotel had 2,000 rooms, making it the largest in the world at the time. Bally's expanded the premises with an additional tower in 1994.

CASINO

It is on the casino floor where Bally's tacky Las Vegas theme really shines. Bally's small casino floor is about 67,000 square feet of games, including slot and table games, a poker room, and a race and sports book section with countless televisions depicting the events.

POOL

(☞ *Swimming Pools*) Bally's pool complex is small. It has one large outdoor pool which, at about 12 feet deep, is one of the deepest in Las Vegas. The pool has not been significantly remodeled since the MGM Grand days. Food and drink service is available poolside. One portion of the pool features a handicap-accessible entrance. The pool is closed during a portion of the winter for cleaning.

Additionally, **The Spa at Bally's** offers different types of massages, sauna and whirlpool facilities, and a beauty salon.

BALLY'S AVENUE SHOPPES

(☞ *Shopping)* Bally's Avenue Shoppes is a small, basic shopping center. The complex features some gift shop-like places, sweet foods, and a flower shop. It serves its purpose to provide guests with basic (mostly impulse) shopping needs.

RESTAURANTS

Bally's down-to-earth collection of restaurants is an easy resort to dine in, whether or not visitors want upscale or casual fare. The finer **Bally's Steakhouse** serves cuts of meat prepared in various ways. **Al Dente** features classic Italian dishes, and **Chang's** serves contemporary Asian food.

The **Big Kitchen Buffet** offers a range of home-style foods in a relaxing environment, served buffet-style.

Over 40% of Nevada's total revenue is from gaming taxes alone.

Resorts: Mid-Strip

At the heart of the Las Vegas strip are some of the most familiar established resorts in the gaming and hospitality industry. It was in this section where the "birth" of the modern Las Vegas strip took place, and the resorts here have become synonymous with luxury travel to the region.

The mid-strip resort area is the most compact resort section of Las Vegas. Though most of the resorts themselves are a bit smaller than South Strip (in terms of casino space, acreage, and number of guest rooms) they are slightly easier to walk between, and contain some of the most historically significant and famous names on the strip.

BARBARY COAST

(3595 Las Vegas Blvd ☎ 702.737.7111 ↻ barbarycoastcasino.com)
Barbary Coast is a tiny resort sandwiched on a corner of giants – Caesars Palace, Flamingo, Bellagio, and Bally's all occupy the same general area. Barbary Coast occupies just over four acres of land. Despite this, however, the tiny resort sticks out among all of its neighbors. The lighting scheme is flashy and loud, more reminiscent of those on Fremont Street in Downtown Las Vegas. Tiny lights adorn the canopies, the signs and the awnings, and flash wildly in a call for visitors. It is this startling contrast – a classic Vegas resort along the otherwise modern strip – that makes Barbary Coast popular. The inside is dark, wooden, a bit musty and claustrophobic, reflecting its prominent Victorian-era décor. Stained-glass windows and antique-inspired light shades are scattered throughout.

Named after the San Francisco neighborhood known for gambling and other "sinful" acts during the late 1800s, the resort got its start on the strip early on, in the late 1970s. When it first opened in 1979 it was under the ownership of Coast Casinos, and was designed as a local's casino (catering to area residents as opposed to tourists). However, in 2004 Boyd Gaming acquired Coast Casinos, and today Barbary Coast attracts tourists from the nearby resorts as well as locals from the area. Despite the massive growth around it, the resort has remained popular and true to its roots.

ACCOMMODATIONS

As mentioned, Barbary Coast is a tiny hotel, with just under 200 rooms in total. However, the location of the hotel allows very easy access (including nearby pedestrian road overpasses) to neighboring resorts that make the main floor much more crowded than such a small selection of rooms might indicate. In other words, Barbary Coast is more of a casino than a resort.

CASINO

At 30,000 square feet, Barbary Coast's casino floor is only a fraction of the size of the nearby giants. However, as an established local's casino, it offers deals that even the largest and most comprehensive resorts never offer, including less expensive minimum bets at tables and different betting options. Therefore, people will frequently visit Barbary Coast for both a taste of that classic Las Vegas and for its gambling perks.

RESTAURANTS

Barbary Coast's décor and friendly ambience carry through to its two notable restaurants, both of which are semi-casual. **Michael's** specializes in steak and seafood. **Drai's**, started by Victor Drai, features basic continental foods, and doubles as a nightclub after hours. Also, the **Victorian Room** offers quicker eats 24 hours a day.

CAESARS PALACE

(3570 Las Vegas Blvd ☎ 877.427.7243 ⌁ caesarspalace.com The story of Caesars Palace begins in 1962, when motel owner Jay Sarno acquired a ten million dollar loan to begin planning a major resort. He would initially rent about 32 acres of barren land from Kirk Kerkorian, who owned much of the property alongside Highway 91 (the land would later be sold to Sarno). Caesars opened to the public in 1966 with an initial complement of about 680 rooms.

In keeping with the design of a combination of classical European style coupled with ancient Rome, Sarno called it Caesars Palace. He also decided that there should be no apostrophe in the word "Caesars"; everybody at the palace is treated like royalty, and thus everybody is a Caesar.

In 1974 the resort had its first major expansion with the addition of a second tower. More expansions occurred in 1979. By the 1980s, Caesars Palace became world-famous for boxing tournaments. In 1993, the Forum Shops, the first themed upscale shopping mall, opened. Expansions to Cacsars continue to this day. Most recently, their most luxurious tower to date, the Augustus tower, was opened.

On a corporate level Caesars Palace has managed to maintain striking consistency, despite having several different owners. It started independently, and eventually was absorbed into Bally's, Caesar's World, Park Place Entertainment, Caesars Entertainment, and ultimately (in 2004) Harrah's. Today Caesars Palace (and the Caesars name) is among the most well-known and upscale resorts on Harrah's massive roster.

ACCOMMODATIONS

The recent addition of the luxurious Augustus tower brings Caesars room count to 3,348; the other towers include the Roman, Centurion, Forum, and Palace towers. There are many levels of suites offered, but the Augustus tower is the most desirable, as it features the largest and most modernly equipped rooms. The towers are scattered somewhat haphazardly around the resort, as they were all built at different times. This can make it difficult to find the rooms in the seemingly infinite casino maze.

CASINO

The Caesars Palace casino is as big as it is upscale. At 129,000 square feet, there is plenty of room for all the table and slot games, including a large race and sports book section, different casino areas, a poker arena, and Baccarat. The Caesars casino is also known to be one of the most expensive casinos in Las Vegas (like Bellagio), catering to the wealthier gambler.

GARDEN OF THE GODS

(☞ *Swimming Pools)* Caesars Palace has a spectacular pool environment. It is as luxurious and beautiful as Mandalay Bay; but with less of a "waterpark" feel. It features four Ancient Roman-style pools adorned with statues and foliage, and two smaller Jacuzzis.

Additionally, the **Spa at Caesars Palace** is one of the largest in Las Vegas. This 23,000 square foot facility features spa and fitness facilities, and treatments include massages, tanning booths, steam and sauna rooms, and a terrace overlooking the pools.

RESTAURANTS

Caesars Palace is famous for its array of "celebrity chef" restaurants. Dining choices reflect the high quality atmosphere of the rest of the resort, and some of the strip's classiest (and most expensive) choices. Topping the list is **Restaurant Guy Savoy**, which features upscale French food. **Empress Court** serves American-inspired Chinese food. Bobby Flay's **Mesa Grill** is hip and trendy, featuring his innovative southwestern style. **808** serves an international variety of foods with Hawaiian influence. **Bradley Ogden** serves American cuisine. **Neros** features fine steaks and seafood.

For more casual choices, Caesars Palace offers the **Augustus Café** with continental choices. **Cypress Street Market** is a cafeteria-style dining area. The Caesars buffet is **Café Lago**, with various continental choices for breakfast, lunch, and dinner.

THE FORUM SHOPS MUST SEE

(☞ *Shopping*) For many people in the Las Vegas area and beyond, a visit to the famous strip is synonymous with a step into the Forum Shops at Caesars Palace. It is one of the most unique shopping experiences in the world. Accessible via outdoors and the main casino floor, the Forum Shops is an indoor mall like no other. It is perpetual twilight in the downtown Ancient Roman Empire. People walk along the streets, among the fountains, statues, and architecture of the past. More than 160 restaurants and shops align this indoor city's "streets", and the domed ceiling and lighting scheme makes it feel like a Roman evening. At night, the lights slowly dim and the ceiling changes to indicate that night has fallen.

Since the opening of The Forum Shops in 1993, other resorts including the Venetian, Paris Las Vegas and Aladdin have followed suit with their themed malls. But The Forum Shops was the first, and is still one of the best.

The shops and restaurants are all generally known upscale chain brands including **Banana Republic, Gap, Coach, Burberry, Abercrombie and Fitch,** , **Brookstone, Gucci,**

Anthropologie, Planet Hollywood and **Cheesecake Factory** to name just a tiny fraction. For entertainment, the **Fall of Atlantis** and the **Festival Fountain** are highlights; these animatronic characters perform at regular intervals throughout the day. It is at heart a mall, but a very unique and entertaining one.

In short, if you do nothing else at Caesars Palace, or even in Las Vegas itself, you must visit The Forum Shops, if only to appreciate its ambience.

APPIAN WAY

(☞ Shopping) Before The Forum Shops, Caesars Palace had the Appian Way, a small collection of boutique-style stores alongside the casino floor. Clothing, fine jewelry, and other such deluxe items are available. It is rarely crowded like The Forum Shops, so visitors can enjoy a quieter, more subdued shopping experience.

THE COLOSSEUM

A large, newer entertainment venue built in the shape of the famous Roman Colosseum, this theater has seen more than its share of superstars. It was built specifically for Celine Dion and her resident show **A New Day**, but others have graced the stage, including **Elton John** and **Jerry Seinfeld**. For show schedules, visit the resort's web site or call their main number.

FLAMINGO

(3555 Las Vegas Blvd ☎ 702.733.3111 ⌁ flamingolasvegas.com) This is the hotel that made Las Vegas famous. The bright pink neon and flowery Caribbean décor seem to have been ripped from the heyday of downtown Las Vegas. It is a flamboyant and colorful tropical collage that has been made famous through its long-standing location and ability to avoid most wrecking balls. Its

most famous symbol – a massive, bright tropical flower in permanent bloom attached to the side of the building – has become somewhat of a landmark for the way Las Vegas was supposed to be. Beneath all the glitz and glitter, the Flamingo's history in Las Vegas is perhaps the most important of any resort in all of Nevada.

When it opened in 1946 (15 years after Nevada legalized gambling), *The Pink Flamingo* had only 77 rooms and a small gambling space. Owned and operated by Benjamin "Bugsy" Siegel, the name purportedly came from his nickname for his girlfriend, Virginia Hill. Its location was utterly desolate; Las Vegas had few commodities to its name, though Siegel was passionate about the financial possibility of legalized gambling. Unfortunately, however, the property's revenues did poorly during the first year, and because of that (coupled with some creative business practices) Siegel was shot and killed by his "investors".

In 1947 it was sold off and re-named *The Fabulous Flamingo*. During the 1950s and 1960s, the resort added various wings and attractions besides gambling, making it one of the first "all-encompassing" resort destinations in Las Vegas; thus helping to pave the way for the mega-resorts to come. Siegel's original resort would eventually be torn down to make way for larger, newer facilities.

Kirk Kerkorian owned the property for a while in the late 1960s. In 1972 the property was acquired by Hilton, and re-named the *Flamingo Hilton*. In 1998, Park Place Entertainment took over all Hilton gaming complexes, and as a result the Flamingo eventually wound up on the Harrah's resort roster. While the original Flamingo that made the town famous is long gone, a plaque in the courtyard of the resort is dedicated to Siegel, who is unofficially credited as the father of Las Vegas.

ACCOMMODATIONS

The Flamingo's pink flamboyant Caribbean style extends to its guest rooms. The resort has about 3,600 rooms in several different tower sections, featuring various levels of rooms and suites, making it one of the largest in this section of the trip – a far cry from the mere 77 rooms it had at the beginning.

CASINO

At 77,000 square feet, Flamingo's casino floor is surprisingly small given that it is one of the biggest resorts in the area. There are flamingo decorations throughout, and it features standard slot and table games, including a poker room and race and sports book area.

POOL

(☞ Swimming Pools) Flamingo's outdoor pool area is an impressive tropical watery wonderland, oftentimes rated among the best in Las Vegas. Complete with palm trees and waterfalls, the area encompasses about 15 acres and features four pools and two Jacuzzis. Seasonally (during the summer months) there is a large waterslide section. Food and drinks may be purchased at the **Flamingo Beach Club Café**.

The Flamingo also has outdoor tennis courts, and a **Spa** which features wet and dry saunas, fitness equipment, all kinds of massage options, and a salon.

RESTAURANTS

For fine steak and seafood, Flamingo has **Steakhouse46**. **Hamada of Japan** serves traditional Japanese foods, and features a sushi bar. **Ventuno** serves classic and contemporary Italian foods in a more lively setting.

Casual dining at Flamingo includes a variety of tropical-themed restaurants. Jimmy Buffet's **Margaritaville** has a lively

Caribbean atmosphere and a selection of steak, fish, and tropical-themed dishes. The **Paradise Garden Buffet** and **Tropical Breeze** have views of the Wildlife Habitat and both serve a variety of dishes.

WILDLIFE HABITAT

(☞ Natural Encounters) Immediately adjacent to the pool area, surrounded by imported tropical trees and shrubbery, is a collection of birds and other "exotic" animals. The outdoor habit showcases Chilean Flamingos, of course, but it also contains penguins, turtles, and about 300 various birds.

IMPERIAL PALACE

(3535 Las Vegas Blvd ☎ 702.731.3311 ⌁ imperialpalace.com) With all the tropical and desert themes of Las Vegas resorts and casinos, Imperial Palace might seem a bit out of place. The quasi-Asian architecture and independent resort ownership make this large resort stand out from its surrounding competitors. It is loosely based on Kokyo, the Japanese Imperial Palace in Tokyo, but its influence is in name only, as it is meant only as a general reference to Asian culture, and less to a specific place. The look is wholly outdated, however, which may add to its charm.

Given its location immediately adjacent to the original Flamingo resort, Imperial Palace began its run in 1959 as the Flamingo Capri (over a decade after Bugsy Siegel started the original Flamingo). In 1979 it was taken over by Ralph Engelstad, and given an Asian theme. Although Engelstad died in 2002, casino ownership has been placed under his trust and operated by Imperial Palace, LLC. Harrah's Entertainment, which owns much of the neighboring properties, purchased Imperial Palace at the end of 2005.

ACCOMMODATIONS

In 1988 the newest tower was added to the skyline of Imperial Palace, adding an additional 18 stories of accommodations, bringing the room total to 2,700 guest rooms and suites. Many of the deluxe rooms feature the **Luv Tub**, which is a private Jacuzzi surrounded by drapery.

CASINO

Imperial Palace's casino floor is 77,000 square feet of the most popular slot and table games, including poker and a race & sports book area. Additionally, the **Dealertainer's Pit** – a unique feature of Imperial Palace – features dealers of table games impersonating celebrities.

POOL

Imperial Palace's outdoor pool environment covers the basics; one large outdoor pool (open seasonally) and a Jacuzzi nearby. The facility has basic Asian touches, but is a mostly functional, "yes we have a pool" complex. Drink service is available around the pool area. Additionally, the **Imperial Palace Spa** features a wide range of spa and massage services, including a fitness center.

RESTAURANTS

The finer establishments at Imperial Palace still reflect the more casual atmosphere of the resort overall. **Fireside** features homestyle foods and barbeque. The more romantic and intimate **Embers** serves steak and seafood. **Ming** serves an array of Asian food.

For casual seafood, the **Cockeyed Clam** has a selection of shrimp, lobster, and more. **Pizza Palace** serves Italian food and sandwiches. The **Emperor's Buffet** has continental cuisine for breakfast, lunch, and dinner.

AUTO COLLECTION

(☞ Museums) Imperial Palace plays host to the largest auto show of its kind. The Imperial Palace Auto Collection is an outside company that uses space at the resort to showcase, buy, and sell classic and vintage automobiles. At the daily show in one of the areas of the parking garage, you can buy or sell classic, vintage, or muscle cars (sometimes costing upwards of five million dollars), or just admire them. The selection of cars on display may vary daily, but there are generally at least several hundred on display at a time. For more information, visit autocollections.com or call 702.794.3174.

HARRAH'S LAS VEGAS

(3475 Las Vegas Blvd ☎ 702.369.5000 ↻ harrahs.com) Despite the lengthy history of William F. Harrah's ventures into casino ownership, Harrah's Las Vegas is actually a rather new resort in its current form (Harrah's actually got its start in Reno). The carnival and party atmosphere that has become so indicative of the Harrah's chain helps this complex stick out as the more "friendly" resort surrounded by a largely upscale crowd.

In the 1950s, the **Tumbleweed Motel** and the **Pyramids Motel** sat next to each other on an unimpressive expanse of road just outside Las Vegas. After some tossing and jostling about, the Holiday Casino, a Holiday Inn hotel, opened in 1973. The dream of Shelby and Claudine Williams, the resort's steamboat theme (the resort was shaped like a large steamboat) became somewhat of an icon on the strip, lasting for almost two decades.

Over the next few years, Holiday Corporation purchased Harrah's gaming casinos, and in 1992 the resort was re-named Harrah's Las Vegas, and ultimately the steanboat theme was abandoned for the carnival theme. Through the magic of paperwork, Harrah's Entertainment separated from the Holiday Corporation, and asked Claudine Williams to stay on board as chairman of Harrah's Las Vegas.

ACCOMMODATIONS

The resort has about 2,500 rooms and suites of various sizes, each with bright decorations and a decidedly "friendly" atmosphere. Harrah's Las Vegas attracts many people to stay at their resort because of their loyalty program, one of the best in the business.

CASINO

It is a perpetual carnival at Harrah's Las Vegas, with lights and decorations that seem just a bit brighter and happier than most. The casino floor is over 86,000 square feet and features many of the latest and greatest slot and table games, as well as a poker room and a small (about 50-seat) race & sports book center.

POOL

(☞ *Swimming Pools*) Harrah's outdoor pool complex is decidedly small; there is only one pool (though it is Olympic-sized). The basics are included here, such as lounge chairs and rentable cabanas. Drinks and massages are available poolside. As the pool is unheated, it is closed during the winter season.

Harrah's also has a small **spa** which features additional massage and body treatments, and a fitness room that overlooks the pool.

RESTAURANTS

Harrah's down-home casual quality and trademark friendliness are reflected in its selection of casual and moderate dining choices. The more upscale **Penazzi Italian Ristorante** serves a wide selection of quality Italian food. The restaurant also features an oyster bar. Asian-inspired foods are available at **Ming's Table**. **The Range Steakhouse** serves steak and seafood in an upscale environment. Harrah's Buffet, **Flavors**, serves a wide array of food choices.

For casual eating, **Winning Streaks** is a sports bar with all kinds of fast, greasy food. Also, the **Café at Harrah's** serves quick bits 24 hours a day.

CARNAVAL COURT
Harrah's major entertainment center is Carnaval Court. A cross between a bar, a restaurant, a small shopping center, a club, and an entertainment venue, this outdoor center is designed to look like a street fair. There is a bandstand with regular performances, a full bar with "flair" bartenders, t-shirt stands and gift shops, and even outdoor blackjack tables (weather permitting). A highlight of the area is the **Ghirardelli Chocolate Company**, the famous San Francisco soda fountain/ice cream parlor/gourmet chocolate shop, which overlooks the court.

THE MIRAGE

(3400 Las Vegas Blvd ☎ 702.791.7111 🖳 themirage.com) It is a tropical oasis in the middle of an uninhabitable desert. It is a glistening paradise far on the horizon. No, this is not a figment of your imagination. It is The Mirage, Las Vegas' first mega-resort. Set with a South Seas theme, the Mirage is that iconic desert oasis with a lush landscape of dense rainforest, beautiful waterfalls, and even volcanic activity.

The Mirage deserves credit in many areas, most notably for ushering in the "new era" of Las Vegas in the early 1990s. When it first opened in November of 1989, it was the world's largest resort, and the first hotel in history to top the 3,000-guest-room mark. Of course, today it is a far cry from being the largest resort, but it helped pave the way for many similar massive undertakings in the few short years that followed. Plus, it proved that a successful resort is possible even with a $680+ million investment.

It started out as a vision for Steve Wynn. As a casino developer, he already had moderate success with other Las Vegas properties, most notably his complete re-design of the Golden Nugget in downtown Las Vegas. However, he envisioned a lavish resort outside of town that wasn't completely centered on the casino. Rather, he saw an upscale resort with as much focus on refinement and luxury as it did on the oftentimes loud and rowdy casino floor. The resort would cater to the wealthiest clients. So, Wynn's Golden Nugget company became Mirage Resorts, and the era of the luxury casino mega-resort had begun.

In 2000, after spearheading the development of several other properties, Wynn sold Mirage Resorts to MGM Grand, which became MGM Mirage, so he would have the money to finance his ultimate dream resort, Wynn Las Vegas.

Mirage is also where, for nearly 14 years, the Siegfried & Roy Show entertained audiences with magic and white tigers. In 2003, a tiger attacked Roy Horn on-stage, and the show closed forever. However, to this day, the influence of the magicians is still apparent in the various exhibitions found in the resort.

ACCOMMODATIONS

Unlike the surrounding always-being-upgraded resorts, The Mirage has had the same 3,049 rooms and suites since its inception. In 2002 the rooms were renovated and updated with modern features, such as Internet access.

Checking into The Mirage is a special treat; the front desk of the resort sits in front of a massive 20,000 gallon **aquarium** filled with all kinds of fish and sea life.

POOL

(☞ Swimming Pools) The pool area of the Mirage is a favorite. It is not particularly large, but it sure keeps to the tropical themes of the resort. There are two outdoor pools, one large and one small. However, the large pool is of such unique character that it can hardly be called a pool; it is more of a tropical South Seas lagoon, surrounded by waterfalls, tiny alcoves, and lush tropical foliage Food and drinks are available in the pool area.

RESTAURANTS

Mirage has all the variety of restaurants to be expected in such a lavish resort. For upscale dining, **Onda** serves an array of contemporary and classic Italian food. **Japonais** serves unique Japanese-inspired choices. **STACK** features the finest all-American dishes. Chinese-inspired food is served at **Fin**, and **Samba** offers steak choices from Brazil.

Even the casual affairs at Mirage are classy. **Caribe Café** has a selection of burgers, salads, and other standards. **Carnegie Delicatessen** serves sandwiches and lighter foods. **Cravings**, the buffet at Mirage, features a wide array of continental and international food.

THE VOLCANO [MUST SEE]

(☞ Free Shows) The Mirage's main entrance on Las Vegas Boulevard has one of the most famous permanent fixtures on the strip – an active "volcano". By day it looks like a regular waterfall. However, on nightly regular intervals (generally about every 30-60 minutes after dark), it becomes a spewing, churning, fiery mass of Vegas-style entertainment. From many great vantage points along the strip, visitors see the volcano spew "lava" as much as 100 feet in the air. The lake in front of the resort then catches fire, and flames and smoke set this once peaceful corner of the South Seas ablaze.

In 1995, the same contractors responsible for the Fountains of Bellagio were hired to give the aging Volcano attraction a much-needed facelift, adding much of the special effects seen today.

SECRET GARDEN

(☞ Natural Encounters) Adjacent to the pool is one of the most popular attractions at The Mirage; Siegfried & Roy's Secret Garden. For a fee, visitors may enter an animal habitat designed to look like a tropical wonderland, filled with exotic animals such as white tigers and white lions, a black panther, and even leopards. It is a lushly foliated "jungle" in the middle of the desert.

The unique "white" animals have been a passion for Siegfried and Roy. They even began an organization which has been breeding them in captivity for many years. ($$)

DOLPHIN HABITAT

(☞ Natural Encounters) Across from the Secret Garden is a 2.5 million gallon tank that offers both underwater and outdoor views of real dolphins as they explore, swim, and play in a habitat designed to look like their oceanic home.

Unlike other dolphin aquariums, there are no performances here, and no tricks to get audiences to cheer. Mirage prides itself on the facility being designed for dolphin awareness, and as such there is no showiness – after all, you can get that almost anywhere else in Las Vegas.

Admission fees for the Secret Garden may include admission to the Dolphin Habitat; inquire when tickets are purchased. ($$)

WHITE TIGER HABITAT

(☞ Natural Encounters) Almost clear on the other side of the resort from the Secret Garden and Dolphin Habitat are the most

famous residents of the Mirage: Siegfried & Roy's white tigers. Although the show no longer exists at the resort, these animals are cared for and exhibited to the public, usually one at a time, free of charge.

MONORAIL TO TREASURE ISLAND
The northern sister resort of the Mirage, Treasure Island, is accessible via a free courtesy tram that goes back and forth between the two resorts. It is on a track and automated, with a total round trip of about ten minutes.

THE VENETIAN

(3355 Las Vegas Blvd ☎ 702.414.1000 ✆ venetian.com) Ah, Venice! It is rich with culture and history. Gaze upon a beautifully painted ceiling. Cross over one of the many bridges of Venice's famous canals, or take a tour of an art museum. Eventually, you may even find your way to a plaza in the middle of a bustling shopping district. No, you're not in Italy – you're in the American desert. The Venetian, one of the newer, best, and most popular resorts along the strip, emulates the arts and contemporary styling of one of the most culturally rich cities in Europe; Vegas-style, of course.

 The Venetian sits on the site of the original Sands hotel, one of the first resort casinos on the Las Vegas Strip. With an opening in December 1952, the Sands was made famous during its near 50-year history by hosting the first group performance of what would later be known as the "rat pack": Frank Sinatra, Sammy Davis, Jr., Joey Bishop, Peter Langford, and Dean Martin. The group would continue to perform regularly at the Sands, and Sinatra at one point even held partial ownership of it. As such, the resort and the rat pack helped pave the way for Las Vegas as being a center for stage entertainment.

Howard Hughes purchased the Sands during his famous slew of casino buy-outs in the 1960s, when he added a 500-room tower. However, as the decades progressed, the Sands fell into disrepair. Even Kirk Kerkorian owned it for a year in the mid-1980s, and it eventually entered the hands of Sheldon Adelson.

In 1996 Adelson's Las Vegas Sands Corporation closed the Sands resort forever. On November 26 of that year, at about 2:00AM, it was demolished in one of the most famous Las Vegas events of recent history. For two years afterwards, at a cost of about $1.5 billion dollars, a new mega-resort was constructed that would be the Venetian.

The resort is a powerhouse, filled with artistic riches. Visitors seem to be naturally drawn to the Venetian, with its impressive architecture and wide array of entertainment options. Its decorative casino, plush accommodations, canals, and museums make this one of the classiest and most beautiful places in Las Vegas.

ACCOMMODATIONS

With the addition of a newer tower, the Venetian hosts a staggering 4,049 guest rooms and suites, thereby surpassing in size all of its neighbors. It features upscale room choices and amenities for the more discerning luxury vacationer.

CASINO

The Venetian's large number of guest rooms naturally demands a large amount of casino gaming space. To that matter, the 120,000 square foot casino has many of the most popular table and slot games, including a baccarat area and race & sports book section. Strolling through the Venetian's casino is at times like strolling through a small town in Italy – save, of course, for the rows of noisy slot machines.

POOL

(☞ Swimming Pools) The Venetian's pool complex is split into two sections, and both have a contemporary design. The main area features four pools and the new **Venezia** section has an additional two pools. The hours of each vary depending on the season (though the pools are heated during colder times of year). Limited drink service may also be available.

RESTAURANTS

More than just Italian food, the Venetian's dining options run the gamut from world class to more casual choices. From New York, **Lutèce** features the finest French cuisine. **Pinot Brasserie** serves French and American-Californian foods and features an extensive wine list. **Valentino** features some of the best contemporary Italian food in the industry. **Zeffirino Ristorante** serves classic Italian dishes. Wolfgang Puck's **Postrio** offers fusion-American food and features a patio in the Grand Canal Shoppes area. **Aquaknox** features a wide away of seafood. Visitors can dine in Saint Mark's Square at **Canaletto**, a noisy but nice Italian restaurant. For steaks, the **Delmonico Steakhouse** features a contemporary setting and a menu by Emeril Lagasse. For Asian-inpired dishes, the Venetian also offers **Royal Star** and **Tsunami Asian Grill**.

Even casual is classy at the Venetian. **Taqueria Cañonita** uniquely serves Southwestern foods while diners overlook the Canals of Venice. **Grand Lux Café** offers a wide array of continental food. For dessert, **Tintoretto Bakery** features pastries, coffees, and more.

CANYON RANCH SPACLUB

For those that like resort spa centers, The Venetian's is top of the line – probably the best on the entire strip. An offshoot of the famed Arizona getaway, The Venetian's spa is just shy of 70,000 feet (the largest in Las Vegas) – the size of a small casino floor, and boasts all kinds of spa and fitness-related amenities. Among the features are a rock-climbing wall, a huge fitness center, the **Canyon Ranch Café** restaurant, dozens of massage treatment rooms suitable for all kinds of massages and other body treatments, saunas, hot tubs, and much more.

THE GRAND CANAL SHOPPES

(☞ *Shopping)* In the spirit of themed malls now peppering the Las Vegas strip, the Venetian hosts a shopping promenade direct from Venice – well, almost. The Grand Canal Shoppes is an indoor mall designed to look like a bustling outdoor Venetian shopping district, complete with **St. Mark's Square**, restaurants, vendor carts, street performers, and a real water "canal" running through several of the sections.

The Grand Canal Shoppes twist and turn around, sometimes making it hard to find one's way – but if you follow the canal or the sound of the clinking slots nearby, you're sure to find your way back.

CANAL AND GONDOLA RIDES

(☞ *Rides and Attractions)* One of the most attractive and unique features of The Venetian is the canal that runs through the resort. The outdoor promenade section of the Venetian is an impressive mix of museum façade, canal bridges, and the shallow canal itself that seems to run forever in several directions. On the inside, the canal twists and turns through a portion of the Canal Shoppes.

On this canal visitors can ride on an authentic Venetian-style gondola, complete with singing gondolier dressed in the classic striped attire and hat. Visitors can choose between an indoor and outdoor (weather-permitting) ride, and can even opt for a private 2-passenger ride. Sights on the gondola include the

Grand Canal Shoppes (with sky-painted ceiling) and outdoor Venetian patio, with architecture inspired by famous sights throughout Venice. The ride is about 12-15 minutes and is less than a half-mile total distance. The outdoor ride is slightly shorter, and may close due to inclement weather.

This is a popular and not very private feature attraction. Be warned – while on this unique attraction, all passersby will be focused on *you* and your singing gondolier. ($$)

THE GUGGENHEIM HERMITAGE MUSEUM

(☞ Museums) With a regular rotation of exhibits, the Guggenheim Hermitage Museum showcases works of art from two of the most famous museums in the world: the Guggenheim and the Hermitage. The facility is managed by the Solomon R. Guggenheim Foundation. More information is available at guggenheim-lasvegas.org. ($$)

MADAME TUSSAUDS

(☞ Museums) In the admittedly specific category of the wax museum, there are two reigning champions. For eerie environments and creepy factoids, the crown goes to Ripley's. But for life-like replicas of famous (and infamous) persons, the royal scepter must go to Madame Tussaud and her small but impressive chain of celebrity waxworks.

At Madame Tussauds Las Vegas, visitors are encouraged to "intermingle" with life-size wax figures of their favorite celebrities. Dubbed an "interactive" museum, the figures are posed so that visitors may shake hands with, be interviewed by, or even play poker with, a whole slew of famous people from yesterday and today; mainly for photo opportunities. Occasionally, the museum may dedicate a special section as a haunted house, where visitors walk around dark rooms getting scared by live actors (the haunted house can be bypassed should you not want the fright). For more information, visit mtvegas.com. ($$)

TREASURE ISLAND

(3300 Las Vegas Blvd ☎ 702.894.7111 🌐 treasureisland.com) The initial success of the Mirage prompted a flurry of resort-building activity. So the idea was simple: take what worked with the Mirage, and give it a family-friendly twist. And what do kids learn about that live in the South Seas? Pirates! Robert Louis Stevenson's book has always been the quintessential pirate book for school children since it was published in the mid-1880s, so the resort was given the same name and a Caribbean theme. Mirage Resorts opened Treasure Island in 1993 with a skull-and-crossbones logo, a huge video arcade, live family-friendly pirate shows, and more. The goal was to attract families, particularly those with young children. Still, the resort was designed to be upscale, just like Mirage.

In 2000 it was acquired by MGM Grand (with the other Mirage Resort properties), and slowly the child-friendly attractions were removed. The arcade, some of the pirate-show features, and other kid-friendly features were phased out. Today (to some disappointment) the pirate theme and the family-friendliness have largely been abandoned, to make a more congruent fit with the neighboring Mirage. They have even shortened the unofficial name to "TI" or even "TI at the Mirage" as an attempt to combine the two resorts into one. Still, Treasure Island is an all-around luxurious resort, and is a permanent fixture on the Las Vegas strip, with plenty to see and do throughout the complex.

ACCOMMODATIONS

Treasure Island has 2,885 rooms and suites, a little bit smaller than the size of its neighboring Mirage. It is a higher-class resort with many amenities expected with higher price tags. However, the resort is actually less expensive on average than the neighboring resorts of similar quality.

CASINO

The casino floor at Treasure Island is about 95,000 square feet of gaming, including slots and the standard table games. There is also a large sports book complex.

POOL AND SPA

(☞ *Swimming Pools*) Treasure Island has a small but pretty outdoor pool complex. It features a large Jacuzzi and a lagoon-shaped pool surrounded by tropical trees. It is only a basic pool complex, and drinks may be available poolside.

Treasure Island also features a newly-renovated spa area. Called **WET – The Spa at TI**, it features many services, including massages and other treatments, and a salon.

RESTAURANTS

Treasure Island has a few fine dining choices. The new **Social House** features Japanese-influenced food in a lively, trendy, and modern environment. **Francesco's** is a cozy restaurant featuring traditional Italian food. **The Steak House** serves fine steak and seafood. **Isla Mexican** has a wide range of Mexican food and an extensive tequila bar.

For a more casual meal, **Canter's Delicatessen** is an open and friendly place serving sandwiches and lighter fare. **Dishes**, the resident buffet, serves a wide array of continental and international foods in a contemporary setting, many made to order.

MONORAIL TO MIRAGE

Treasure Island offers a free tram service that connects the resort to its sister to the south, Mirage. The tram runs about every ten minutes and allows for a quick jaunt back and forth between the resorts.

SIRENS OF TI

(☞ *Free Shows)* At the main entrance of Treasure Island there is an outdoor open-air stage that looks like it was ripped from Disneyland. Formerly a pirate-themed family show, Sirens of TI has been recently re-invented with a much more adult, lusty theme. The performance is free to watch and has regular nightly shows.

At the north end of the strip, the Stratosphere Hotel and Tower stands at 1,100 feet tall. It is the tallest building west of the Mississippi.

Resorts: North Strip

As visitors travel north on the strip, they will notice that resorts get older and the pedestrian traffic decreases. In fact, the North Strip is the only part of the strip that is partially contained within the Las Vegas city proper. The resorts here have a more spread-out, isolated feeling and have managed to maintain a "classic Vegas" appeal as opposed to the more modern decorative approach. Famous North Strip names like New Frontier and Stardust echo with Las Vegas history. With one notable exception, the north strip generally offers the least expensive resorts and hotels in the area.

WYNN LAS VEGAS **MUST SEE**

(3131 Las Vegas Blvd ☎ 702.770.7100 🖰 wynnlasvegas.com) The crown jewel of the north strip (and vying for top resort of Las Vegas, nay, the world) is the Wynn Las Vegas. Located on a staggering 215 acres of land on Las Vegas Boulevard and rivaling, perhaps even surpassing, the mega-resorts further south, the new Wynn Las Vegas is the most ambitious single project in Las Vegas history. Funding for the resort was one of the main goals of Steve Wynn's sale of Mirage Resorts to MGM Grand in 2000. With its sleek, dark architectural design, it has a contemporary look which sticks out as one of the tallest buildings in Nevada.

Unlike other mega-resorts on the strip, Wynn Las Vegas beckons visitors inside rather than having free outdoor shows. The entrance features a cascading waterfall and promenade that brings visitors through a luxuriously appointed shopping arcade of high-end stores and art exhibits on their way to the casino floor. From there, visitors can admire the first-rate décor of the resort, and enjoy one of the most full-featured facilities in Las Vegas.

The Desert Inn once dominated this portion of the strip when it was first constructed in the 1950s. Though the resort had its own 18-hole golf course, one of its real claims to fame was Howard Hughes' purchase of the resort in 1966 – he rented the hotel's top floor and stayed there for four years (eventually purchasing the resort to stop them from kicking him out).

After the sale of Mirage Resorts, Steve Wynn (as Wynn Resorts Limited) acquired the still-operational Desert Inn and the adjoining golf course, and closed it down shortly thereafter. For the next five years, development of the new resort began including a remodel of the original golf course. The property eventually opened to the public in April 2005. It has been said that this resort was a very personal project for Wynn, and is the flagship for other Wynn Resorts worldwide. At a cost of $2.6 billion, it is America's most expensive privately-funded construction project.

ACCOMMODATIONS

Wynn Las Vegas has over 2,700 rooms and suites within the single building. Guest room sizes at the resort begin at about 600 square feet – among the largest standard room sizes in the hospitality industry.

The guest rooms themselves are top-notch and feature floor-to-ceiling windows, flat-screen televisions, and high-speed Internet access. They all feature the contemporary décor and artistic flair prominent throughout the rest of the resort, and are destined to become some of the highest-rated accommodations in Las Vegas.

CASINO
Wynn's casino floor is about 111,000 lavishly decorated square feet. It features favorite slot and table games, including a poker room and sports & race book center. Many of the slot games are Wynn-branded.

WYNN ESPLANADE
(☞ *Shopping*) Beyond the waterfall of Wynn's entrance, along the corridor connecting the Las Vegas strip to the main casino of Wynn is the indoor Esplanade, which features upscale shops and small eateries, and some Wynn-branded retail opportunities. It is a small mall complex, but decorated with a contemporary-natural feel that serves as a good introduction to the resort itself. Shops along the Esplanade include **Chanel**, **Louis Vuitton** and other luxury retailers.

RESTAURANTS
Wynn Las Vegas showcases several upscale restaurants. Topping the list is **Alex**, one of the most upscale and finest French restaurants in the city. **Tableau** serves classic American foods in an open, relaxing environment. **Bartolotta** serves classic Italian dishes, and specialize in seafood. **Corsa Cucina** also serves Italian food, including pizza. The **Daniel Boulud Brasserie** features French cuisine. The **SW Steakhouse** offers steak and seafood choices. **Red 8** features Chinese-inspired dishes, and **Okada** offers Japanese dishes.

For more casual choices, the **Terrace Pointe Café** offers lighter food overlooking Wynn's pool area. **The Buffet**, one of the best in Las Vegas, features an array of continental and international choices served for breakfast, lunch, and dinner.

POOL
(☞ Swimming Pools) The pool area at Wynn Las Vegas features several pools and Jacuzzis, including one larger pool. There is also the **Spa at Wynn Las Vegas**, which is over 35,000 square feet of luxury spa and fitness services.

THE WYNN COLLECTION
(☞ Museums) Steve Wynn's love of art is no surprise to those familiar with the other resorts he spearheaded (such as Bellagio). However, the Wynn Collection is comparatively small; there are seldom more than 15 different works on display at any given time. However, the works are from Wynn's private collection and feature some of the best-known art and artists of any art museum. The admission price is relatively inexpensive, and it won't take a lot of time to explore the collection. ($)

WYNN GOLF AND COUNTRY CLUB
The only golf course on the Las Vegas strip, located behind Wynn Las Vegas, is a beautiful and staggering 18-hole golf course. Taking up most of Wynn's 217-acre resort and available only to resort guests, the course has a full-service country club complete with practice areas, golf cart rentals, caddies, and a pro shop. Most holes are par 4 (the total course is par 70), and most feature some kind of water obstacle. It is indeed a luxurious choice for golfers willing to shell out $500 per person for a tee time. For those who want to see the course but not play, consider a ride on the Las Vegas Monorail which circles the course and offers great views. ($$$$)

PENSKE WYNN FERRARI MASERATI
(☞ Shopping) Within the Penske-Maserati showroom is a collection of some of the world's most expensive new cars, many of which are over $600,000. Cars include rare models, and even a

glimpse of Steve Wynn's personal $1.4 million Ferrari. Most people simply come in to look, but cars are available to purchase should you have the need and financial resources for such an automobile.

NEW FRONTIER

(3120 Las Vegas Blvd ☎ 702.794.8200 ⁻∂ frontierlv.com) Located in an area where the resorts are much more spread out, the New Frontier has kept its classic luster throughout its 60+ years of continuous operation. As the second major hotel on the Las Vegas strip (it even still has part of the original building), visitors entering the property immediately feel as though they are stepping into Vegas' past – even if it does look a bit weathered and aged. Still, this is an inexpensive and historic hotel that deserves a look-see.

Although New Frontier is known as the second hotel built on the strip, its history begins nearly a decade earlier. In 1930, it opened as a private nightclub called *Pair O' Dice*. As this was a year before gambling was legalized in Nevada, the club was secretive about its internal activities (primarily gambling and drinking). In 1931, only minutes after gambling was legalized, they reopened as a public nightclub. Thus, Pair O' Dice was the first legal gambling establishment in Nevada.

In 1942 the nightclub opened as a hotel and became *Hotel Last Frontier*, and in 1955 became *New Frontier*. In 1956, Elvis made his first public appearance in Las Vegas at the resort. In 1967, during his string of resort buyouts, Howard Hughes purchased the resort. In 1998, Phil Ruffin purchased it with intentions to tear it down and build a bigger resort; plans which have yet to come to fruition.

ACCOMMODATIONS

The New Frontier is just about the only major resort that has not yet passed the 1,000-room mark, and features about 980 guest rooms and suites. The rooms are generally well maintained but they naturally feel more aged. Rooms are generally inexpensive, and certain ones have modern amenities, such as Internet access.

CASINO

The New Frontier's casino floor is officially about 100,000 square feet. However, it feels very small, and as a result sources vary widely about the size of the New Frontier's casino, sometimes estimated to be as small as 40,000 square feet. In any case, it *feels* small and cozier, which may be advantageous for gamblers looking for a more intimate surrounding. It features the standard casino games and a race & sports book. New Frontier also features a **bingo** parlor.

POOL

(☞ *Swimming Pools)* New Frontier has a small pool area, with one large oddly-shaped pool, small Jacuzzi, and a few tropical trees scattered about for good measure. The pool itself has a deep end of twelve feet; one of the deepest pools in Las Vegas.

RESTAURANTS

The New Frontier's restaurants have an overall casual atmosphere and showcase the resort's Southwestern and country hospitality. **Phil's Steakhouse** serves steaks prepared in various ways. **Phil's Deli** features American foods like hamburgers and sandwiches. **Margarita's Cantina** offers Mexican food. **The Orchard Coffee Shop** has continental foods and buffet-style dining.

The Riviera

(2901 Las Vegas Blvd ☎ 702.794.9451 ⁀ rivierahotel.com) The Riviera is a stretch of land along the Mediterranean Sea that is part French and part Italian. It is a wealthy and beautiful coastline attractive to tourists all over the world. As such, "Riviera" has become synonymous with wealthy coastlines worldwide, such as the Mexican Riviera and the California Riviera. In Las Vegas, however, only the name remains – there is no scenic coastline here. Instead, the 23-story Riviera provides the glitz of classic Las Vegas with the larger-than-life starry décor and the appeal of a 1950s Vegas resort (modernized, of course).

The Riviera Hotel first opened in April 1955. The building was the first towering hotel on the Las Vegas strip, as well as the first hotel to feature inward-facing rooms (as opposed to motel-style, where rooms opened up to the outdoors). Its well-publicized construction brought the attention of many investors, including two of the Marx Brothers. Vegas legend Liberace's classic performance graced the resort during the opening ceremony, and he continued to perform there for years.

Despite some problems and ownership changes, the Riviera has made a real name for itself along the strip. Today, the hotel is owned and operated by the Riviera Holdings Corporation, which controls a small number of casino resorts. Another major investment is the Riviera Black Hawk, about 40 miles outside of Denver.

Families please note: with its eccentric performances and some thoroughly "adult" entertainment options, the Riviera is just about as far from a family-friendly resort as you can get. Even for Las Vegas.

ACCOMMODATIONS

The Riviera has about 2,100 guest rooms and suites within four towers. The rooms have been dated since their opening over 50 years ago, so in 2000 they were refurbished with modern amenities.

CASINO

There is over 100,000 feet of gaming space within the resort, featuring all the favorite slot and table games, as well as a smaller race & sports book area. Additionally, the casino is one of the more popular ones in the North Strip area, as it houses many penny slots and otherwise caters to the more budget-minded player.

POOL

(☞ Museums) There is one outdoor lap pool at the Riviera. It features limited services in a somewhat confined space. Bar service is available in the pool area. **Executive Fitness** offers a Jacuzzi, a fitness center and various kinds of massage and body services.

RESTAURANTS

Riviera has several upscale restaurants on-premises. **Ristorante Italiano** features classic and contemporary Italian food, while **Kristofer's Steak House** offers traditional steak and seafood.

More casually, **Kady's Coffee Shop** has a wide range of faster-food choices. The **World's Fare Buffet** offers continental and international food for all meals of the day.

RIVIERA COMEDY CLUB

(☞ Live Shows) A small venue fitting about 350 people, the Riviera Comedy Club hosts a regular rotation of comedy acts, most

local and some headliner. Call in advance for scheduling. Teenagers are allowed to attend performances. ($$)

RIVIERA SHOPPING ARCADE
(☞ *Shopping)* Riviera features a small selection of impulse shops ranging from gifts to finer cosmetic items to sweets and clothes. The **Riviera Arcade** has some of the latest video arcade and redemption games.

CIRCUS CIRCUS

(2880 Las Vegas Blvd ☎ 877.224.7287 ✆ circuscircus.com) Las Vegas has fluctuated from adults-only to family-friendly and back to adults-only once again. However, one resort that has stuck to its thematic principles since its opening, and has become a fixture as one of the few "true" family havens in Las Vegas, is Circus Circus. The more northerly location, endless rows of slot machines, and inexpensive minimum bids might lead the layperson to believe that this is a casino for the masses. But *no* – many of the customers are not here for the gaming alone; they are here for the family, and this is *the* family resort of Las Vegas. And the theme couldn't be simpler – spend a day at the circus!

The Circus Circus casino first opened without a hotel in October 1968. It was intended to be the family-friendly alternative to Caesars Palace. Jay Sarno, who opened Caesars just two years earlier, wanted to build a Roman circus next to Caesars for families. Instead, however, he opened it a few miles uptown and gave the theme of the more familiar *circus* circus.

After changing corporate hands many times, it landed in the lap of Mandalay Bay Group, and ultimately into the MGM Mirage roster. Ironically, despite the fact that they opened as sister resorts by Sarno, Caesars and Circus Circus are now owned by two directly competing companies; Harrah's and MGM Mirage.

Altogether, Circus Circus is an inexpensive mega-resort that attracts budget-minded families to the Las Vegas strip. It is a bit run-down and does show its age, and it doesn't have the shiny new quality of the resorts further south. However, Circus Circus delivers a classic Vegas vacation that the whole family can enjoy.

ACCOMMODATIONS

There are about 3,770 guest rooms and suites at the affordable Circus Circus, making this the largest moderately-priced resort on the Las Vegas strip. Most of the rooms are located in the tower, with about 800 in the manor section; both offer standard rooms and suites, and have their own amenities. Additionally, the resort is home to a **Kampgrounds of America** (KOA)-operated RV park (the only one on the strip), with about 400 full hook-ups, laundry facilities, a swimming pool, and more.

CASINO

The casino floor is a circus in and of itself. At a large 107,000 square feet of slot and table games, a race & sports book, and a poker room, there is always activity at Circus Circus.

POOL

(☞ *Swimming Pools*) The pool facilities at Circus Circus are small and functional, but with 3 pools and Jacuzzis scattered throughout the premises (one of which is in the adjacent campground), they are readily-available. Snacks are available in the pool area, but otherwise the place has few frills.

RESTAURANTS

The primary finer dining choice at Circus Circus is **The Steak House**, which serves steak, fish, lobster, and more. More casually, **The Garden Grill** features many favorite American foods. **Westside Deli** offers quick bites, such as sandwiches and donuts. **Mexitalia** has fast Mexican and Italian-inspired dishes. The large **Circus Buffet** serves standard choices of buffet-style foods all day.

THE CIRCUS

(☞ *Free Shows*) At a staggering 120,000 square feet, the main attraction at the resort is listed in the Guinness Book of World Records as being the "World's Largest Permanent Circus". Yes, the circus here is larger even than the casino. Every 15-30 minutes from early in the morning until late at night, spectacular stunts commence, including a high-wire act, swings, acrobatics, and more. And the best part is, watching the circus acts is always free.

ADVENTUREDOME

(☞ *Rides and Attractions*) Theme parks have come and gone in Las Vegas, but the Adventuredome is here to stay. Attached directly to the hotel, this five-acre *indoor* glass "dome", which opened in 1993, is a small but jam-packed amusement park with thrill rides and family-friendly attractions.

There are some top-quality rides here: **Canyon Blaster**, an indoor roller coaster, is the only one in the world with a double-corkscrew and double-loop. **Slingshot** shoots people up 100 feet straight into the air, only to have them free-fall back down a few seconds later. Also on the premises is an **IMAX Ride** motion simulator which offers a rotating schedule of movies. Of course, classics like a small **carousel**, a **Ferris Wheel**, **bumper cars,** and even a water flume ride can be found here.

The Adventuredome is a unique family treat on the otherwise adult-oriented strip, and adds greatly to an already fun-filled family resort. It is free to walk around the facility. However, ride experiences within the park may be purchased individually or as an all-day pass. For more information, visit the website adventuredome.com. ($/$$)

MIDWAY

(☞ Rides and Attractions) With an impressive array of 200+ video arcade, redemption, and midway games, the Circus Circus Midway draws throngs of families, teens, and children. Located above the casino floor and near the permanent circus, the Midway is always bustling with activity, and the regular circus performances make this section of the resort very popular.

SAHARA

(2535 Las Vegas Blvd ☏ 702.737.2111 ⌁ saharalasvegas.com) The "Hollywood" version of the African desert has made its way into Nevada – sort of. Loosely based on romantic images of Morocco, Sahara sits on a lonely but large site on the northern Las Vegas strip. It is one of the northernmost hotels on the contiguous Las Vegas Strip (only Stratosphere on Las Vegas Boulevard is further north).

Sahara first opened in 1952 on the site of Club Bingo, which had opened a few years earlier, in 1947. Sahara has had its hand in several ownership situations, but it has largely been privately controlled. In 1995 William H. Bennett purchased the troubled Sahara and gave it a major face-lift (including adding new restaurants and attractions), hoping to attract more visitors to the north strip. Though he passed away in 2002, his efforts gave Sahara the momentum it needed to keep up with the mega-resorts and compensate for its out-of-the-way location. Today it is one of the oldest continuously-operating resorts on the strip.

ACCOMMODATIONS
Sahara boasts about 1,700 rooms and suites, which were all remodeled in the late 1990s. It is an inexpensive yet relatively remote hotel choice for your Las Vegas stay.

CASINO
The casino at Sahara is about 80,000 square feet of gaming space, including slots and tables. The resort also features a sports book and poker facility.

POOL
(☞ *Swimming Pools*) Sahara's outdoor pool is large – about 5,000 square feet. However, it is not heated and only open during the summer seasons, leaving off-season visitors a bit high and dry. The complex as a whole is small and functional, with little shade offered by some scattered trees and a snack and drink bar.

RESTAURANTS
The **House of Lords** is Sahara's fine dining choice and features a range of foods, including steak and seafood. For casual food, **Paco's** serves classic Mexican dishes. The **NASCAR Café** serves classic American food. The **Caravan Café** has a wide variety of fast American food choices, and the large **Buffet** offers a range of choices for breakfast, lunch, and dinner.

CYBER SPEEDWAY
(☞ *Rides and Attractions*) Video game racing enthusiasts will delight at Sahara's Cyber Speedway. Here, they can drive 7/8 size stock cars on a virtual racetrack, while competing with other drivers in real-time. In this 35,000 square foot entertainment center, participants sit in hydraulic-powered vehicles while watching a screen that simulates a racecourse. The whole experi-

ence is designed to be an accurately-simulated racing experience. Participants are clocked as they compete to win first place. ($$)

SPEED – THE RIDE
(☞ *Rides and Attractions*) A newer addition to Sahara is its resident roller coaster, Speed. This modern thrill starts off inside the resort and proceeds to twist and turn its way around the main exterior entryway. When it reaches its high point, it does the whole course in reverse. Much of the coaster's track is visible from the sidewalk as visitors walk by the resort. ($$)

STRATOSPHERE

(2000 Las Vegas Blvd ☎ *702.380.7777* 🖰 *stratospherehotel.com)* The unmistakable landmark needle at the northern tip of the Las Vegas strip, Stratosphere's remote location is no detriment to its popularity. In addition to some of the best panoramic views of Las Vegas from 1,149 feet skyward, Stratosphere is the tallest building not only in Las Vegas but also in the United States west of the Mississippi River, as well as the nation's tallest freestanding observation tower. Plus, it is the only resort complex on the Las Vegas strip that is actually in the City of Las Vegas.

Of course, the most prominent feature of the resort is the tower, which can be seen for many miles. Though the casino itself is not located in this tower, the resort takes great advantage of its vertical stature by doing something no other resort in the world has done: in addition to a restaurant, lounge, and observation deck, the Stratosphere tower has an *outdoor amusement park* 1,149 feet above ground, on the roof! This unique feature has made the resort a popular one for those who visit Las Vegas with no intention of gambling.

With an opening in 1996, Stratosphere sits on the site of Bob Stupak's Vegas World Casino. Despite some financial hardship early on, it is doing well. Today it is operated by American Casino & Entertainment Properties.

ACCOMMODATIONS
The Stratosphere is a relatively large strip hotel, despite its more remote location. It features about 2,400 guest rooms and suites. The rooms are not located in the tower itself, but rather in a collection of several smaller, surrounding buildings. The towers have had recent renovations.

CASINO
The casino at Stratosphere, located on the ground floor of the resort, features about 80,000 square feet of gaming space. It includes all the popular slot and table games and a race & sports book. The décor is vaguely reminiscent of the 1960s spaceage — kind of like you're stepping into a neon-retro-cyber wonderland, but with slot machines.

RESTAURANTS
Stratosphere's dining choices reflect the kind of colorful fun found throughout the resort. **Naga** serves Asian-inspired foods and has a sushi bar. For casual food, **Lucky's Café** and **Roxy's Diner** serve a wide range of classic American food in vintage Vegas settings.

Crazy Armadillo is a mix of restaurant, bar, and club, with a wide range of casual food and drink choices, and features a tequila bar. The **Courtyard Buffet** allows diners to enjoy a wide range of buffet-style foods for breakfast, lunch, and dinner.

THE TOWER
(☞ *Rides and Attractions*) The skyscraping needle at the northern tip of the Las Vegas strip can be seen for many miles in all directions. The Stratosphere's tower, one of the most recognizable

icons in Las Vegas, is filled to the brim with things to do. Tower attractions must be planned in advance, and tickets for the attractions, when applicable, are purchased on the ground floor before taking the elevator up to the 900-foot-high observation area.

At the top are several different kinds of attractions. The most popular is the basic **observation deck**, which allows visitors to see the entire Las Vegas valley at 360-degrees. The amusement park features regular rides in a unique location, from **Insanity**, which dips riders over the edge, to the **Big Shot** on top of the tower, which blasts thrill-seekers over 100 feet *straight up*.

The upscale **Top of the World** restaurant is also located in the Tower. The restaurant's main floor slowly revolves around the tower, giving diners a great view of the Las Vegas valley no matter where they are seated. Dining choices include steak and fish, and dress is business casual. ($/$$$)

POOLS AT STRATOSPHERE

(☞ *Swimming Pools*) Stratosphere is home to two separate pool areas. The main pool area, an outdoor facility on the eighth floor, offers a very large pool and spectacular sweeping views of the surrounding Las Vegas area, surpassed only by views from the tower itself. The pool area features snack, food service, and pool-related sundries.

Beach Club 25, another outdoor pool area located on the 25th floor, is much smaller, but is designed exclusively for adults over age 21. The facility includes fitness equipment and drinks.

ENTERTAINMENT

Stratosphere's largest theatrical venue is the Theater of the Stars. It is home to **American Superstars**, a tribute show featuring celebrity impersonations. Also available is the afternoon show

Viva Las Vegas, a musical-comedy which is regularly mentioned as being one of the best afternoon shows in the city. For tickets, contact the resort directly.

Resorts: Downtown Las Vegas

Before the strip, even before legalized casino gambling, there was Downtown Las Vegas. Commercially centered on Fremont Street, the downtown section was the birthplace of the glitz, glamour and gambling that made the Las Vegas image famous to begin with. Today, the area serves as a bustling, bright retrospective of the old days, and is well worth a visit by any tourist.

Downtown Las Vegas is north of the strip, about three miles from the north end of the Stratosphere, and it has a fundamentally different atmosphere from the strip resorts. It is glittery, congested, cramped and smoky, with a faded antique quality. It feels like an area filled with old locals' casinos, yet the crowds are decidedly tourist. The famous signs and awnings sparkle with countless lights, just as they have for many years. Nevertheless, Fremont Street has been beautifully updated to attract visitors, yet it still manages to stay true to its classic roots.

Unlike the separate areas of South Las Vegas Boulevard, Downtown Las Vegas is not accessible on foot from the strip. Taxicabs, shuttle services and public transportation are readily available to transport visitors, but the trek involves leaving the comfort of the strip, and venturing into the "real" city of Las Vegas.

Fremont Street itself dates back as far as 1905. Fremont and the surrounding neighborhood were home to many of the hotels and gaming establishments of the city's first golden age. There was gambling on Fremont long before it was officially legalized, and the bright neon signs adorned with countless flashing lights to attract visitors eventually earned it the nickname "Glitter Gulch." It used to be that when you went to Las Vegas as a tourist, you went to Fremont Street.

However, with the popularization of strip hotels in the 1950s and 1960s, crowds were drawn away from the congested downtown area and onto Las Vegas Boulevard, where the room to grow seemed almost infinite. As a result, poor Fremont Street fell into disrepair as tourism to the once glamorous area declined.

THE FREMONT STREET EXPERIENCE 🔲

Until recently, Fremont Street and the surrounding neighborhood attractions were all but avoided by tourists to Las Vegas, who instead opted for the newer resorts of the strip a few miles away. However, in a much-anticipated plan to revitalize the neighborhood, in 1994, the street was closed to automobile traffic forever. A year later a new high-tech upgrade was well underway, turning a portion of the once rusty Downtown Las Vegas into The Fremont Street Experience, an outdoor pedestrian mall of sorts with all the great tacky casino and gift shop greatness of yesteryear.

Sheltered from the blistering desert heat by a 15,000-foot canopy stretching four blocks along the street, visitors can enjoy the Fremont Street of old not with the rugged urban glow of yesteryear, but as a theme park. Visitors park their cars (or take public transportation) to the street, and spend their day strolling along the sun-sheltered district, exploring the many gift shops and gift carts, entering some of the world's most famous casinos just as people have for decades.

Of course, the famous signs and lights are still there, including those for the landmark **Binion's Horseshoe**, **Golden Nugget**, and **4 Queens**, which collectively grace many a postcard.

Downtown vs. The Strip

There are in fact two very different kinds of Las Vegas casino-hotels. There are the newer, larger, more expensive and more full-featured strip hotels. And then there are the resorts that glitter with the shine of yesteryear, calling out to patrons not with a theme or special restaurants, but with good old-fashioned casinos; small, smoky, claustrophobic and charming. Sometimes built for locals and sometimes built for tourists, these are the places that made Las Vegas famous, and they are predominantly in the downtown area.

This section describes some important differences between the two different resort types. Sure, some resorts blur the line (Barbary Coast and Golden Nugget could easily switch their respective places on the strip or downtown), but there are distinct differences between the two experiences.

THE LOCALS' CASINO
Though decidedly tourist-driven, downtown resorts have the feel of locals' casinos. Elsewhere in Vegas (and indeed Nevada) locals' casinos cater away from the tourists by offering unique and less expensive games and (sometimes markedly) better gambling odds. Downtown and Fremont Street gives tourists the "local" experience.

DÉCOR
Downtown casinos are smaller, more claustrophobic and aged than the big new resorts of the strip. Visitors will immediately notice the more antiqued look of the resorts. Decorative themes is virtually nonexistent; the resorts rely much on the gambling and games to draw visitors.

HOTEL SIZE

Hotels in the downtown area contain fewer guest rooms on average than the hotels along the strip. More for the budget-minded, suites and special room types are rare, frills and amenities (such as a swimming pool or upscale restaurant) may lack in quality or be nonexistent. In fact, many people who play at a downtown casino are not spending the night downtown.

DINING CHOICES

If Las Vegas is known for great inexpensive buffets and steak dinners, it is largely because of the downtown resorts! Dining and buffet specials abound; even if you're not staying at the resort, the cheapest buffets are almost always highly advertised.

On the other hand, there is far less choice of restaurants in a downtown resort, and far less variety of dining styles and food options.

CASINOS

Downtown-area casinos are considered by many to have the flavor of "locals casinos" – small (40,000 feet or less), less expensive, and occasionally unique games. Most of them have some kind of loyalty program. They are cramped, often crowded and flashy, sometimes darker and well worn. Tourists regularly prefer Fremont Street gaming establishments when they have had enough of the expensive table games of the strip.

EL CORTEZ HOTEL

(600 East Fremont Street ☎ 702.385.5200 ✆ elcortezhotelcasino.com)
Though it officially dates back to as early as 1941, the El Cortez Hotel & Casino began its claim to fame in 1945 when Benjamin Siegel purchased it. Being one of his first Las Vegas investments,

he sold it a mere six months later, using the profits in part to establish his famous Flamingo on the strip a few miles away.

In the early 1960s, it was purchased by Jackie Gaughan, who already had interests in several other area casinos. He would eventually gain control (either by purchasing or building) several casinos in the downtown area, including the Plaza Las Vegas. In 2004, he sold off most of his properties to Barrick Gaming, but maintained control of the El Cortez.

While still on Fremont Street, the El Cortez Hotel is just off the Fremont Street Experience section of town, rendering it a more budget-minded approach to downtown Las Vegas. However, the Fremont Street light show may be seen from certain locations in this smaller complex. There is no swimming pool, no resident show, and only a few restaurants. Though it has grown, it is still a small resort (with limited or no frills) and an ideal fit for those wishing to experience Fremont Street on a tighter budget, and stay in one of the oldest resorts in Downtown Las Vegas.

ACCOMMODATIONS

El Cortez houses about 300 guest rooms. With no pool, health club, or entertainment options other than casino gambling, (though a hair salon is located on-property) this is an extremely reasonably-priced resort with no frills.

CASINO

The casino floor at El Cortez is about 50,000 square feet. El Cortez is truly a locals casino – very few players spend the night. Additionally, the minimum bids and slot machine denominations are small, with the most expensive slots being around five dollars. It is a smoky and congested facility (common in Downtown), with some of the standard table and slot games, and a race & sports book.

RESTAURANTS

El Cortez has about three casino bars scattered around the facility. The hotel also offers banquet and catering capabilities on the premises. **Roberta's** is the most upscale restaurant on-site, has reasonable prices (entrees are under $20) and a standard chicken and steak menu. Additionally, the **Chinese Kitchen Buffet** is open for breakfast and dinner.

FITZGERALDS LAS VEGAS

(301 Fremont Street ☎ 702.388.2400 🖰 fitzgeraldslasvegas.com) For those entering The Fremont Street Experience from its far eastern end, they will first come across Fitzgeralds Las Vegas; the Irish-themed resort-casino which is adorned with shamrocks. One of the newer hotels in the Downtown area, Fitzgeralds first opened in 1980 as the Sundance Hotel. After some renovations about a decade later it eventually became Fitzgeralds. It was renovated again in 2003 with more modern casino resort amenities.

Today, there are several Fitzgeralds establishments, including ones in Colorado and Tunica, Mississippi. Collectively, this small chain is owned by Majestic Star Casino.

ACCOMMODATIONS

The canopy above Fremont Street masks the towering 34-floor hotel rising above Fitzgeralds casino. The resort features about 630 guest rooms and a few suites. Rates are reasonable, and the resort caters to the budget-minded traveler.

CASINO

The casino at Fitzgeralds is small (compared to guest room count) at 42,000 square feet. Its prime location on Fremont Street makes it almost always crowded, and it is the only casino within the Fremont Street Experience that is on two floors. The standard table games and slots are represented here, as well as a race and sports book.

THE POOL AT FITZGERALDS
Fitzgeralds features one small outdoor pool and Jacuzzi, with several lounge chairs. Located near the back of the resort, the pool is purely functional and is only open during the warmer months of the year.

RESTAURANTS
Fitzgeralds has a few casual restaurant choices. The **Limericks Steakhouse** serves steak and seafood. **Molly's Buffet** offers continental buffet-style dining for all meals of the day.

LUCKY LOOKOUT BALCONY
(☞ *Rides and Attractions*) For a nice view of the surrounding Fremont Street Experience, including the light show, the Lucky Lookout Balcony is hard to beat.

THE FREMONT

(200 East Fremont Street ☎ *800.851.1703* ↻ *fremontcasino.com)* Located on the street of the same name, the Fremont Hotel and Casino was the tallest building in downtown Las Vegas when it first opened in 1956. As of 1985, the Fremont Hotel & Casino is a part of Boyd Gaming. As such, it is also called "Sam Boyd's Fremont".

Like most of the downtown hotels, amenities and services are limited at Fremont. However, with an established relationship with the California Hotel a short walk away, many of the amenities not readily available at Fremont can be experienced just around the corner at this "sister property".

ACCOMMODATIONS

The hotel has about 450 rooms. Though the resort lacks many of the frills found on the strip a few miles away, its almost unprecedented location in the middle of the Fremont Street Experience gives visitors many activities which are only a few steps away. However, guests of the hotel may be permitted to use the pool facilities of the nearby California Hotel, which is also a Boyd Gaming establishment (contact the hotel for more information).

CASINO

Fremont has about 32,000 square feet of crowded gaming space, including slots and table games in a typical downtown environment. The facility also has a race and sports book.

RESTAURANTS

Dining at the Fremont is a more casual experience. The **Second Street Grill** serves continental foods. **Tony Roma's** features ribs, chicken, and other comfort foods. The **Paradise Buffet** offers continental buffet-style foods in a tropical setting.

FOUR QUEENS

(202 East Fremont Street ☎ 702.385.4011 ⁂ fourqueens.com) In the center of Fremont Street is one of the most photographed street corner decorations in Las Vegas: the "4 Queens" entryway awning. It is a popular subject for good reason – it looks like the brightest casino sign on Fremont Street, and has been a permanent fixture and symbol of downtown Las Vegas since its opening in 1966. Named not for the playing cards, but in respect of the founder's four daughters, the Four Queens Hotel and Casino draws large crowds despite its small casino floor.

ACCOMMODATIONS

The nineteen-story Four Queens Hotel has about 690 guest rooms in two towers, including suites and Jacuzzi rooms. The hotel is without many amenities (such as pool or fitness center) but it does have a gift shop, which has basic gift items and sundries.

CASINO

With a modest New Orleans French Quarter theme, Four Queens' casino floor is about 32,000 square feet, and has the standard slot and table games represented. Additionally, Four Queens is one of the only casinos in Las Vegas to have a player's club specifically devoted to senior citizens: **Club 55**.

RESTAURANTS

Hugo's Cellar, a fine dining establishment, is constantly rated as one of the best gourmet restaurants in Las Vegas – a major accomplishment in this restaurant-centric city! Wine, cheese, steaks, fish, and dessert are served.

Four Queens also offers a few more casual restaurants. **Magnolia's Veranda** serves continental foods overlooking the casino floor. The **Chicago Brewing Company** features a micro-brewery and comfort foods such as pizza.

BINION'S GAMBLING HALL

(128 East Fremont Street ☎ 800.937.6537 ⏃ binions.com) Benny Binion first opened up his casino on Fremont Street in 1951, calling it *Binion's Horseshoe*. Being the first casino in Las Vegas with widespread complimentary offerings and higher table game limits, it became a popular casino with high rollers. However, Binion's true claim to fame was the popularization of poker as a casino

game. In fact, it was at Binion's Horseshoe where the first *World Series of Poker* tournament was held in 1970.

In the late 1990s, Binion's began cutting costs and eventually closed. In 2004 it was purchased by Harrah's and quickly resold. However, Harrah's retained the "Horseshoe" name and thus new owners in 2005 changed the name to *Binion's Gambling Hall*.

Though in the middle of the modern *Fremont Street Experience*, Binion's Gambling Hall is painstaking classic Vegas. Though the World Series of Poker has moved out, Binion's poker legacy still lives on in this strictly classic casino-resort.

ACCOMMODATIONS
Binion's Gambling Hall's hotel is 25 stories tall and features 360 rooms. While the rooms offer no-frills value (relative to the strip resorts), various levels of suites are also available.

CASINO
The casino floor at Binion's is 50,000 square feet and includes many of the popular slot and table games. Of particular note is the multitude of single-deck and double-deck blackjack tables and, of course, its world-famous poker room. To this day, the casino holds regular and very popular poker tournaments.

ROOFTOP POOL
(☞ *Swimming Pools*) The outdoor pool at Binion's is a basic one; simply for swimming and resting (no food or drink service, no cabanas, etc). However, as it is located on the 25th floor (the roof of the resort), the facility offers unparalleled panoramic views of Las Vegas and surrounding countryside. The pool is open seasonally.

RESTAURANTS

With one of the best steak dinners in Las Vegas, Binion's **Ranch Steakhouse** is hard to beat. It serves up several different cuts of steak. Also on the property is **Binion's Original Coffee Shop**, open 24 hours a day.

GOLDEN NUGGET

(129 East Fremont Street ☎ *800.846.5336* ✆ *goldennugget.com)* If Fremont Street had a single definitive resort, one that attracted as much attention as the most popular resorts of the strip, one that upped the ante – so to speak – of this otherwise exhausted section of Vegas, it would be the Las Vegas Golden Nugget.

The Golden Nugget opened in 1946. When Steve Wynn got control of the resort in 1973, he created the Golden Nugget Companies, Inc. and opened several other Golden Nugget resorts in Laughlin and Atlantic City. In 1989 it became part of Wynn's Mirage Resorts. Poster Financial Group owned the resorts briefly in 2004. Finally, in 2005, Golden Nugget Las Vegas was purchased (and is now owned) by *Landry's Restaurants*; the same company that owns *Rainforest Café*.

Today, the Las Vegas Golden Nugget is a AAA Four Diamond Award winner, the oldest recipient of the award in Las Vegas, and the only one in the Downtown area. It is classy, upscale, elegant, and a complete change of pace from its neighbors.

ACCOMMODATIONS

With an impressive 1,900 rooms and suites in three towers, Golden Nugget is the largest hotel in the downtown area of Las Vegas. It is also the most luxurious and most expensive, as it is the only hotel downtown with the AAA Four Diamond award (a distinction it has had for the past three decades – more than any other Las Vegas hotel).

CASINO

The Golden Nugget casino is very small relative to the size of the hotel. Even though it is only 36,000 square feet, it has all the popular table games and slot machines. It also has a large race and sports book, and a poker room.

HAND OF FAITH

(☞ Rides and Attractions) On permanent display in the lobby at the Golden Nugget is what gives the resort the right to its name. Discovered in 1980, the Hand of Faith is the largest golden nugget viewable by the public in the world. It weighs 61 pounds.

THE POOL

(☞ Swimming Pools) Golden Nugget features one outdoor pool and one Jacuzzi. It is the most comprehensive pool facility of the downtown Las Vegas hotels, but still lacks that ultimate aquatic experience of strip pools. Even so, Golden Nugget's has heated water and is open year-round, but poolside drink and food service is only available in the summer.

RESTAURANTS

The Las Vegas Golden Nugget contains some of the best restaurants in the entire Downtown section of Las Vegas. For fine dining, **Vic & Anthony's Steakhouse** serves a wide range of steak and seafood dishes. **Lillie's Noodle House** offers Asian-inspired cuisine.

More casually, **Carson Street Café** serves American food, and **The Buffet** at Golden Nugget serves buffet-style continental food for breakfast, lunch, and dinner.

ENTERTAINMENT
Golden Nugget has several venues for live performances, including the **Theatre Ballroom** and **The Lounge**. Contact the hotel for specific shows, times, and ticket information.

THE VEGAS CLUB

(18 East Fremont Street ☎ *702.385.1664* 🖱 *vegasclubcasino.net)*
Located on the western edge of The Fremont Street Experience, the Vegas Club offers inexpensive accommodations, a few thrills, and a couple unusual extras. It is a scaled-down version of the neighboring Plaza Las Vegas, both of which are managed by the same company, PlayLV. As such, the Vegas Club uses many of the entertainment options available at the Plaza as an incentive to stay here.

ACCOMMODATIONS
The Vegas Club features about 410 rooms and a limited number of suites. The rooms offer limited frills and cater to budget-minded travelers. Those staying at The Vegas Club may have access to various amenities (including pool and fitness center) at the neighboring Plaza Las Vegas.

CASINO
The Vegas Club features a 49,000 square foot casino. The casino, though a bit cramped and congested, has all the standard slots and table games.

RESTAURANTS
The more casual **Upper Deck**, a casino burger joint, is one of the best hamburgers in town according to several sources. However, the big daddy of this restaurant is the tremendous nine-

pound "Big Daddy Burger", which measures a foot in diameter and requires two whole tomatoes and 12 slices of cheese.

GOLDEN GATE HOTEL

(1 Fremont Street ☎ 702.385.1906 ✆ goldengatecasino.net) With regard to slices of history, the hotel at One Fremont Street (on the western edge of the Fremont Street Experience) in downtown Las Vegas is hard to beat. It is here that the tiny Golden Gate hotel sits. Dwarfed by its neighbors in every aspect except its age, this ancient gem has stood its ground almost as long as Las Vegas itself, and unlike most of the rest of the city, it remains nearly exactly as it stood over 100 years ago – almost two decades before Fremont Street itself was paved. It also houses the oldest casino in Las Vegas.

In 1906, a year after Las Vegas was founded, Golden Gate Hotel opened as Hotel Nevada, a name it held for over 50 years. In 1959, it was changed to Golden Gate Hotel after the bridge in San Francisco. A few years later, in 1959, the hotel introduced a Las Vegas first – the ninety-nine cent shrimp cocktail; a deal it still has to this day.

ACCOMMODATIONS
Golden Gate hotel is one of the smallest hotel-casinos in Las Vegas, and certainly the smallest on Fremont Street. At only 109 rooms, it is an aged, budget-minded facility offering almost no amenities other than a great location on Fremont Street.

CASINO
Golden Gate Hotel's tiny casino floor is less than 10,000 square feet. Plus, it has that "classic Vegas" look and feel and has not changed much (if at all) over the years. It looks and feels old and

intimate. The casino features popular slots and table games, as well as a small race and sports book.

RESTAURANTS
Golden Gate Hotel has a limited selection of restaurants and drink options; namely the **San Francisco Shrimp Bar & Deli** and the **Bay City Diner**. However, the "ninety-nine cent shrimp cocktail" is promoted throughout, and is reason enough to visit this tiny corner of Fremont Street. The shrimp is small (larger sizes with larger prices are also available), and includes cocktail sauce.

PLAZA LAS VEGAS

(1 Main Street ☎ 702.386.2110 ✆ plazahotelcasino.com) Book-ending the four-block stretch of the Fremont Street Experience on the western end is the relatively skyscraping Plaza Las Vegas Hotel. One of the largest hotels in the Fremont Street area, the resort is managed by **PlayLV** (playlv.com), who also manages the nearby Vegas Club.

ACCOMMODATIONS
Plaza Las Vegas offers just over 1,000 guest rooms and suites. Though the hotel (like much of downtown) has good options for the budget-minded traveler, the larger size allows it to offer more amenities and perks than the smaller hotels of the area.

CASINO
The 60,000-foot casino floor at Plaza Las Vegas features all the popular table games and slots, a larger race and sports book, and even a bingo parlor and poker room which hosts occasional tournaments.

POOL AND FITNESS CENTER
There is a year-round outdoor pool on the roof of Plaza Las Vegas. During the summer season, snacks and drinks may be available poolside, as well as scheduled entertainment. There is also a fitness center with modern equipment and a running track.

RESTAURANTS
The resident upscale restaurant of the Plaza/Vegas Club resort complex is **Center Stage**. Taking advantage of its prime location at the western end of the Fremont Street Experience, Center Stage has huge windows and a dome shape, allowing diners to overlook all the outdoor action, lights, and glitter of the gulch down below. Specialties include various cuts of meat and lobster.

MAIN STREET STATION

(200 North Main Street ☎ *800.634.6255* ↻ *mainstreetcasino.com)* Located about two blocks north of Fremont Street is the Main Street Station Hotel and Casino. Though it has a more remote location, it still allows for easier walking distance to the other downtown resorts. The resort is a bit more upscale than most of those in the Fremont Street Experience area, while still staying more affordable.

The theme here is Victorian antique – the resort is decorated with all kinds of turn-of-the-century knickknacks, from lighting fixtures to doors and more, and even a portion of the Berlin Wall (located in a rather unique place). Additionally, the resort has a full-featured brewery on-site, where visitors can enjoy several home-grown tastes.

Main Street Station does not have a swimming pool, however access to the neighboring California Hotel is easy, and guests may be permitted to use that hotel's facilities. The two properties are directly connected via an overpass. Main Street

Station, California, and nearby Fremont Hotel and Casino are all managed by Boyd Gaming.

ACCOMMODATIONS
Main Street Station has about 400 rooms on 17 floors with a limited number of suites. Though facilities at the resort are more sparse, guests staying here may have access to facilities (such as a swimming pool) in the nearby California Hotel.

CASINO
The Main Street Station's casino, at about 29,000 square feet, is small for the resort's size. However, it is decorated with all kinds of Victorian antiques, and features all the popular slot and table games.

ANTIQUITIES TOUR
(☞ *Museums*) Main Street Station is loaded with antique artifacts. Therefore, the resort provides interested parties with information on the various antiquities scattered throughout the property. Brochures are available for a self-guided tour that points out and explains the various pieces from the collection. The "tour" gets visitors acquainted with specific pieces, and is a nice way to walk through the casino without gambling.

RESTAURANTS
In addition to standard American fare such as hamburgers and sandwiches, pizza and fish, the **Triple 7 Restaurant** serves its very own home-brewed beer. Choose from at least five different varieties as well as "special" limited-edition brews. The restaurant is open late and offers a laid-back and sometimes noisy atmosphere; it is the most popular place in the resort other than the casino itself.

CALIFORNIA HOTEL

(12 Ogden Avenue ☎ 800.634.6255 ⌁ thecal.com) The California Hotel opened in 1975 and would eventually become the first property owned and operated by Boyd Gaming. Nicknamed "The Cal", it is about one block north of the Fremont Street Experience, and one of the largest resorts in the downtown Las Vegas area. As such, it contains many upscale amenities that aren't available at its smaller neighbors. The resort features a tropical island motif that alludes to a Hawaiian paradise.

ACCOMMODATIONS
The California has about 790 rooms and a generous number of suites that maintain the tropical illusion throughout the resort. The room prices are generally reasonable, and the resort caters to budget-minded travelers.

CASINO
The casino within the California is a decent size, at 60,000 square feet. It features the slots and table games in an environment a bit less cluttered than surrounding resorts. The casino also has a sports book.

THE POOL
(☞ Swimming Pools) The California has one medium-sized pool on the roof of the resort. The pool is outdoors and very basic, and it is only open during the summer months. Guests at several other area hotels, lacking a pool, have access to the pool at California.

BRIDGE AVENUE SHOPPING

(☞ Shopping) The California has a small shopping area. Called "Bridge Avenue", the area features a few snack shops, gifts and branded merchandise, and a small video arcade.

RESTAURANTS

With a selection of porterhouse, steak, and fish, the **Redwood Bar & Grill** is a middle-of-the-road dining establishment: casual but upscale. The restaurant also features live piano entertainment on select occasions.

The Cal also has the **Market Street Café**, open 24 hours, and the **Pasta Pirate**, which serves Italian and seafood dishes.

Resorts: Off-Strip

Las Vegas Resorts aren't confined to just the downtown and Strip areas. In fact, casinos and casino games can exist in many places in the Las Vegas area – bars and restaurants, gas stations, and even airports. This section highlights a few of the major casino resorts around town that aren't specific to either of the two main areas. Some of these resorts are located just off the strip, in the downtown area, or are further away from the main tourist areas of the city.

As visitors will notice, the resorts in this section predominately fall under the "locals" category. Although tourists are free (and encouraged) to use the facilities, the marketing, promotion, and activities generally cater to those living within the Las Vegas area.

PALACE STATION

(2411 W. Sahara Ave ☎ *702.367.2411* 🌐 *palacestation.com)* The Palace Station, one of the largest and most visible locals casino in Las Vegas, opened in 1976 as a bingo parlor. It was the first and flagship resort for the Station Casinos chain. It is also the closest major locals casino to the Las Vegas strip, providing easier access (with an automobile) to North Strip hotels via Sahara Avenue.

ACCOMMODATIONS
Palace Station has just over 1,000 rooms of varying types. The rates are reasonable, and the hotel caters to those who are more budget-conscious.

CASINO

The casino at Palace Station is about 84,000 square feet and features all the favorite slot and table games. It also has a large bingo parlor and a race & sports book. There is a section devoted to Asian-themes casino games as well. Despite it being a locals casino, the floor at Palace Station is large and more open, and does cater to tourists as well as locals.

POOL AREA

Palace Station features two small outdoor pools. It is a minimal facility that gets the job done (of having an on-site pool) with no frills. There may also be limited drink service. There is also a small fitness center.

RESTAURANTS

Dining at Palace Station is a more casual affair. The **Broiler** restaurant offers continental food choices in a relaxed environment. The **Grand Café** features a very wide selection of lighter food. **Pasta Palace** has Italian-inspired dishes, and **Guadalajara** features Mexican food. The **Gourmet Feast** has buffet-style dining for breakfast, lunch, and dinner.

SOUND TRAX

The Palace Station's resident entertainment venue is Sound Trax, a small comedy club that has a regular schedule of performers, predominantly comedians.

LAS VEGAS HILTON

(300 S. Paradise Rd ☎ 888.732.7117 ⌂ lvhilton.com) Though the property is technically off the strip (*not* located on Las Vegas Boulevard), this mammoth resort is so close and so similar to the strip resort design that it can easily be grouped with all the

nearby North Strip resorts. Plus, its prime location immediately adjacent to the Las Vegas Convention Center, coupled with easy monorail access, makes this a very accessible location.

The Las Vegas Hilton began as the International Hotel. Started and owned by investor Kirk Kerkorian, it was the largest hotel in the world when it first opened in 1969. It was also at the International Hotel where Elvis Presley broke performance records as the resident entertainer throughout much of the 1970s, up until the end of his life – he even lived in the penthouse suite for eight years. In 1971 the resort was re-named the Las Vegas Hilton when Kerkorian sold it to Hilton Hotels.

ACCOMMODATIONS

The staggering size of the Las Vegas Hilton, about 3,100 rooms and suites, makes it one of the biggest hotels in Las Vegas; bigger even than many of its nearby strip neighbors. There are regular rooms as well as themed suites, and many other kinds of accommodations. However, the penthouse suite occupied by Elvis in the 1970s is rarely (if ever) available.

CASINO

The 100,000 square-foot casino has it all: favorite slots, popular table games, a poker room, and more. Plus, the **Race & Sports SuperBook** is 30,000 square feet, and the world's largest race & sports book.

RESTAURANTS

Like the best strip resorts, dining options at the Las Vegas Hilton run the gamut of upscale to trendy to casual. Upscale choices: **Andiamo** serves eclectic Italian dishes. **Benihana** features classic and contemporary Japanese food, and **Garden of the Dragon** serves Chinese-inspired dishes. **The Hilton Steakhouse** has steak, chicken and seafood.

More casual choices: **Margarita Grille** features classic Mexican food. Paradise Café serves light fare, and is open 24 hours a day. Also, **The Buffet** serves a wide range of buffet-style continental food for breakfast, lunch, and dinner.

STAR TREK: THE EXPERIENCE

(☞ Rides and Amusements ✆ startrekexp.com) When in Las Vegas, Star Trek fans descend in droves to one of the city's most popular attractions. At the Las Vegas Hilton, **Star Trek: The Experience** is a theme park and museum of sorts dedicated entirely to the perpetually-popular television shows, movies, and cultural phenomenon that is Star Trek. Visitors enter the facility and are immediately swarmed with possibilities to explore and live the show.

The **History of the Future** museum features over 200 different articles from the actual television shows. On display are costumes, set pieces, props, and other memorabilia that was used in the movies and shows.

For a less educational experience, there are two major theme park-type attractions: **Borg Invasion 4D** and **Klingon Encounter**. Using motion simulation, 3D effects and sensory stimulation, these attractions transport visitors into the world of Star Trek for some neat (and scary) special effects and motion simulation.

Eating in the world of Star Trek involves a stop at **Quark's Bar & Restaurant**. Here, visitors enjoy a futuristic drinking and dining experience and upscale food choices. To top off the experience, visitors stroll through a massive shopping promenade featuring a seemingly limitless supply of branded merchandise, and can even have souvenir photos taken aboard the Enterprise bridge.

Star Trek: The Experience is a worthy visit, especially for those who enjoy the series. As the attractions are priced separately (packages are available), this is a pricey outing, and costs for a family or group can soar into many hundreds of dollars.

POOL

The third floor pool deck at the Las Vegas Hilton features one mid-sized pool, a Jacuzzi, and lots of patio space. The pool area is outdoors and open seasonally. Occasionally the area plays host to "pool parties" which features live music, poolside casino table games, and a cover charge. The best part of the pool, however, is its view of the Las Vegas strip.

Also nearby are a fitness center, spa facilities, and tennis courts. Drinks may be available in the area at the **Cabana Bar** when the pool itself is open.

HILTON THEATER

The Hilton's major performance venue is the Hilton Theater. With 1,700 seats, this large theater plays host to popular names in music and other entertainers. The Hilton Box Office has information about performers and schedules.

GOLD COAST

(4000 W. Flamingo Rd. ☎ *888.402.7278* 🕆 *goldcoastcasino.com)* Coast Casinos opened the Gold Coast Hotel and Casino in 1986. Less than two miles west of the Mid-Strip hotels and resorts, the Gold Coast markets itself almost exclusively to locals, and features a few key entertainment options not available in a tourist's casino. Today, Coast Casinos is managed by Boyd Gaming, and Gold Coast pairs itself with the nearby Barbary Coast (on the Strip) and The Orleans.

ACCOMMODATIONS
Gold Coast is a larger locals hotel. The 700+ rooms at Gold Coast offer basic amenities and cater largely to the budget-minded traveler.

CASINO
The casino at Gold Coast is surprisingly large. In fact, at 120,000 square feet it is one of the larger casinos in Las Vegas. The casino features many of the favorite slot and table games. It also features a large Bingo parlor, a poker room, and a large race & sports book.

POOL
Gold Coast has a midsized outdoor pool that is open year-round. Located in the back area of the resort, the area offers basic pool amenities, including limited drink service.

RESTAURANTS
There are several more casual dining choices at Gold Coast. The **Cortez Room** serves steak and seafood. **Arriva** features classic Italian dishes. Open 24 hours, the **Monterey Room** offers lighter continental choices. **Ping Pang Pong** serves Chinese food. The **Ports O' Call Buffet** has a wide range of buffet-style food.

BOWLING
A unique feature not found in tourist resorts, Gold Coast features a very large on-site bowling alley. The center has 70 lanes, lockers, food, a pro shop, shoe and equipment rental, and more. This full-featured establishment has regular bowling hours, league bowling, and even "cosmic" (dark-lit) bowling. For specific times, prices, and availability, contact the resort.

RIO

(3700 W. Flamingo Rd ☎ *866.746.7671* ✆ *playrio.com)* Billed as an "all-suite" hotel, Rio Hotel and Casino opened in 1990 as a locals casino. In 1999 Rio was taken over by Harrah's Entertainment, which would ultimately combine with Caesars to be the largest gaming company in the world. Today, even though it is located just off the strip, it is considered by many to be an on-strip property with the same kinds of amenities and entertainment to be found at the neighboring strip resorts.

Like much of Harrah's roster, Rio exhibits a perpetual party, a carnival and festival atmosphere, with a bit of Mardi Gras. Overall, however, Rio is one of Harrah's more upscale properties, with luxurious amenities and large guest rooms.

ACCOMMODATIONS
Rio's major claim to fame is its upscale and roomy accommodations. Each and every one of the 2,500 rooms is listed as a "suite". They are each over 600 square feet (more than twice that of an average hotel room) with a living area and floor-to-ceiling windows. Of course, additional levels of suites are available.

CASINO
The casino floor at Rio is about 120,000 square feet and features the latest popular slot machines and table games, as well as a race & sports book.

POOL
The outdoor, year-round pool facility at Rio – called Ipanema Beach, and one of the better of these in Las Vegas – is thoroughly themed to resemble a tropical beach. In fact, one of the area's four pools actually has a sandy bottom, and the design of

an ocean shore. Oddly-shaped pools, tropical trees, umbrellas, waterfalls, a wide selection of poolside beverages, and more add to the ambience of an ocean resort. Rio also has a **Spa** and **Fitness Center** with a wide range of services.

RESTAURANTS

Rio has a wide range of restaurants from which to choose. Fine dining: the **Fiore Steakhouse** features upscale steak and seafood choices. **Antonio's Italian Ristorante** serves a wide range of classic Italian dishes. **Gaylord India Restaurant** offers Indian meat and vegetarian foods. **Bamboleo** serves classic and contemporary Mexican-inspired dishes.

Casual dining: **Mah John Chinese Kitchen** features traditional Chinese food, and **Hamada's Asiana** serves Japanese food, and has a sushi bar. The **All-American Bar & Grille** offers quality American food. **Buzio's Seafood Restaurant** serves seafood and features views of the pool area. The **Carnival World Buffet**, one of the best buffets in the city, offers a wide range of seafood, continental and international buffet-style food.

PALMS

(4321 W. Flamingo Rd. ☎ *702.942.7777* 🖰 *palms.com)* One word best describes this newer entry into the Las Vegas upper class: "sexy". Less than two miles west of the mid-strip area is Palms, one the most upscale and trendy off-strip establishments in Las Vegas. It opened in November of 2001, and has since become known as a sleek, sophisticated destination for the young and rich. So much so, in fact, it hosted the 12th season of MTV's youth-centric television show "The Real World". The activities,

from several posh nightspots to many themed suites, show that "youth", at Palms, means "young and rich".

Palms is owned by the Maloof Family, whose primary investments include ownership of basketball teams in both the NBA and WNBA. As such, there is a sports theme to the resort, although much of it is understated or expressed in a stylish way.

ACCOMMODATIONS

The Palms has a relatively small number of rooms, about 450, given its immense recent influx of interested tourists. However, recent expansions have given the resort a boot of rooms and it is likely that the guest room count will increase over time. There are many unique room types and suites (the most lavish of which are called "fantasy suites") available, for everything ranging from regular oversize rooms to romantic outings to bachelor parties.

CASINO

The casino floor at the Palms is about 95,000 square feet and features the most popular slot and table games. Palms also has two different poker rooms, one for low stakes and one for high stakes, and a race & sports book.

POOL AND SPA

The Palms has a large outdoor pool facility that has, like the rest of the hotel, been expanding and re-inventing itself since its opening. The pool area here has one outdoor pool and several smaller wading pools. Food and drink service may be available, as well as poolside casino games and even massages. The **Spa at the Palms** is a three-story facility that features popular massage and relaxation treatments, and a fitness center. Portions of the spa overlook the pool.

RESTAURANTS

Dining choices at the Palms are some of the trendiest, hippest, and contemporary joints in Las Vegas. Fine dining: **Alizé**, serving fine French food, is located on the 56th floor of the resort and offers spectacular city views. Other choices include **Garduño's**, which serves Mexican food and **Blue Agave**, with oysters and other seafood choices. **N9ne Steakhouse** offers steaks, seafood, and a comprehensive wine selection. **Little Buddha** has fusion Asian-inspired cuisine and a sushi bar. The **Fantasy Market Buffet** offers a wide selection of buffet-style continental and international cuisine.

THE ORLEANS

(4500 W. Tropicana Ave. ☎ *800.675.3267* ♺ *orleanscasino.com)* The spirit of New Orleans, and with a hearty helping of Mardi Gras-style festive atmosphere, is captured in this locals casino operated by Boyd Gaming. Located a few miles west of the south strip casinos, The Orleans opened in 1998 and has had significant revamping and expansion since then. The resort is large and features a few key amenities that make it unique.

ACCOMMODATIONS

The Orleans features about 1,900 rooms and suites in several towers. The facility has been extensively renovated since its opening, including the addition of a new tower, and touts that its regular rooms are "oversized". The rates cater to a more budget-minded traveler, with fewer frills.

CASINO

The casino floor of The Orleans is an impressive 135,000 square feet. The floor consists of many favorite table and slot games, and there is also a poker room and a mid-sized race & sports book.

POOL AND SPA

The Orleans has an outdoor pool facility, which is open year-round. It features a standard pool and a wading pool. Drinks are available poolside. Also nearby is a **spa**, which includes various spa treatments and a fitness center.

RESTAURANTS

The festive atmosphere of the Orleans continues with its Cajun-influenced dining choices. The **Prime Rib Loft** overlooks the casino and features various specialty prime rib dishes. **Canal Street** serves steak and seafood. **Big Al's Oyster Bar** serves fresh oysters and other seafood. The **French Market Buffet** serves a wide range of buffet-style continental, French, and other international foods for breakfast, lunch, and dinner.

CENTURY ORLEANS 18

One of the perks of being a locals casino is access to a few unusual resort amenities. As with several other Coast Casinos in the area, within the walls of The Orleans is a full-featured 18-screen movie theater, which has a rotating schedule of the latest movies.

BOWLING

An unusual addition to a Vegas casino resort, the bowling center within The Orleans features 70 full-size lanes. The facility is used for leisure bowlers as well as for tournaments and leagues. It also has shoe rental, snacks and drinks, and more. For pricing and information, contact the hotel.

ORLEANS ARENA

(*orleansarena.com*) One of the newest and largest entertainment and event venues in Las Vegas is the impressive 9,000-seat Orleans Arena. It is the home stadium of the Las Vegas Wranglers hockey team, but it also hosts various other sporting and entertainment events. For ticket information and prices, contact the resort or contact **Ticketmaster** (✆ *ticketmaster.com*).

TERRIBLE'S

(4100 Paradise Rd ☎ 702.733.7000 ✆ terribleherbst.com) For tourists not used to Nevada's gaming laws, companies like Herbst Gaming plays an odd, odd role in gambling commerce throughout the state. In addition to the several casinos and resorts in Nevada and across the country run by the Herbst family, they also place slot machines into many non-casino high-traffic locations, such as gas stations and convenience marts. They even own the "Terrible Herbst" gas stations, which accounts for the casino's name. Decorated with a quasi-Southwestern and desert motif, it is a true locals company.

ACCOMMODATIONS
As the resort caters exclusively to locals, the room count is small – about 370. Frills and room choices are minimal. The hotel provides budget-minded accommodations at a location relatively close to the strip.

CASINO
The small casino at Terrible's has a limited number of slots and table games, without a lot of the choice that other, larger casinos have. However, Terrible's does have a large **Bingo** parlor and a race & sports book.

POOL
Terrible's has a small outdoor pool facility, which includes a limited-service spa. The pool is medium-sized, and the surrounding

decorations and foliage, like the rest of the hotel, emulates that of a desert paradise.

RESTAURANTS
The eclectic **Bougainvillea Café** serves a mix of Chinese, Mexican, and American food. The **Terrible's Buffet** offers buffet-style dining and a rotating menu.

HARD ROCK HOTEL

(4455 Paradise Road ☎ *702-693-4455* ⌁ *hardrockhotel.com)* The Hard Rock Café franchise began in 1971 in London and has since spawned well over a hundred restaurant offspring around the world. However, its recent stride of hotels and casino properties is very recent. The Hard Rock Hotel & Casino opened in 1995 just off the Las Vegas strip.

The hotel's theme is just as obvious as the restaurant chain: "anti-establishment rock & roll". Inside, nearly everything is dedicated to popular music, from recording artist paraphernalia to the trademark guitar logo. It is dark, loud, brash, and filled with the youngest, hippest party-seekers allowed to partake in the parties of Las Vegas.

For an off-Strip property, it has many of the amenities and much of the atmosphere of an on-Strip resort. It is small, but packed with activity. Plus, the mid-Strip area is nearby.

ACCOMMODATIONS
There are about 650 rooms at Hard Rock Hotel. There are various levels of suites available, and have a more contemporary style. It is an upscale hotel, with the same service and cleanliness as would be expected from the nicer hotels along the Strip.

CASINO
Like the hotel itself, the casino floor at Hard Rock Hotel is small. The floor is a tiny 30,000 square feet, but features many favorite slot and table game choices.

POOL
The Pool at Hard Rock Hotel is famously one of the best pool areas in Las Vegas. With a tropical desert-style ambience, two large outdoor pools, scattered palm trees, food and drink service, and even a small arm of the casino, it is no wonder that the 5-acre area is almost always crowded.

The pool area offers several gambling choices, including **swim-up blackjack**, one of Las Vegas' few of such offerings. Other blackjack tables are available nearby. The **Palapa**, designed like a breezy tropical gazebo or hut, houses more blackjack tables and a poolside bar. On certain nights, the area becomes a non-stop pool party called **Rehab**, complete with a dance floor and live musical entertainment.

The resort also has a **health club** with the latest fitness equipment. Like the rest of the resort, Hard Rock Hotel's pool area caters to the younger-of-age and beautiful-of-exterior visiting the city.

RESTAURANTS
Hard Rock Hotel's restaurants reflect the resort's more casual and youthful clientele. Fine dining: **AJ's Steakhouse** features steak and seafood in a California-inspired setting. The trendy **Nobu** serves Japanese-inspired food. **Pink Taco** is both bar/club and restaurant serving Mexican food. For lighter food, **Mr. Lucky's 24/7** offers basic American cuisine 24 hours a day.

HOOTERS CASINO

(115 East Tropicana Ave ☎ 866.584.6687 🖱 hooterscasinohotel.com)
Making its debut into the casino industry is the Hooters Casino Hotel, located just east of the South Strip area.

The Hooters restaurant chain began with its first establishment opening in Clearwater, Florida, in 1983. Today, the Hooters Casino Hotel embodies the "south Florida" theme of all Hooters restaurants.

ACCOMMODATIONS
The Hooters Hotel has about 700 guest rooms and a limited number of suites. Like the restaurants, the hotel is designed to be accessible, friendly, a little bit sinful, and entirely accommodating.

CASINO
The casino space at Hooters Hotel is small, with only about 30,000 feet of gaming space. It features many popular slot and table games. Poker is available, as well as a race & sports book combined with a bar atmosphere.

POOL
Hooters has a small outdoor pool area. Open seasonally, the pool features a relaxed atmosphere and swim-up bar. There is also an on-site **spa** with various massage services and treatments.

RESTAURANTS
Of course, Hooters Casino contains the classic **Hooters** restaurant, serving greasy comfort food in a south Florida setting. For more upscale dining, **Dan Marino's Fine Food** offers steaks, seafood, and American comfort food. **The Dam Restaurant** offers lighter fare and a buffet.

BOULDER STATION

(4111 Boulder Hwy ☎ *800.683.7777* ⌁ *boulderstation.com)* The casino section of Boulder Highway – or "Boulder Strip", as it is known, is home to the Boulder Station Hotel Casino. While this strip is known for its locals and smaller casinos and resorts, Boulder Station, part of the Station Casinos repertoire, is a popular choice for tourists as well.

ACCOMMODATIONS
Boulder Station has 300 guest rooms in a 15-story building, including regular rooms and suites. The hotel is more upscale than the modest budget-minded hotels in the area.

CASINO
The casino floor at Boulder is rather large; 75,000 square feet – more space than many locals casinos. It features all the latest slot and table games, plus a huge **bingo** parlor (more common in locals casinos), a poker room, and a race & sports book.

POOL
Boulder Station's single outdoor pool is small, with limited amenities. There may be food and/or drink service, but this is a no-frills pool area.

RESTAURANTS
Boulder Station has a more casual and relaxed approach to dining. **The Broiler** steakhouse serves steak and lobster. **Guadalajara Bar & Grille** features Mexican-style food. **Pizza Palace** and **Pasta Palace** serve casual Italian food. **China Express** offers fast Chinese food. **The Feast** is Boulder Station's buffet, serving a wide range of buffet-style continental food.

KIDS QUEST

(🕾 kidsquest.com) In the tradition of several Las Vegas locals casinos, Boulder Station features Kids Quest, a chain of child care centers designed to give kids supervised activities while parents enjoy the nearby casino. The center features many activities, from video games to indoor slides, and is designed for various age groups.

THE RAILHEAD

A small entertainment venue with about 270 seats, the Railhead at Boulder Station features a schedule of performers and headlining entertainers throughout the year. Show information can be obtained directly through the resort.

SAM'S TOWN

(5111 Boulder Hwy ☏ 702.456.7777 🕾 samstownlv.com) Named after Boyd Gaming founder Sam Boyd, Sam's Town has the distinct recognition of being the first casino hotel in the Las Vegas area that "officially" marketed itself towards locals as opposed to tourists. With an opening in 1979, the Sam's Town Hotel & Gambling Hall maintains its locals atmosphere to this day, with flashy décor and claustrophobic casino ambience.

ACCOMMODATIONS

Sam's Town has about 650 rooms and a limited number of suites. The resort is more budget-friendly than most strip resorts without compromising the quality. Many of the rooms are built around a large ten-story indoor atrium, complete with live trees, a waterfall, and a glass roof.

CASINO

The 150,000 square foot casino at Sam's Town takes up three floors. It features standard slot and table games, a bingo parlor, and a poker room.

POOL

Though Sam's Town has an outdoor pool area, it is small and basic, with only a single pool and Jacuzzi, and limited amenities. However, it is generally open year-round.

RESTAURANTS

Sam's Town has a selection of casual restaurants. **Billy Bob's Steak House and Saloon** offers steaks, chicken, and more in an Old West setting. **Fresh Harvest** has lighter food and late hours. **Willy and Jose's Cantina** serves Mexican-style food. **The Firelight Buffet** offers buffet-style dining and a wide selection of food.

BOWLING CENTER

As a predominantly locals casino, Sam's Town has a bowling center which features 56 lanes open 24 hours a day. On certain nights, the center has **Extreme Bowling**, turning the alleys into a club with lights, loud music, and fog effects. Shoe and equipment rentals are available.

TEXAS STATION

(2101 Texas Star Lane ☎ 702.631.1000 ⌘ texasstation.com) The neighboring city of North Las Vegas holds Texas Station Hotel and Gambling Hall, a massive locals casino with a thorough "Lone Star State" atmosphere. The resort is one of the northernmost casino resorts that is part of the Station Casinos chain.

ACCOMMODATIONS

There are about 200 guest rooms at Texas Stations, making it one of the smallest hotels of the Station Casinos chain.

CASINO

As is common with locals casinos, the small number of guest rooms is no match for the whopping 125,000 square-foot casino. Texas Station features the standard slot and table games, as well as a larger race & sports book, keno center, a poker room, and a large bingo parlor.

BOWLING

Texas Station has a large 60-lane bowling alley with all kinds of flair, including **Cosmic Bowling**. Open 24 hours, the center is very popular with locals, and there are regular **league bowling** sessions. Shoes and other equipment may be rented on-site.

DALLAS EVENTS CENTER

Named after the city in Texas, the 2,000-seat Dallas Events Center is the resident event venue. Events vary; contact the main resort number for specific shows, show times, and prices.

CLUB ARMADILLO

A small venue for music and various live performances, Club Armadillo primarily features local performers and cover bands with weekend and sometimes evening performances.

KIDS QUEST

(kidsquest.com) For those wishing to turn casino gambling into a family outing, Texas Station offers Kids Quest. This supervised child daycare features fun activities for very young children, and is available on an hourly basis.

GREEK ISLES HOTEL & CASINO

(305 Convention Center Drive ☎ 702.752.8000 ⌁ greekislesvegas.com)
With a location oh-so-close to some of the best entertainment on the strip, and even closer to the Las Vegas Convention Center, this tiny resort transports visitors to the Greek Isles with calming Mediterranean-inspired décor.

ACCOMMODATIONS
The Greek Isles features about 200 rooms, including suites.

CASINO
Tiny! The casino at Greek Isles is a mere 7,000 square feet, and features only slot machines (no table games). Luckily, the strip is nearby.

POOL AND SPA
Greek Isles does have an indoor pool and spa facility that is open 24 hours a day. The pool is outdoors, but it is heated.

RESTAURANTS
The only major restaurant at Greek Isles is **Yanni's**. It features a casual ambience and a mixture of Greek and Mediterranean food.

RESORT ATTRACTION GUIDE

Adventuredome	Circus Circus	An indoor amusement park with a roller coaster and midway-style rides.	Rides / Amusements
Auto Collections	Imperial Palace	A showcase of famous and infamous cars, including celebrity vehicles.	Museums
Bellagio Conservatory	Bellagio	An indoor garden of exotic plants arranged in innovative visual displays.	Natural Encounters
CBS Television City	MGM Grand	Participate in audience screenings for test television shows and markets.	Free Shows
Circus	Circus Circus	Regular shows featuring real circus performers defy gravity and nature.	Free Shows
Cyber Speedway	Sahara	Compete in a virtual NASCAR driving experience.	Rides / Amusements
Desert Passage	Aladdin	A desert village and bazaar comes to life with shopping and eating possibilities.	Shopping
Eiffel Tower Experience	Paris Las Vegas	Ascend to the top of a miniature Eiffel Tower's observation deck.	Rides / Amusements
Exotic Cars	Caesars Palace	Collection features a showcase of classic and not-so-classic cars and memorabilia.	Museums
Fall of Atlantis	Caesars Palace	An animatronic show with lights, sounds, and a real aquarium set.	Free Shows
Forum Shops	Caesars Palace	Shop in the twilight of a perpetual Roman evening.	Shopping
Fountains	Bellagio	A programmed display of lights and water dance to music.	Free Shows
Gallery of Fine Art	Bellagio	A collection of classic and contemporary visual art.	Museums

RESORT ATTRACTION GUIDE

Gondola Rides	The Venetian	Take a relaxing gondola ride through the "canals" of "Venice".	Rides / Amusements
Grand Canal Shoppes	The Venetian	See "Venice", from the famous canals to Saint Mark's Square, and do some shopping along the canal.	Shopping
Guggenheim Hermitage	The Venetian	A small but comprehensive exhibition center with a rotating collection of art.	Museums
IMAX	Luxor	Enjoy one of several IMAX filmed attractions, including several in 3D.	Rides / Amusements
King Tut's Tomb	Luxor	Walk through a re-creation of the tomb of King Tutankhamen.	Museums
Le Boulevard	Paris Las Vegas	Spend time in downtown Paris amidst the quaint shops.	Shopping
Lion Habitat	MGM Grand	See lions up close in a glass-enclosed naturalistic environment.	Natural Encounters
Madam Tussaud's Wax Museum	The Venetian	Celebrities and famous scenes of the past and present are re-created as life-size wax figures.	Museums
Mandalay Place	Mandalay Bay	Shop for famous name brands in a contemporary setting.	Shopping
Manhattan Express	New York - New York	A white-knuckle indoor and outdoor steel roller coaster.	Rides / Amusements
Masquerade Show in the Sky	Rio	Tilt your head up and watch an eclectic costumed show reminiscent of Carnivale.	Free Shows

RESORT ATTRACTION GUIDE

Merlin's Magic Motion Machines	Excalibur	Ride inside a motion simulator.	Rides / Amusements
Motion Rides	Luxor	Ride one of several motion simulator attractions.	Rides / Amusements
Secret Garden and Dolphin Habitat	The Mirage	See unusual animals, dolphins, and other creatures in an exotic oasis.	Natural Encounters
Shark Reef	Mandalay Bay	View sharks and other aquatic creatures in a large, elaborately themed walk-through aquarium.	Natural Encounters
Sirens of TI	Treasure Island	Sexy sirens seduce a group of hapless pirates in a cavalcade of music and stunt action.	Free Shows
Speed - the Ride	Sahara	A fast roller coaster that goes backwards and forwards.	Rides / Amusements
Star Trec: The Experience	Las Vegas Hilton	Ride **BORG Invasion** and **Klingon Encounter**, two state-of-the-art simulator attractions.	Rides / Amusements
Stratosphere Tower	Stratosphere	Experience vertigo on some of the world's highest rides.	Rides / Amusements
Via Bellagio	Bellagio	Luxury brand stores in an opulent setting.	Shopping
Volcano	The Mirage	Watch a spectacular volcano erupt several times every night.	Free Shows
White Tiger Habitat	The Mirage	Home of Siegfried and Roy's famous white tigers.	Natural Encounters
Wildlife Habitat	Flamingo	A habitat of exotic birds and other small animals.	Natural Encounters
Wynn Esplanade	Wynn	Browse upscale shops and boutiques in a luxuriously appointed promenade.	Shopping

The Hoover Dam

Wynn Las Vegas

Riding a Gondola in The Venetian

4 Queens on Fremont Street

Select Live Shows

Las Vegas is all about the show: in this town, showier is always better. As such, aside from casinos and vibrant nightlife, one of Las Vegas' most famous attributes is its unique selection of live shows. Nearly every major resort has at least one resident show, sometimes with a run of several years or more. With an array of celebrity shows, magic, circus acts, comedy, artistic, and (more recently) Broadway-style shows, Las Vegas is second only to New York City in terms of United States' live performance venues. Many people visiting Las Vegas must make the decision: *which show do we see?*

Following is a list some of the more well-established (not ephemeral) live shows in Las Vegas. Remember, however, that there are many more shows than are listed here.

SEEING A LIVE SHOW

Unlike most other attractions in Las Vegas, attending a live show requires a bit of advance preparation. Tickets need to be purchased well in advance, as they are regularly sold out, or given as complimentary items to gamblers. Shows can also be expensive; good seats for popular shows can be upwards of $100 per ticket or more.

While most shows are family-friendly, there are a few key ones that are not suitable for children under 18 (or 21), who may not even gain admittance. *You are advised to contact the resort hosting the show for additional information.*

DISCOUNT TICKETS

(Various Locations ✆ tix4tonight.com ✆ tickets2nite.com) Of course, there are ways to get around paying box office prices. For visitors not picky about seats or which show they wish to see, two companies, **Tix4Tonight** and **Tickets2Nite** sell show tickets for

the same night for up to 50% off the box office prices. There are four Tix4Tonight stands located throughout the city, check their website or call 877.849.4868 for more details. Tickets2Nite is located at the Showcase Mall.

RESIDENT AND TOURING SHOWS
Oftentimes, resorts will host resident shows (shows that have a venue for an indefinite period) and touring shows (shows scheduled for a specific time only). A few times, resident shows will have custom-built theaters that will be used by touring shows during the resident's "dark days" (days without a performance). Sometimes it is difficult to tell between a resident show and a touring show. *This section deals only with resident shows*, as they have a longer life and thus warrant entry in a travel book. For touring shows, just check with your resort for whatever happens to be in performance for the day(s) of your visit.

THE CELEBRITY SHOW

There are few things more fleeting than a Las Vegas Celebrity Show. Headliners – big-named stars whom everybody recognizes – will grace a stage, fill the city with billboards, and be the biggest thing since sliced bread. Before you can say "flash in the pan", however, the billboards will be gone, and a new show will have magically taken its place in the limelight. Because of the fleeting nature of these shows, *this book does not talk about celebrity shows, which tend to be touring and thus temporary, unless they are well-established in the city.* Prior to your trip, contact your resort for current show information.

EXOTIC SHOWS

Showgirls in sequined dresses. Elaborate sets. Flash and "razzle dazzle". There is nothing more quintessentially Vegas than the glitzy, glamorous, showy, and oftentimes erotic "Exotic" Las Vegas show. Many times epitomized, often imitated but never duplicated, these unique entertainment offerings are principle examples of the Vegas "pursuit of pleasure". Note, however, that these shows are primarily adult-themed and may feature nudity or other such material inappropriate for children.

CRAZY GIRLS
(☞ *Riviera*) One step away from being a full-fledged strip club, Crazy Girls is among the most sexually explicit resort-hosted shows in town. The women are all topless (and might as well be bottomless) dancing on poles, jiggling their "femininity", and other such acts of Vegas-friendly sin. The show is revue-style, with choreographed dance numbers and some comic relief; there is even some tongue-in-cheek humor as the girls dance to humorous lampoons. Only about 400 people can fit into the theater, making the experience even more intimate than the larger-scale topless shows. Absolutely no children are allowed; only patrons aged 18 and up (although 21 might even be too young).

AN EVENING AT LA CAGE
(☞ *Riviera*) When you spend an evening at La Cage at the Riviera, you are sure to see some of the most glamorous divas and goddesses the entertainment industry has ever known... or so the *men* who are playing these roles want you to think! That's right, you are in the midst of a genuine drag show. French for "The Cage", the term La Cage has – in pop culture - become synonymous with drag shows (remember the play "La Cage Aux Folles"). Despite the mature subject matter and slight off-color

naughtiness, there is no nudity and children over the age of 12 are admitted.

FOLIES BERGERE

(☞ Tropicana) When envisioning the classic Las Vegas show, what comes to mind? Scantily clad showgirls? Glittery costumes with huge feathers? Lavish yet pointless musical numbers? Even if you're not consciously aware of it, you're thinking about the quintessential Vegas showgirl of Folies Bergere, Las Vegas' longest-running stage show. Though it changes as time passes, with the additions of new numbers and acts, it still maintains the classic Vegas flair that fits so well into Tropicana's glitzy ambience.

Although certain performances are specially designed to be family-friendly, parents must be aware that portions of some shows contain topless female dancers; though the acts are generally done tastefully, families may want to avoid these "steamier" shows.

JUBILEE!

(☞ Bally's Las Vegas) When it comes to a show dedicated to Vegas, what better host venue than the 1,040-seat **Jubilee! Theatre** at Bally's? Here, the ongoing revue show features the glitzy dresses, feather props and costumes, bright lights and big production numbers so indicative of classic Las Vegas. This show is strictly adult; the performance features topless dancers, and no one under age 18 is admitted. It doesn't really need to be topless, however, because the elaborate sets and costumes (some weighing 16 pounds or more) draw such attention to themselves.

For an additional thrill, on occasion a **Backstage Walking Tour** of the show is offered, which gives visitors a glimpse into the vast efforts being put into the production during every performance. *Adults Only.*

LA FEMME

(☞ Bally's Las Vegas) In Paris, Crazy Horse is one of the most famous cabaret theaters around. Nude female dancers in erotic performances have attracted millions of patrons to the establishment since it opened in 1951. At MGM Grand, La Femme is an original production from Crazy Horse, brought to Las Vegas. In classic cabaret style, dancers perform to musical numbers and in artful and erotic skits. *Adults Only.*

SPLASH

(☞ Riviera) Here is a Las Vegas show about Las Vegas. It is a revue of revue shows. Touted as a tribute to the Las Vegas of yesterday and today, Splash is a cornucopia of acts that highlights the best of Vegas through the years. The show features topless showgirls in glitzy gowns, skating and motorcycle stunts, rock 'n' roll performances, and other Vegas-inspired images. The theater has room for a thousand people. Though certain performances of the show may cut down on some of the skin to draw more families, it is primarily an adult show intended for *Adults Only.*

THUNDER FROM DOWN UNDER

(☞ Excalibur ☙ thunderfromdownunder.com) A kind of adult variety and male revue show, Thunder from Down Under is an Australian-originated show featuring a regular rotation of skits showcasing men – oftentimes scantily clad – strutting their stuff on stage. Don't expect a strip show, however; these men are legitimately talented and put on quite the performance. The show is also a popular outing for bachelorette parties.

CIRQUE DU SOLEIL

Among the most recognized shows in Las Vegas are those created by **Cirque du Soleil** (cirquedusoleil.com). French for "Circus of the Sun", the company has turned the international idea of a "circus" upside down with its stunning acrobatic displays, fascinating stage sets, and trademark "contemporary" visuals. Cirque shows in Las Vegas are perfect for families, *with one notable exception* (Zumanity is adults-only). Most Cirque du Soleil shows follow the same basic plot ("fish out of water" or "naïve person learning about the world"), but the principle draw is the unique performance art.

MYSTÈRE

(☞ Treasure Island) Mystère was the first permanent fixture of the Cirque du Soleil chain in Las Vegas, and it has been playing for over 10 years. It is a singing, dancing, musical and acrobatic stage show with all kinds of unusual twists on classic circus acts.

KÀ

(☞ MGM Grand) KÀ plays with the performance stage and offers a very modern production, which makes sense for an MGM Grand-hosted show. In fact, the entire set is a kind of futuristic prop that moves as the show progresses. The basic storyline follows a pair of twins ("Ka" can mean "double" in Egyptian folklore) as they battle enemies for control of their empire.

LOVE

(☞ Mirage) Siegfried & Roy's legendary stage performance will be a hard act to follow, but the Mirage seems to have the answer with Cirque's newest Vegas show, LOVE. A mixture of classic music from The Beatles and Cirque du Soleil contemporary ar-

tistic styling and set in theater-in-the-round, LOVE takes audiences on a journey through the colorful worlds of Beatles music.

'O'

(☞ *Bellagio*) Cirque du Soleil has managed to shorten the name of one of its Las Vegas shows to a single letter – a play on the French word for water "eau" (pronounced "o"). This family-friendly (though not intended for kids) show features all the acrobatics, mood-setting music, artistic stunts and performances that one expects, but this time in and out of a giant pool. It is an aquatic, water-centric performance with a stage flooded with water. Performed in an 1,800-seat theatre, 'O' is a visually stunning and beautiful show.

ZUMANITY

(☞ *New York – New York*) *Do not bring the kids to this one!* Billed as "another side of Cirque du Soleil", Zumanity has all the entertaining acts and performances that have made the chain a Las Vegas hit, but with one notable exception: this time it is geared strictly for adults. Zumanity has topless performers and extra erotic "spice". The show itself, a glimpse into the "Human Zoo", is a cabaret-inspired performance that has no storyline but rather showcases the human body in all its acrobatic beauty.

MAGIC SHOWS

Magic acts have been in Las Vegas for decades, and (in most cases) they are perfect entertainment for adults and families alike. Making large props disappear, sawing people in half, and levitation are all performed regularly in Vegas. They are rarely just magic tricks, and often feature lavish sets, impressive props and occasionally even singing and dancing! Following are a few of the more established and popular magic-shows.

LANCE BURTON, MASTER MAGICIAN

(☞ *Monte Carlo ⌁ lanceburton.com*) The long-running magic show starring Lance Burton calls Monte Carlo its home. The star, Lance Burton, performs his magic acts of wonder and awe regularly in the **Lance Burton Theatre**, which seats about 1,200 people (and the show is frequently crowded). The show is absolutely family-friendly, and the magic is large and show-stopping, yet with that classic Las Vegas glitz. This show and the "magic" theme throughout much of the Monte Carlo experience are partly what bring families to this resort. In fact, this is widely regarded as the best family show in Las Vegas.

MAGIC OF RICK THOMAS

(☞ *The Orleans ⌁ rickthomas.com*) With a bevy of props, beautiful assistants, and exotic animals, the Magic of Rick Thomas has all the lavish stage mystery to be expected. Plus, the show stands out because he performs in the afternoon, thus freeing up evenings, or allowing the younger family crowd to enjoy a predominately kid-friendly show.

PENN & TELLER

(☞ *Rio ⌁ pennandteller.com*) The talkative Penn and silent Teller have been performing as a magic act for many years, and have earned a sour reputation in the magic world since they actually *reveal* many of their techniques during their shows. At Rio, they mix comedy, a bit of politics, and lots of great magic in a very down-to-earth and hilarious routine. Kids might not understand much of the humor, but they are certainly allowed to attend.

WORLD'S GREATEST MAGIC SHOW

(☞ *Greek Isles*) A different idea for a Las Vegas magic show: let the tricks speak for themselves. Instead of one headlining magician performing many tricks, this show offers many magicians performing their favorite(s). The magicians and tricks may rotate, but all magicians featured are at the top of their game.

XTREME MAGIC STARRING DIRK ARTHUR
(☞ *Tropicana*) What makes Dirk Arthur's magic so "Xtreme"? It is probably the magician's use of exotic tigers. The performance features larger-than-life stage props and sets, animals, beautiful assistants, and of course many classic acts of magic and mystery.

IMPERSONATION SHOWS

It is hard to picture Las Vegas without an Elvis or other celebrity impersonator. And so we have the Celebrity Impersonation Show – shows dedicated to paying homage to (or in many cases making fun of) the celebrities of yesterday and today.

AMERICAN SUPERSTARS
(☞ *Mirage*) Dressed in their trademark garb and performing their hit songs, American Superstars features impersonators of popular singers and groups. Though the show focuses primarily on current popular acts, there are some stars of yesterday sprinkled in (think Elvis).

DANNY GANS
(☞ *Mirage* ☏ dannygans.com) Danny Gans is a celebrity impersonator, and one of the best ones around. Instead of mastering one or two celebrities, his roster of hundreds and hundreds of voices makes his show just about as wild as can be. The show first opened in the 1,250-seat theater where the Siegfried & Roy show once performed. Gans' performance is eclectic, hilarious, and

oftentimes ripped from the political headlines. He is an impressionist, a singer, a comedian, and more.

LEGENDS IN CONCERT
(☞ Imperial Palace) Legends in Concert has been at the Imperial Palace for over 20 years and is one of the major draws to the resort. The show features live musicians and a regular rotation of celebrity impersonators playing the songs that made them famous. Impersonators rotate on a regular basis, so the show changes frequently. Legends in Concert is a chain of shows, with productions in Branson and Myrtle Beach.

THE RAT PACK IS BACK
(☞ Greek Isles) Where would Las Vegas entertainment be today without the original crooners? "Frank Sinatra," "Joey Bishop," "Dean Martin," and "Sammy Davis, Jr." perform all the songs we have loved, just as they had during the Las Vegas golden years.

BROADWAY SHOWS

Okay, the name is a bit misleading. "Broadway Shows" don't have to be on Broadway in New York City. They can be off-Broadway, at London's West End, or anywhere else, touring or resident. They all, however, have that "Broadway-style" production value.

The "act" (so to speak) of bringing Broadway-style shows to Las Vegas is a fairly new occurrence. Until recently it was nothing more than a rare experiment. Though a few shows that were a hit in New York City have completely tanked when brought here, there are several gems that were able to withstand the prejudice that New York City shows have no place in Las Vegas.

Well, it is too late. They are already here, and many more are coming.

BLUE MAN GROUP

(☞ Venetian) This energetic, percussive, artistic romp through the creative world of characters – literally, men painted blue – is a fun-filled delight. The blue men, performing in mime, play unique drums, tubes, and other drum-like instruments as color and light jump around in beautiful and fun-filled skits. Spoken dialog is all but nonexistent, but the energy is high and the audience is, at times, part of the show.

The show also demonstrates that music can be created from just about anything. From the get-go, the audience is encouraged to participate, shout and cheer as they enter the 1,760-person theatre. Those in the front row may get splashed with paint, water, or other kinds of goop.

MAMMA MIA!

(☞ Mandalay Bay) With so much music of the classic 1970s pop band ABBA infused into the show, Mamma Mia! is as much a tribute show as it is a Broadway-style musical. Nonetheless, one of the most popular musicals in recent years follows the story of a girl who tries to find her father. Most notably, however, is the way the show uses classic ABBA songs in one of the sweetest, happiest shows in Las Vegas.

PHANTOM: THE LAS VEGAS SPECTACULAR

(☞ Venetian) The longest-running Broadway show in history is Andrew Lloyd Webber's "The Phantom of the Opera". Having run for over 20 years, when seen in New York today, it is an aged and tired production. Therefore, when brought to Las Vegas, the show got a bit of a makeover. New sets and special effects gives the show a more modern, technologically advanced

look. Some creative editing has also cut the run-time to 90 minutes (the show runs 2.5 hours in New York).

THE PRODUCERS

(☞ Paris Las Vegas) The show that won a dozen Tony awards on Broadway has found a home at Paris Las Vegas. Comedic director Mel Brooks created both the original movie and this musical staged version of the Broadway producers determined to make millions of dollars by putting on the worst show in history. It is legitimately hilarious, particularly for fans of Brooks-style humor, and has a well-deserved Vegas home. This is one of Las Vegas' most popular shows – get your tickets well in advance.

TONY N' TINA'S WEDDING

(☞ Rio) Basically, Tony n' Tina's Wedding re-enacts a real-time wedding ceremony and reception for lovebirds Tony and Tina, both from very different families. However, instead of attending the show, the audience of Tony n' Tina's Wedding are actually treated like guests to their wedding and reception. The event follows the wedding ceremony and reception, including a wedding toast and full reception buffet. Throughout the production, hilarity ensues as the families bicker, get drunk, and bicker some more.

OTHER SHOWS

One impressive thing about the Vegas show life is the sheer diversity in entertainment options. As such, this catch-all category has a few of the more popular shows that don't really fit anywhere else.

CELINE DION: A NEW DAY

(☞ *Caesars Palace*) Popular singer Celine Dion has her very own permanent venue at Caesars Palace. The Colosseum, built especially for her, features the multimedia music concert *A New Day* and showcases many of the singer's famous songs, and a few new ones as well. The set itself, designed by Cirque du Soleil's Franco Dragone, is a bright collage of stimulation, flash, and just plain coolness.

LE RÊVE

(☞ *Wynn*) Subtitled "A Small Collection of Imperfect Dreams", Le Rêve (French for "The Dream") was created by the mind behind Mystère and O, Franco Dragone. The show is a mix of acrobatics, water, smoke, fire, stunts, and special effects. Its overall artistic sensibility, flair and loose sense of plot resemble Cirque du Soleil. There is some nudity.

THE SECOND CITY

(☞ *Flamingo*) Live sketch comedy is doing well at Flamingo, with ongoing performances of the famous Second City (the comedy troupe with roots in Chicago as well as national tours) on a regular schedule. The theatre is intimate and almost has a coffeehouse feeling, with small round tables and chairs. From improvisation to skits to full-on audience participation, Second City has mastered the art of the live sketch comedy show; turning ordinary situations into hilarious ones. The show is suitable for older teens, and only ages 15 and up are admitted into the performances.

TOURNAMENT OF KINGS DINNER SHOW

(☞ *Excalibur*) The **Tournament of Kings** is Excalibur's resident ongoing dinner show. Like a Medieval battling tournament, the crowd cheers loudly as good battles evil with some nice stunt action. The 900-seat theater has regular performances. The show tickets are expensive, but dinner is included.

VIVA LAS VEGAS
(☞ Stratosphere) The long-running afternoon show Viva Las Vegas is not so much a tribute show about Las Vegas as it is a mix of comedic Vegas-style skits. From magic to comedy, the lively show is entertaining for families as well as adults, and is one of the most inexpensive quality shows in the city.

More than 35% of the days each year in Las Vegas have temperatures which exceed 90° F.

Select Restaurants

Las Vegas loves to eat! Though all the major resorts have more than enough dining choices for even the most criti-

Price Guide: (Per Entrée, in USD)		
$$$	-	More than $40
$$	-	$20 to $40
$	-	Less than $20

cal food enthusiast, many visitors like to find the very best dining experience, both on and off the strip. Following is a rundown of a small selection of the top restaurants in Las Vegas. Although more restaurant information can be found within the individual resort sections of this book, here are some of the city's dining highlights. *Please know that there are many, many more restaurants in Las Vegas than are listed here.*

GOURMET

There are many, many gourmet restaurants from which to choose in Las Vegas. What follows is but a small selection of these places that have regularly been cited as being among the best in the city. These restaurants offer some of the finest dining in Las Vegas, coupled with upscale ambience.

3950 RESTAURANT
(☞ *Mandalay Bay*) Named after Mandalay Bay's street address on Las Vegas Boulevard, the newly renovated 3950 is a cross between a traditional Vegas steakhouse and a gourmet restaurant. It features a wide range of classic American and continental cuisine in a contemporary setting. ($$$)

ALEX 🆂

(☞ *Wynn*) Chef Alessandro Stratta moved from Renoir in the Mirage (a now-closed top restaurant) to Wynn, with a venue dedicated to him. Featuring a diverse French, Italian and Mediterranean menu, Alex serves up the very best of Las Vegas in a romantic and luxurious setting. ($$$)

ALIZÉ

(☞ *Palms*) Located atop the Palms resort, on the 56th floor, Alizé offers sweeping views of the Las Vegas skyline, and a fine French selection of food to enjoy. This romantic restaurant serves lobster and seafood, duck, shrimp, escargot, and much more. ($$)

ANDRE'S FRENCH RESTAURANT

(401 South Sixth St ☎ 702.385.5016 ⌂ andrelv.com) Chef Andre Rochat has several restaurants in Las Vegas, including one in Monte Carlo and one in the Palms. His original, which opened in 1980, is still the best. Featuring top-quality French cuisine in quaintly-decorated dining rooms, menu items include caviar, lobster, salmon, chicken, and specialty salads. ($$)

AUREOLE

(☞ *Mandalay Bay*) From the best dining scene in New York City comes this gourmet and contemporary American Restaurant. Housed in a modern, four-story room and headed by chef Charlie Palmer, the eclectic food choices include steak, duck, and seafood. A highlight of the unique décor is a tower of wine, and an extensive wine list is available. ($$)

BOUCHON

(☞ Venetian ⁓ bouchonbistro.com) Modeled after classic French bistros, with a menu by Chef Thomas Keller, Bouchon offers a wide range of fine Food and features an Oyster Bar. Also noteworthy are the desserts, pastries and lighter foods available at the Bouchon Bakery. ($$)

CARLUCCIO'S TRIVOLI GARDENS

(1775 East Tropicana Ave ☎ 702.795.3236) For visitors interested in dining at a restaurant designed by Liberace himself, Carluccio's is the place to go. The restaurant is located next to the Liberace Museum, and features autographed pianos, elegant décor, and an Italian menu. ($$)

CHINOIS

(☞ Caesars Palace ⁓ wolfgangpuck.com) In the Forum Shops, Wolfgang Puck has come up with a fusion of Asian and French cuisine that only he could have created. Chinois, from Santa Monica, is a bit on the trendy side. It has a menu ranging from Asian-inspired lobster to chicken, served family style. The restaurant also features a sushi bar. ($$)

COMMANDER'S PALACE

(☞ Aladdin / Planet Hollywood) Located in the Desert Passage complex, Commander's Palace offers Cajun-style food choices. Additionally, live music is performed on select occasions. ($)

EIFFEL TOWER RESTAURANT

(☞ Paris Las Vegas) A romantic dinner in the Eiffel tower is closer than you think. Located atop the 50% scale model of the Eiffel Tower, this unique French restaurant offers great food and great views, particularly of the Bellagio fountains across the street. ($$$)

EMERIL'S NEW ORLEANS FISH HOUSE

(☞ MGM Grand) Emeril Lagasse is no stranger to the Las Vegas dining scene, but his New Orleans Fish House in MGM Grand is a favorite. Featuring the chef's famous Cajun-inspired dishes, menu items include seafood and steak, as well as an extensive wine list. ($$$)

HUGO'S CELLAR

(☞ Four Queens) Romantic gourmet restaurants in Las Vegas are indeed plentiful, but Hugo's Cellar, located on Fremont Street in the Four Queens resort, is among the city's best. The food includes lobster and steak, and the intimate setting is perfect for couples or close friends. Plus, as upscale dining goes, this is among the more affordable. ($$)

JOËL ROBUCHON AT THE MANSION

(☞ MGM Grand) Joël Robuchon is an unsurpassed French chef that has created one of the most intimate and upscale dining experiences in Las Vegas. With a limited and constantly changing menu of the finest French cuisine available, coupled with limited seating, a dinner at Robuchon is indeed a memorable one. ($$$+)

LE CIRQUE [MUST SEE]

(☞ Bellagio) Sometimes the best food is hard to come by, but not at Le Cirque. Hailed by many as being the best French restaurant in Las Vegas, and recipient of the coveted AAA Five Diamond Award, Le Cirque comes to Las Vegas as an extension of the much-praised New York City original and features an intimate circus-like surrounding, and a wide range of the best food money can buy. ($$$+)

MESA GRILL

(☞ *Caesars Palace*) Bobby Flay's original trendy New York City restaurant has found its way to Las Vegas. The contemporary setting features Flay's unique Southwestern-influenced food including steak, duck, and seafood. ($$)

MICHAEL'S

(☞ *Barbary Coast*) Barbary Coast's Victorian theme is at its pinnacle within the tiny, 50-seat Michael's. Serving steak, seafood, and continental foods in a romantic and intimate environment, this superb restaurant makes Barbary Coast worth a visit. ($$$)

NOBHILL

(☞ *MGM Grand*) Named after the affluent San Francisco neighborhood and restaurant, Nobhill is chef Michael Mina's creation. The menu features a wide array of food from San Francisco, including shellfish, steaks, specialty salads, and more in a secluded and romantic setting. ($$$)

PICASSO

(☞ *Bellagio*) Where else in America, nay, the world, can you dine while surrounded by original artwork of one of the world's most famous artists? Winner of the AAA Five Diamond Award, Picasso allows for just that. This extremely intimate and classy experience features a range of European foods, decadent surroundings, and of course, world-class works of art. ($$$+)

PIERO'S ITALIAN CUISINE

(*355 Convention Center Drive* ☎ *702.369.2305* ⌁ *pieroscuisine.com*) Despite the plethora of Italian restaurants on the strip, one of Las Vegas' finest isn't even in a resort. Piero's Italian Cuisine offers classic and contemporary Italian food in a more relaxed and quiet environment than the clamoring resort activity nearby. ($$)

ROSEMARY'S RESTAURANT
(8125 W. Sahara Ave ☎ 702.869.2251 ⌁ rosemarysrestaurant.com)
Located just off the strip, Rosemary's menu is comprehensive, featuring lamb, steak, pasta, fish, and other continental and international foods. Wine is also a specialty here, featuring a large list. Rosemary's may also have special "ladies only" specials; contact the restaurant for details. ($$)

SPAGO
(☞ Caesars Palace) Many consider Spago to be Wolfgang Puck's signature restaurant in Las Vegas. Located in the Forum Shops, the food is Puck at his best; a fusion of flavor with fish, steaks, chicken, and more. The restaurant also features a patio section located right on the floor of the Forum Shops. ($$+)

TOP OF THE WORLD RESTAURANT
(☞ Stratosphere) Located within Stratosphere's tower high above the city, and offering top-notch American cuisine, this pricey gourmet restaurant showcases the resort's location by providing diners with one of the best views of the Las Vegas strip. ($$$)

BUFFETS

As far as food goes, Las Vegas is famous for its buffets. In fact, any resort in Las Vegas worth its weight in salt and pepper has an on-property signature buffet. From the expensive array of fine buffet-foods along the strip to the cheap buffets of Fremont Street, most visitors will enjoy at least one buffet during their trip. Following is a list of select buffets, *but keep in mind that most resorts have at least one buffet.*

BAY SIDE BUFFET
(☞ Mandalay Bay) The Buffet at Mandalay Bay is a tropically themed paradise that overlooks the garden area of the resort. The food is standard continental and international cuisine. ($+)

THE BUFFET
(☞ Bellagio) A little more expensive than most resort buffets, the extravagant buffet at the Bellagio is one of the best in the city, featuring a wide range of classic international and continental cuisine. ($$)

THE BUFFET
(☞ Golden Nugget) By far the most extravagant buffet in Downtown Las Vegas, The Buffet at Golden Nugget features the wide array of foods normally reserved for large strip resorts. It features continental buffet-style food, and a room that glistens with brass and gold. ($+)

THE BUFFET
(☞ Wynn) The Wynn's resident buffet features decorative surroundings. The buffet has a wide array of continental and international food, including many stations where the food is cooked or prepared to order. ($$)

CRAVINGS
(☞ Mirage) By many accounts, Cravings at the Mirage is one of the best buffets in all of Las Vegas. The contemporary room itself was designed by the same person responsible for Mandalay Bay's Aureole restaurant. The food is a mix of continental and international food, much of which is cooked to order. ($$)

CARNIVAL WORLD BUFFET

(☞ Rio) A wide assortment of international foods are available, notably Asian and south-of-the-border choices. Much of the food is cooked-to-order, and the festive yet serene atmosphere is pleasing. ($$)

DISHES

(☞ Treasure Island) Treasure Island's buffet offers the standard buffet-style food, including continental and international choices. As far as buffets go however, the atmosphere is much more in tune with a traditional contemporary "sit-down" restaurant. ($$)

DOWNTOWN RESORT BUFFETS

More often than not, the location of the buffet is the main factor for visitors. In Downtown Las Vegas, buffets both in a resort or a neighboring facility will be much less expensive (oftentimes less than $10), more limited serving hours, and less choice. Notable Downtown buffets include the **Backstage Buffet** at the Plaza, **Molly's Buffet** at Fitzgeralds, and **Paradise Buffet** at the Fremont. Unlike buffets on the strip, visitors to Downtown Las Vegas and Fremont Street will oftentimes base their buffet choice on an impulse: price, special, advertisement, or other factor. They may simply decide to visit "a buffet" on Fremont Street and make their final selection upon arrival. ($)

FANTASY MARKET BUFFET

(☞ Palms) There is nothing at Palms that isn't swanky. The Fantasy Market is small and somewhat loud, but the tasty buffet features standard American and continental food. It is a popular and relatively inexpensive buffet. ($+)

FRENCH MARKET BUFFET

(☞ Orleans) In addition to French, Cajun, and Creole-inspired dishes, the French Market Buffet offers a range of continental and international food. This is a relatively inexpensive buffet despite its closer proximity to the strip. ($+)

THE GRAND BUFFET

(☞ MGM Grand) The largest hotel in the world deserves a large buffet. The MGM Grand delivers a stunning family-friendly selection of American food, from hamburgers and chicken, salads, carving stations, desserts, and delights. ($$)

LE VILLAGE BUFFET

(☞ Paris Las Vegas) Like much of the rest of Paris Las Vegas, the décor of Le Village Buffet is incredibly cute. Designed to look like an outdoor street market, food offerings are predominantly French, but other continental food choices (seafood, carving stations, etc.) may be available. ($$)

TODAI

(☞ Aladdin / Planet Hollywood ☙ todai.com) Located in the Desert Passage, Todai is one of the most comprehensive Japanese buffets around. The buffet has sushi, a hibachi grill, an udon station, and many specialty Japanese dishes, both hot and cold. Todai is a chain buffet, with additional locations across the country, including New York City and Chicago. ($$)

VILLAGE SEAFOOD BUFFET

(☞ Rio) A rarity in Las Vegas: a mostly-seafood buffet. The buffet features all the favorite top-quality fish choices: crab and lobster, sushi, shrimp and more. There are meat and veggie choices as well, but most of the delight comes from the extravagant oceanic choices. ($$)

THEME RESTAURANTS

Even average food seems to taste a whole lot better when enjoyed amidst the glaring show of celebrity memorabilia, loud music, screaming children, and kitschy décor. Welcome to the theme restaurants of Las Vegas. These places aren't necessarily known for quality cuisine; in fact, the ambience detracts much from the menu, which is oftentimes just average. Nonetheless, these are special places that deserve nothing less than superb placement within Las Vegas. Plus, for family trips to Vegas, theme restaurants are generally a great place to bring the children!

CHEESECAKE FACTORY

(☞ *Caesars Palace* ✆ *cheesecakefactory.com*) What started as a restaurant devoted to specialty desserts has become known not just for its sweet tooth, but for true gourmet American cuisine. Pizza and Pasta, steak and fish, sandwiches, and of course, indulgent desserts make up a bevy of comfort foods served in heaping portions. The restaurant is located in the Forum Shops. ($+)

ESPN ZONE

(☞ *New York – New York* ✆ *espnzone.com*) Big screen televisions, greasy comfort food, sports-themed video games, and shouting fans all make up the recipe for success at ESPN Zone. Many television sets of varying sizes, each tuned to a sporting event, are scattered throughout the room. It is a sports bar, expertly executed. ($+)

HARD ROCK CAFÉ

(*4475 Paradise Rd* ☏ *702.733.8400* ✆ *hardrockcafe.com*) Hard Rock Café has over 120 locations worldwide, but its Las Vegas branch (which opened in 1990) and the gigantic neon guitar landmark make this one perhaps the most famous of them all. Food here is basic American: burgers, fries, chicken, and the like. The delight, of course, is the loud rock music and insane amount of popular music memorabilia (and an entire "Elvis" section). It is a cluttered, loud and vibrant, perfect for music fans. ($)

HARLEY-DAVIDSON CAFÉ'
(3725 Las Vegas Blvd ☎ 702.740.4555 ⌁ harley-davidsoncafe.com) Fans of the Milwaukee-based Harley-Davidson Motor Company will feel right at home in this motorcycle-themed shop. On display are over a dozen motorcycles (many of which were owned by celebrities), photographs, and even a mammoth-sized motorcycle. Food is good old-fashioned American grease: burgers, chicken wings, fries, ribs, and other such delights. ($)

HOOTERS
(☞ Hooters Hotel ⌁ hooters.com) Within the walls of Hooters Hotel, naturally, is a branch of the original restaurant that carries the name. The "Hooters Girls", fried food, South Florida décor and a relaxing atmosphere make this one of the most controversial and well-recognized restaurant chains of recent years. Despite the somewhat risqué nature of the restaurant, families with children are welcome to dine. ($)

HOUSE OF BLUES
(☞ Mandalay Bay ⌁ hob.com) Part restaurant and part entertainment venue, one of the most successful and popular themed chains is the House of Blues. Influenced by southern blues music dives, Creole and Cajun cooking, House of Blues features regular live, on-stage performances by popular names in blues and rock. Diners enjoy the performance while they eat jambalaya and other such foods. ($$)

MARGARITAVILLE

(☞ *Flamingo ⌀ margaritavillelasvegas.com)* Not just for Parrot Heads! Jimmy Buffet's song ideal of tropical relaxation is realized in this restaurant of the same name. Modeled after Floridian bars and restaurants, Margaritaville serves American comfort food in a relaxing, front-porch-style environment. At night, the restaurant becomes a bit of a family-friendly nightclub, with regular live musical performances. ($)

NASCAR CAFÉ

(☞ *Sahara ⌀ nascarcafelasvegas.com)* Speed and racing are the themes at NASCAR Café. Complete with checkered decorations and even a racing simulation "Cyber Speedway", fans of NASCAR and racing in general will enjoy the lively and loud atmosphere. The restaurant serves American food (burgers, hot wings, sandwiches) surrounded by NASCAR paraphernalia. The complex is large, taking up two floors. ($)

PLANET HOLLYWOOD

(☞ *Caesars Palace ⌀ planethollywood.com)* The inside is reminiscent of a large, haphazardly-constructed movie set. The interior walls and pillars are plastered with movie and celebrity memorabilia, and the menu is just as diverse. The food is thoroughly American (hamburgers and such), with a few exotic twists thrown in. ($+)

RAINFOREST CAFÉ
(☞ MGM Grand ⌁ rainforestcafe.com) Step into a huge simulated rainforest, complete with rain and lightning, dense trees, a real aquarium, and even robotic jungle creatures. Food choices at Rainforest Café are a bit more exotic than other theme restaurants, with dishes including shrimp, chicken, crab, pasta, and burgers. ($+)

STEAKHOUSES

One principle ingredient separates steakhouses from regular restaurants: fine steaks (of course). Like buffets, many Las Vegas resorts feature a resident steakhouse with top-of-the-line steaks and seafood. These restaurants frequently represent Las Vegas dining at its finest, and usually provide an intimate but upscale atmosphere. Following is a selection of a few of the city's resort steakhouses but, again, *there are many more in Las Vegas than are listed here.*

BALLY'S STEAKHOUSE
(☞ Bally's Las Vegas) Featuring a wide array of steak and seafood choices, Bally's Steakhouse is decorated like a hunting club. Menu items include lobster, steak, chicken, shrimp, and an array of desserts. ($$+)

BINION'S RANCH STEAKHOUSE
(☞ Binion's Gambling Hall) A favorite and popular steakhouse for tourists and locals who know the city well, Binion's Ranch has some of the best steaks and seafood on Fremont Street. Also, it is located on the 24th floor of the resort and offers spectacular views of the Las Vegas skyline. ($$)

THE CAPITAL GRILLE

(3200 Las Vegas Blvd ☎ 702.932.6631 🖰 thecapitalgrille.com) Located on the third floor of the Fashion Show Mall, the upscale Capital Grille offers a wide selection of steak and seafood. They also feature hundreds of wine choices, and also hosts a relaxing bar area. The restaurant is a chain, with locations across the USA. They are generally open for lunch and dinner. ($$$)

FIRESIDE

(☞ Imperial Palace) Fireside crosses a traditional Las Vegas steakhouse with a casual southwestern grill. In addition to steaks (and some seafood), barbequed ribs, pork chops, and more are also available. ($$)

GALLAGHER'S STEAKHOUSE

(☞ New York – New York) Originally from New York City, Gallagher's Steakhouse has a wide selection of steaks and seafood, including lobster and crab. ($$$)

GOLDEN STEER

(308 West Sahara Ave ☎ 702.384.4470 🖰 goldensteerlv.com) The Golden Steer Steakhouse is among the oldest in Las Vegas. With an opening in 1958, it was a celebrity hangout in its heyday. Today it serves fine steaks and seafood in a somewhat upscale and retro environment; a throwback to steakhouses of yore. ($$$)

HILTON STEAKHOUSE

(☞ Las Vegas Hilton) Hilton's resident steakhouse features the tried and true recipe for success. In addition to steak and seafood, the restaurant features chicken, lamb, and other standard choices. ($$+)

NEROS

(☞ Caesars Palace) The main steakhouse in Caesars Palace is naturally one of the city's best. Steak, lobster, and other dishes are served. An extensive wine list is also available. ($$$)

THE PRIME RIB LOFT

(☞ Orleans) The Prime Rib Loft at the Orleans offers traditional steaks and seafood dishes overlooking the casino floor. It provides a less intimate dining experience but a wide choice of steaks, chicken, and Cajun foods. ($$)

STEAKHOUSE46

(☞ Flamingo) Not really established in 1946 (the year Flamingo opened), Steakhouse46 offers a more nostalgic take on the classic steakhouse. The restaurant offers gourmet steak and seafood dishes, and an extensive wine selection. ($$$)

THE STEAK HOUSE

(☞ Circus Circus) A surprising find within this otherwise casual resort, The Steak House serves top-of-the-line steaks and seafood. The environment is un-intimidating and casual, and the food (particularly the steaks) is among the best in the city. ($$)

Select Night Clubs

Las Vegas thrives on nightlife. Not only are most of the casinos open 24 hours a day, 7 days a week, there is always somewhere else to go, somewhere to eat, play, party, and party some more.

Of course, casinos are the most famous nightlife option available. No matter what time of day or what time of year, there is always, always action on the casino floor. However, for those wishing to explore other all-night venues within the city, the following is a selection of popular nightlife options in and around town. This section includes trendy nightspots, and for the even more adventurous, the strip clubs.

BARS AND CLUBS

In Las Vegas, it is very common for daytime bars (and sometimes restaurants) to become hot nightspots when the sun sets. After certain times, restaurants may charge covers and stop serving food. Following is a rundown of several of the more prominent bar and lounge venues in the city. *As admission prices fluctuate, sometimes even hourly, price indications are not listed here.*

COYOTE UGLY

(☞ *New York – New York*) This nightclub and bar within the resort is designed to look like the bar from the movie of the same name (unlike the New York City original). It features bar-top dancing and is very popular, featuring all the great rowdy fun from the movie. There is generally a cover charge.

GHOSTBAR

(☞ *Palms*) High atop Palms, on the 55th floor of the resort, is Ghostbar. Like the rest of Palms, it has a sleek, contemporary design reminiscent of the hippest New York City nightspots. Inside, Ghostbar offers a panoramic view of Las Vegas and the strip. Ghostbar also has an outdoor patio, which offers even greater skyline vistas. Part of the patio even has a glass bottom, where you can look straight down several hundred feet.

GILLEY'S

(☞ *Hotel New Frontier*) There is only one real country bar on the Las Vegas strip, and it is Gilley's. The bar has it all; it is dark and claustrophobic, has country music blaring, serves all kinds of down-home beverage choices, and even features a mechanical bull. Dancing on the floor is common on weekends and late at night. They even occasionally have mechanical bull contests, unlimited beer nights, and other such activities.

LIGHT

(☞ *Bellagio*) Bellagio's nightclub is about 7,000 square feet and features hip dance music, a dance floor, very limited table seating and several bars. It feels very much like a New York City club (the interior was designed and decorated by New York City artists), except without the bothersome bouncers and velvet rope. Nevertheless, the steep prices and eclectic design (not to mention five-star location) ensure good crowd-control. The drinks are reasonably priced and it is rarely "too crowded".

MONTE CARLO PUB & BREWERY

(☞ *Monte Carlo*) Right on the Las Vegas strip is a microbrewery; patrons can try out their very own brand of Monte Carlo beer. Plus, as one of the most popular places within Monte Carlo, the pub is also an established dining and nightspot; regularly bustling with activity. Children are allowed at the establishment for casual dining during the daytime.

PURE

(☞ Caesars Palace) This huge, 40,000 square-foot club has several faces. It is a bar, a lounge, a nightclub, a dance floor, and an entertainment venue. Divided up into several different areas, portions of the club feature different styles of music and dancing. Highlights include a year-round outdoor Terrace, which offers great views of the Las Vegas strip.

RAIN

(☞ Palms) When it comes to the nightlife of youth, Palms is positively cutting-edge. The Rain Nightclub, the resort's major night venue, is a mix of all things nightclub. Rain is 28,000 square feet, dark and cavernous, with pumping music and a seemingly endless supply of booze, flashing lights, and young hipsters. It was designed for locals but clearly attracts much from the tourist sect as well.

What sets rain apart is its sleek look and special effects, which is a mix of fire and water above and around the dance floor. Rain can also be converted into an entertainment venue, which has hosted popular names in music.

SHADOW

(☞ Caesars Palace) About as close as you can get to a strip club without seeing actual nudity, the Shadow Bar offers the next best thing: the silhouettes of stripping women. Behind the bar, women behind screens proceed to seductively "undress" while still leaving most to the imagination. Patrons see only their projected shadow.

Shadow is a standard bar in every other way. Located just off the casino floor, Shadow is frequently crowded, but offers decent viewing of the dancers without being in the bar itself.

STUDIO 54

(☞ MGM Grand) The original Studio 54 in New York City today has been remodeled to host Broadway shows, but the spirit of one of America's most famous nightclubs lives on at the MGM Grand. With a total of 22,000 square feet divided into four dance floors, bar areas, and limited table service, this mega nightclub is consistently rated as one of the best in Las Vegas. The minimum age is 21, and proper attire is required.

TANGERINE

(☞ Treasure Island) Named after the overwhelming shades of orange that cover the facility's interior, this indoor and outdoor club is frequently swarming with people. Other then the drinks and party music, the most popular attraction of the club is its regular burlesque shows, which feature scantily-clad females dancing it up in classic speakeasy style. Tangerine's outdoor seating area offers views of the strip as well as the nearby Sirens of TI show.

TAO

(☞ The Venetian) Tao is a 10,000 square-foot club with a distinctly Asian style. Divided into several sections, the club features various musical styles and a terrace with a view of the strip.

VOODOO LOUNGE

(☞ Rio) On par with a splendid location to view the Las Vegas strip is the VooDoo Lounge. Located on the 51st floor, this sleek bar/lounge features unique drink selections and a spectacular view of the strip. There is both an indoor and outdoor patio section. On some nights, the lounge turns into a dance club.

STRIP CLUBS

Where would Las Vegas nightlife be without the sin of strip clubs? Almost as famous (or perhaps infamous) in the Las Vegas pleasure-seeking vacation realm as the casinos themselves are the city's numerous strip clubs. Some clubs feature nude girls, and some clubs are topless. Contact the establishment for more information. Also, *please, the websites listed here are not appropriate for children or those who object to strip clubs, so use caution.*

CHEETAH'S
(2112 Western Ave ☎ 702.384.0074 ⌁ cheetahsnv.com) One of the most famous strip clubs in Las Vegas, Cheetahs' claim to fame is its appearance in the feature film *Showgirls*. The club is small by Vegas standards, and open 24 hours a day.

CLUB PARADISE
(4416 Paradise Rd ☎ 702.734.7990 ⌁ clubparadise.net) Close to the strip, Club Paradise is as much performance venue as it is a strip club. Here, the dancers perform choreographed "routines" in addition to simply stripping.

CRAZY HORSE TOO
(2476 Industrial Rd ☎ 702.382.8003 ⌁ crazyhorsetoo.com) In the adult entertainment world, the name "Crazy Horse" carries with it a lot of weight, being named after the famous (or perhaps infamous) nightspot in France. But the similarities end there. This strip club has the theme of Ancient Rome (but is *not* to be confused with Caesars Palace!).

DÉJÀ VU SHOWGIRLS
(3247 Industrial Rd ☎ 702.894.4167 ⌁ dejavu.com) Déjà Vu is somewhat of a large national chain of strip clubs that includes

Larry Flynt's Hustler Club, so the fare here is basic cookie-cutter strip club. The girls dance basic "routines" on stage. The club features various kinds of dances. Adjacent to the club is a popular adult toy store.

SAPPHIRE

(3025 South Industrial Rd ☏ *702.492.3960 ✆ sapphirelasvegas.com)* By far the largest and most popular strip club in Las Vegas, Sapphire is exactly what a Las Vegas strip club should be. Some sources say this is the largest strip club in the world. At about 70,000 square feet, it is bigger than many area casinos. The stage is huge, and the girls and the drinks are aplenty. It is a glitzy, glamorous, and almost kitschy destination. Skybox suites – a rare luxury – are available which overlook the entertainment down below. Bachelor parties are popular here as well.

TREASURES

(2801 Westwood Drive ☏ *702.257.3030 ✆ treasureslaevegas.com)* Calling itself "the world's most luxurious Gentlemen's Club," Treasures is indeed opulent, decorated with chandeliers, paintings and other "erotic" art, the overall look is of a Victorian-era gentlemen's club. Of course, there is a main showroom as well. And a steak house restaurant. And a wide selection of cigars and wine.

Located downtown, the oldest hotel in Las Vegas still in operation is the **Golden Gate Hotel** *– it opened in 1906.*

Area Attractions

Despite the overwhelming draw to the flashing lights and tinsel and entertainment of Las Vegas strip and its many casinos and entertainment options, there is more in Las Vegas than resorts and gambling!

Though much of the Las Vegas Valley is desert, there are more than a few tourist oases to explore in the region. This section describes some of the attractions available throughout Las Vegas and the surrounding area. *For specific directions and price information for many of these places, contact the establishment directly.*

MUSEUMS

Las Vegas contemporary history is rich and storied. And what better way to learn about it than by visiting one of the area's many museums, depicting everything from the area's geological history, to the religious roots and even the Vegas signage legacy? Following is a list of a few of the more popular museums.

LIBERACE MUSEUM
(1775 East Tropicana Ave ☎ 702.798.5595 ⌁ liberace.org) A true landmark of Las Vegas, the Liberace Museum opened in 1979 as a way for the performer to showcase his vast collection of stage and show paraphernalia and earn money for his own **Liberace Foundation for the Performing and Creative Arts**. Today the museum still works on a non-profit basis, securing money for the charity while providing visitors with a peek at the extraordinary life of one of Las Vegas' most famous showmen.

The building's gaudy exterior – a cartoonish architectural style mixing sheet music, piano keys, and other musical staples – is a good indication of the wonders to behold inside. Visitors exploring the museum will see all kinds of memorabilia from large pianos (uniquely decorated) and extravagant cars in warehouse-size showrooms to smaller costumes and stage props. One section even features a re-creation of one of Liberace's own living quarters in Palm Springs.

The museum also features a small café and gift shop that sells Liberace memorabilia, audio and video recordings, and more. The museum is open year-round. ($$)

ATOMIC TESTING MUSEUM

(755 East Flamingo Rd ☎ *702.794.5161* ✆ *atomictestingmuseum.org)* A far cry from the otherwise upbeat attractions surrounding Las Vegas, the Atomic Testing Museum teaches visitors about the history of the nearby Nevada Test Site, and America's nuclear endeavors. The museum is operated by the **Nevada Test Site Historical Foundation** (ntshf.org), which is dedicated to preserving this particular place in American history.

Visitors to the museum will be presented with video presentations regarding the history and functions of the Nevada Test Site. Artifacts on display include scientific equipment, photographs and documents showing various tests and explosions. The museum is located on the Desert Research Institute (dri.edu) campus, and is open year-round. ($/$$)

LAS VEGAS NATURAL HISTORY MUSEUM

(900 North Las Vegas Blvd ☎ *702.384.3466* ✆ *lvnhm.org)* Unlike most of the educational exhibits around Las Vegas, the Las Vegas Natural History Museum has, among other things, information on the history of Las Vegas thousands of years before humankind decided to turn it into a vacation destination.

The museum is divided into several exhibits, or "galleries", which feature displays and information on various facets of area history: marine life, dinosaurs, and other wildlife are on display.

The "Wild Nevada" gallery showcases wildlife from Nevada and the Las Vegas region.

In addition to the displays, the museum features a collection of live animals native to the region, including reptiles such as snakes and lizards. The museum is targeted to a younger sect, particularly local families, children, and school field trips. ($)

NEON MUSEUM
(Fremont Street Experience ☎ *702.477.7751* ⌂ *neonmuseum.org)* A museum that would only fit in a city like Las Vegas, the Neon Museum, located at the Fremont Street Experience, is a collection of old, restored Las Vegas signs from decades past. The museum is easily accessible from Fremont Street, and visitors walking through the area are bound to catch more than a glimpse of these larger-than-life historical pieces, some dating back as early as 1940.

However, for those truly interested in Las Vegas signage, a trip to the nearby **Boneyard** is a real treat. On this three-acre parcel rests old, un-restored signs. Like an automotive junkyard for signs, this impressive outdoor collection features a wide array of old Vegas memorabilia, slowly bleaching in the sun, waiting to be restored. Visitors must schedule an appointment for a tour of the Boneyard.

OLD LAS VEGAS MORMON FORT
(500 E. Washington Ave ☎ *702.486.3511* ⌂ *parks.nv.gov/olvmf.htm)* Though the Las Vegas Valley was inhabited for hundreds of years prior to Western influence, the first permanent native settlement in the area was constructed by Mormon missionaries in 1855. This small adobe fort was used as a rest station for those traveling through as well as a starting post to convert the native population to Christianity. It was abandoned just two years later.

Today, portions of the original fort have been preserved as part of the **Nevada Division of State Parks** (parks.nv.gov). Located near the center of Downtown Las Vegas, visitors may tour the remaining portions of the small fort, as well as learn about the history of the area. ($)

SOUTHERN NEVADA ZOOLOGICAL – BOTANICAL PARK

(1775 North Rancho Drive ☎ 702.647.4685 ⁻᷉ lasvegaszoo.org) Also known as simply the "Las Vegas Zoo", the Southern Nevada Zoological – Botanical Park is a tiny retreat within the congestion of modern Vegas. Although only three acres in size, it has about 200 different species of plants and animals on display. Attractions are diverse and include alligators, birds, lions, and many endangered species.

However, the park also offers what it calls **Desert Eco-Tours** – full day excursions to some of the neighboring landscape's most famous attractions. Via bus group tour, visitors are brought to several area hotspots, including the famous **Groom Lake**, the ghost town of **Delamar**, old mining facilities, and more. Excursions may last eight hours or more. Reservations are required for the tours, which may cost upwards of several hundred dollars for the day. ($)

LAS VEGAS ART MUSEUM

(9600 West Sahara Ave ☎ 702.360.8000 ⁻᷉ lasvegasartmuseum.org) Las Vegas is no stranger to exhibits of fine art. The Las Vegas Art Museum, first established in 1950, was the first of its kind in Southern Nevada. Today it is affiliated with the Smithsonian Institution, and offers a rotation of art exhibits, primarily from the local artistic community. It also plays host to numerous educational programs and occasionally displays art projects from

local students. Visit their website for more information on current exhibits. ($)

LIED DISCOVERY CHILDREN'S MUSEUM
(833 North Las Vegas Blvd ☏ *702.382.3445* 🖰 *ldcm.org)* The Lied Discovery Children's Museum first opened in 1990, and has since become a staple of local education for Las Vegas area youth. It features science, technology, and humanities exhibits designed for a mix of school-aged children and their teachers or families.

Much of the museum specializes in helping children discover aspects of the adult world, such as daily routines and different careers. Some of the highly interactive exhibits include the **Discovery Market**, where children can learn to shop and value merchandise. They can also learn about music, tornados, electricity, plants, animals, and even space travel.

The museum is highly geared towards younger children and their families, with a special area for people under 5 years old. Packages and rentals may be available for special events, such as birthday parties. ($)

SHOPPING

Though most shopping for tourists occurs with the Las Vegas resorts, there is a nice selection of shopping centers catering to tourists that exist outside the resort system. Following are a few select shopping experiences around Las Vegas.

NEONOPOLIS
(450 Fremont St ☏ *702.477.0470* 🖰 *neonopolis.net)* At the southeastern end of the Fremont Street Experience rests a building that more closely resembles an Orlando shopping mall. Loosely influenced by successful tourist malls such as San Diego's Horton

Plaza and the Universal CityWalk complexes, the new outdoor Neonopolis is less about shopping and more about attracting a different, more family-oriented crowd to Downtown Las Vegas. Though Neonopolis is new, the facility is an impressive 200,000 square feet and features a nice selection of family entertainment options.

The most visible entertainment option at the center is **Jillian's Las Vegas** (jillianslasvegas.com). Encompassing about 43,000 square feet, Jillian's is a huge multi-faceted sports-themed gaming center which features video games, a high-tech bowling alley, billiards, several places to eat and drink, and even a small concert venue.

Also at Neonopolis is a multiplex **Crown Theatre** featuring regular movies on some of Las Vegas' largest movie screens. Also on site is a food court and several smaller shops and restaurants.

FASHION SHOW MALL

(3200 South Las Vegas Blvd ☎ 702.369.0704 ✆ thefashionshow.com)
Nestled amongst the resorts between the Mid and North Strip sections is one of the largest malls in the United States, and certainly the largest on the strip. With over 200 stores and ten million visitors annually, the Fashion Show Mall has undergone recent extensive renovations, making the retail shopping experience more akin to the neighboring "themed" resort malls. The décor is flashy and contemporary.

Despite the modern look, however, the mall features standard fare for retail shopping. **Macy's**, **Neiman Marcus**, **Nordstrom** and **Saks Fifth Avenue** are among the anchor stores, as well as many smaller store chains and high-end boutiques. Occasionally fashion shows are held on site.

SHOWCASE MALL

(3785 South Las Vegas Blvd ☎ 702.597.3122) Hardly a traditional mall at all, the Showcase Mall is a cartoonish entertainment complex reminiscent of a larger-than-life Disney building. Ideally situated next to the MGM Grand and across from New York New York (one of the most heavily-trafficked sections of the strip), it features several well-known brands of entertainment, including some headlining attractions.

Topping the list is **GameWorks** (gameworks.com), a large video and arcade game complex. A chain of arcade centers with facilities across America, GameWorks features top-of-the-line arcade games and other interactive experiences. The center also has several eating establishments.

Also featured at the Showcase Mall is **M&M's World** (mmsworld.com), a four-story fun complex dedicated to the M&M candies. While much of the store is dedicated to selling M&M's products, some of which are not available anywhere else, the facility also features a 3D movie attraction and some neat surprises.

LAS VEGAS OUTLET CENTER

(7400 South Las Vegas Blvd ☎ 702.896.5599 ⌂ premiumoutlets.com) While much of the Las Vegas consumer shopping experience is through expensive retail markets, there is hope yet for the bargain-hunter. Located just south of the southernmost section of the Las Vegas Strip is Premium Outlets' Las Vegas Outlet Center. This sprawling complex features about 130 common outlet stores, including many major brands such as Tommy Hilfiger, Casual Corner, Liz Claiborne and Geoffrey Beene. No overtly fancy or kitschy décor or Las Vegas experience here; just bargain shopping.

LAS VEGAS PREMIUM OUTLETS
(875 S. Grand Central Pkwy ☎ 702.474.7500 ⌂ premiumoutlets.com) Over 120 outlet stores are located at this other bargain-hunters paradise. Retailers are generally higher-end than those found at the **Las Vegas Outlet Center** (the word "premium" gives that away, and include Dolce & Gabbana, Banana Republic, Kenneth Cole, Brooks Brothers, Nike, Lacoste and many more.

THE BOULEVARD MALL
(3528 South Maryland Pkwy ☎ 702.732.8949 ⌂ boulevardmall.com) With so many large facilities in Las Vegas, it is no surprise that Nevada's largest mall would be located just a few short minutes from the strip. The Boulevard, a retail shopping center, is a functional establishment with about 150 retail shops. The mall caters more to locals than to tourists.

GOLF COURSES

In recent years, Las Vegas has become very much a golfer's paradise. There are courses all across the Las Vegas metropolitan area, some with very extensive services and facilities. Following is a breakdown of a few popular area public golf courses.

ALIANTE GOLF CLUB
(3100 West Alcorn ☎ 702.399.4888 ⌂ aliantegolf.com) Located in North Las Vegas, Aliante Golf Club is a newer daily use course that features a 72-par, 18-hole professional course, a driving range, and other golf amenities. Visitors may book online up to four months in advance for a tee time.

ANGEL PARK GOLF CLUB
(100 South Rampart Blvd ☎ 888.629.3929 ⌂ angelpark.com) Angel Park is a large and full-featured golf course that offers two com-

plete 18-hole courses, and a smaller course. The **Palm Course** and the **Mountain Course** offer mixed-level holes but are generally easier and less competitive than other area courses. The 12-hole **Cloud Nine** is more for practice or fun. There is also an 18-hole putting course and a comprehensive pro shop.

BALI HAI GOLF CLUB
(5160 South Las Vegas Blvd ☎ 702.597.2400 ⌁ balihaigolfclub.com)
Leave it to Las Vegas to host a themed golf course. Just south of the Las Vegas Strip on Las Vegas Boulevard, the Bali Hai Golf Club is a real Vegas course. Designed to look like a tropical Asian paradise, the par 71 course opened in 2000 and is a luxurious and heavily themed (but expensive) experience. Individual day rates are available for particular tee times. The upscale **Cili Restaurant** on-site serves Asian-inspired cuisine.

DESERT PINES GOLF CLUB
(3415 East Bonanza ☎ 888.427.6678 ⌁ desert-pines-golf-club.com)
About five miles from the strip, the more secluded and wooded Desert Pines Golf Club gives golfers an opportunity to get away from the bustling city. This 18-hole, 71 par course also features a comprehensive **Practice Center**. Casual golfers may book individual tee times online or by phone.

LAKE LAS VEGAS GOLF COURSES
(1600 Lake Las Vegas Pkwy ☎ 877.698.4653 ⌁ lakelasvegas.com) A short drive from the strip is Lake Las Vegas, a luxurious golf-lovers paradise. Courses in Lake Las Vegas include award-winning **The Falls**, a par-72 course known for its vistas and great view of the Las Vegas strip in the distance. **Reflection Bay Golf Club**, designed by Jack Nicklaus, offers views of Lake Las Vegas and is home to **The Golf Institute**, which offers lessons.

LAS VEGAS NATIONAL GOLF CLUB
(1191 East Desert Inn Rd ☎ 702.734.1796 ✆ lasvegasnational.com) The Las Vegas National has been tied in with several of the area's resorts for much of the time since it opened in 1961, including the Stardust, the Sahara, and the Hilton. The course features a wide mix of skill-levels (par 3, 4, and 5). The facility also has a driving range that is open days and evenings, and an on-site restaurant and pro shop.

TPC – "THE CANYONS"
(9850 Canyon Run Drive ☎ 702.256.2500 ✆ tpc.com) The Tournament Players Club offers amateur golfers the chance to play on the same course as the professionals.

WYNN GOLF AND COUNTRY CLUB
(☞ Wynn, See the resort section "Wynn Las Vegas") Part of Wynn Las Vegas, this expensive golf course is available to Wynn hotel guests only.

LAKE MEAD

One of the most visible and famous rivers in America is the Colorado. Cutting through the eastern portion of the Las Vegas Valley and blocked off by the Hoover Dam, the river at this point, on the border of Nevada and Arizona, forms Lake Mead – the largest man-made lake in the United States. This section describes a few of the attractions around this unique area.

LAKE MEAD NATIONAL RECREATION AREA
(601 Nevada Way ☎ 702.293.8990 ✆ nps.gov/lame) A branch of the **National Park Service** (nps.gov), the Lake Mead National Recreation area encompasses nearly all of Lake Mead and the

surrounding areas and facilities. The dry, desert-y landscape surrounding Lake Mead makes it one of the most unusual and picturesque locations for a lake. The area also includes nearby **Lake Mohave**, which follows the state border between Nevada and Arizona.

Established in 1964, the Lake Mead National Recreation Area has about 500 miles of shoreline and sees as many as 10 million visitors each year. In fact, it is the fifth most visited National Park. People can enjoy fairly free access to the lake and surrounding area. Activities are numerous and include boating, hiking, camping, fishing, bird watching, and even horseback riding. Permits may be needed for some activities.

The area features easy (paved road) access to the most popular campgrounds, picnic sites, and other outdoor-centric amenities. For specific information, visit their web site. A fee is charged for park entrance. ($)

HOOVER DAM MUST SEE

(Lake Mead Area ⌁ usbr.gov/lc/hooverdam ☎ 702.494.2517) On the border of Nevada and Arizona is one of the region's most popular attractions outside of Las Vegas. Even though it is over 70 years old, the Hoover Dam draws over a million visitors exploring the vast countryside, and countless more motorists driving over it.

In recent years, the dam has expanded its tourism operations to include more exhibits about the dam's history with a more leisurely atmosphere. The **Discovery Tour**, which replaced the original "hard hat" tours some time ago and (unfortunately) gives visitors less of an internal tour, showcases the workings and history of the dam. Highlights include the power plant generators, the intake, and the overlook. The tour includes numerous informative exhibits, including theater presentations.

Though security around the dam is high, visitors may be able to stroll up to the brink on both sides of the dam, even without going on a tour, and even drive across it; one side has the Colorado River, the other has the backed-up water forming Lake Mead.

Visitors may not be able to drive over the dam for much longer, however – an impressive undertaking, The Hoover Dam Bypass Project, is currently underway to build a bridge to eventually halt all traffic over the dam. The project is slated for completion in 2008. ($$)

NEARBY CITIES

The Las Vegas area has been growing quickly in population over the past several decades. This section describes a few of the neighboring cities around Las Vegas, and any key interests of note for tourists.

BOULDER CITY

(bcnv.org) The Hoover Dam was originally to be called "Boulder Dam", and Boulder City was created specifically by the Bureau of Reclamation to house the workers of the project – and to keep them out of the debauchery of nearby Las Vegas. To that end, during the dam's construction, gambling and liquor sales were made illegal. In 1968 the city gained independence and a year later alcohol was legalized. However, to this day, Boulder City is the only place in Nevada where gambling remains illegal. And to many residents of Boulder City, this is indeed a breath of fresh air.

Today there are about 15,000 residents in Boulder City. In an effort to keep the city "small" and "peaceful", the local government maintains strict control over hotels (no more than 35 guest rooms per hotel), building permits, and other city growth aspects. While visitors may appreciate the quaint atmosphere of the city, for many it serves as a stepping stone to nearby Lake Mead and Hoover Dam, which draws many more visitors per year.

HENDERSON

(cityofhenderson.com) Recently, Las Vegas has become famous (or perhaps infamous) for becoming a sprawling suburban jungle of residential and commercial development. In fact, much of this development is part of the City of Henderson, which has become one of the fast-growing cities in the United States.

Built for the war effort and later incorporated in 1953, the City of Henderson is the second largest city in Nevada. Located almost immediately adjacent to Las Vegas and the nearby strip, Henderson's location gives it some of the Las Vegas tourist runoff. While driving or shuttling through town, visitors will most likely drive through Henderson, especially when on their way to Lake Las Vegas or Lake Mead. Additionally, for the golf enthusiast, Henderson has a nice supply of public and municipal golf courses.

LAKE LAS VEGAS

(1600 Lake Las Vegas Pkwy 702.564.1600 lakelasvegas.com) Although officially located within Henderson, Lake Las Vegas is almost a world apart. Sometimes called the "Lake Las Vegas Resort", the 320-acre private man-made lake is located on the western edge of the Lake Mead National Recreation Area. Development of the lake and resort began in 1987, and has built up over the years to become a secluded high-class resort community for vacationers and full-time residents.

Designed to look like a small Italian village (visitors of the Bellagio resort will recognize the style), Lake Las Vegas is a planned community. Within Lake Las Vegas are some of the area's most upscale resort hotels, golf courses, shopping and water-related activities. It is a luxurious (and expensive) low key alternative to the loud tackiness of the strip and downtown resorts 17 miles away. The entire complex is about 3,600 acres.

ACCOMMODATIONS
Surrounding the waters of Lake Las Vegas are some of the most upscale resorts in Nevada, including the **Hyatt Regency** and the ultra-lavish AAA Five Diamond **Ritz-Carlton**. The Las Vegas Vacation Villas are owned by residents of the area, but may be rented by tourists (lakelasvegasrentals.com). The **MonteLago Village Resort** (montelagovillage.com) is a combination of hotel and villa. All area resorts are designed after a Tuscan-influenced model, and all offer very upscale accommodations. For reservations, contact the Lake Las Vegas resort at the web site or phone number above.

CASINOS
There are two casinos in the Lake Las Vegas Resort complex. The **Casino Baraka** is at the Hyatt Regency, and the **Casino MonteLago** is at the MonteLago Village Resort. Casino MonteLago features about 40,000 square feet of gaming space but without the strip traffic crowds. The much smaller Casino Baraka is only 10,000 square feet. It is entirely intimate, with only a few tables and slots, although it is a very upscale and classy environment.

SPA FACILITIES
There are two spa facilities at Lake Las Vegas; **Spa Moulay** in the Hyatt Regency and **Spa Vita di Lago** in the Ritz-Carlton. Both feature various spa treatments, fitness facilities, and other

relaxing and invigorating experiences. Spa Moulay is the smaller of the two.

MONTELAGO VILLAGE

(🖰 montelagovillage.com) In addition to being a first-rate resort community, MonteLago Village features a beautiful outdoor promenade with shopping, Italian villa-style architecture, and of course beautiful views of Lake Las Vegas. Within the village are dozens of upscale shops, boutiques, and eateries. There is even ample space available for weddings and other special events. The village is within easy walking distance to much of the resort portions of Lake Las Vegas.

GONDOLA ADVENTURES

(Lake Las Vegas Resort ☎ 877.446.63652 🖰 gondola.com) One of the most romantic outings available in the entire Las Vegas valley is a gondola ride on Lake Las Vegas. Experienced gondoliers take passengers out onto Lake Las Vegas where they can partake in a pre-selected array of foods (from snacks to drinks to a full dinner) while the gondolier gently brings the boat around the pristine lake. The gondolas themselves hold as many as 12 people and are 36 feet long, the same size as the gondolas of Venice. The excursion is expensive and can last for up to an hour and a half. Couples may book a gondola for themselves or bring along extra people. Reservations are required. ($$$$)

LAKE LAS VEGAS MARINA

(☎ 702.568.6024) A true marina in the desert, the Lake Las Vegas Marina provides watercraft rentals for use on Lake Las Vegas. With advanced reservations, visitors and residents may rent various kayaks, canoes, sailboats, fishing equipment, and other boats for use on Lake Las Vegas. ($$/$$$$)

OTHER ADVENTURES

Beyond the Las Vegas metropolitan area lies a vast desert of beautiful landscapes, and not much else. Visitors wishing to travel greater distances by car will find some unique treasures in and around southern Nevada.

AREA 51 / EXTRATERRESTRIAL HIGHWAY
(Take U.S. 93 north) A distant 150+ miles from Las Vegas lies one of the most controversial and mysteriously famous roads in America: a special 90-mile stretch of Highway 375, or, more commonly, the Extraterrestrial Highway. Curious onlookers will find a whole lot of nothing up here except vast desert scenery and an occasional gas station. It is a lonely and desolate stretch in the vast Nevada desert. So why do people visit here?

In addition to being the closest major civilian road to **Groom Lake** and the infamous **Area 51** part of the **Nevada Test Site**, the E.T. Highway has long been one of the best places to spot alien life – or so those devoted would swear to. More UFO sightings have occurred around this area than any other place in America. In all honesty, there is nothing else here; if you like Nevada desert scenery this is an ideal day trip. If not, consider a more accessible nearby trip to Lake Mead, the drive to which offers similar scenery.

MOUNT CHARLESTON
(Take U.S. 95 North to Nevada 157) About 45 miles from Las Vegas is a year-round outdoor enthusiast's paradise. In the summer, many hiking and camping activities are available. And in the winter, honest-to-goodness skiing! Granted, a skiing season in Nevada is much like a swimming season in Alaska. Nonetheless, if you happen to be a skier on a Las Vegas vacation between about December and March, then downhill skiing may be a pos-

sibility at Lee Canyon's **Las Vegas Ski & Snowboard Resort**, www.skilasvegas.com.

For those who want to spend the night in a rustic but full-featured environment, the **Mount Charleston Hotel** (mtcharlestonhotel.com) offers standard hotel amenities, and the **Mount Charleston Lodge** (mtcharlestonlodge.com) offers individual log cabins high up on the mountain.

RED ROCK CANYON
(redrockcanyon.blm.gov) A short drive west from Las Vegas towards Nevada 159 will bring visitors into the Red Rock Canyon National Conservation Area, operated by the U.S. Department of the Interior. The excursion is ideal as a quick trip because it is relatively nearby (about 20 miles from Las Vegas) and it offers many ways to see the red rocks and the landscape – including nice and driving tours. The area is known for its unique layered rock formations and color. Hiking, biking, and other outdoor activities may be available, contact the **Red Rock Canyon Visitor Center** at 702.363.1921.

The Grand Canyon

Las Vegas is a world-renowned attraction based on artificiality. However, the relatively close Grand Canyon is a feature of natural wonder unlike anything else on the planet. It dwarfs Las Vegas on almost every scale. As much as a mile deep, about 277 miles long and 18 miles wide, it is an unbelievable sight. It is located in a remote destination in the middle of the vast American desert. However, lucky for us, the National Park Service has made the Grand Canyon much more accessible.

At about 275 miles from Las Vegas, the Grand Canyon is not around the corner, but with so many tour opportunities departing from Vegas by both air and on land, it is a very easy one-day or overnight excursion. It is a great place to take a break from tinseltown and see some of Mother Nature's most awesome work. Located largely within the Grand Canyon National Park, one of the first National Parks, the Grand Canyon has grown from an isolated and seldom-viewed formation into a haven for hikers, naturalists, families, and plain old tourists.

The Grand Canyon is a paradise for nature lovers, and an entire world of outdoor athletic possibilities is available. Hiking, camping, mule riding, animal watching, and so much more are available. There is a lot to do and discover, but this book will only cover the basics, specifically, enjoying the Grand Canyon from a Las Vegas vacationer's perspective.

ABOUT THE GRAND CANYON

The Grand Canyon is the world's largest gorge. It is a gorge of immense proportions – 18 miles across and a mile straight down, it follows the Colorado River for 277 miles as it traverses the terrain of northern Arizona.

HISTORY AND GEOLOGY

During its 1,450-mile journey from the Rocky Mountain National Park into northern Mexico, the Colorado River travels through a particular stretch of land in northern Arizona that has become one of America's most recognized natural landscapes. It is here where, over the course of millions of years, the river carved a deep gorge through the rocks and sediment, creating the Grand Canyon. This exposed rock, colorful and layered, can be seen almost as far west as Lake Mead and reveals over 1.4 billion years of the Earth's evolution.

Even though the Grand Canyon is a mile deep at times, with the Colorado River following through the path, the river is still about 2,800 feet above sea level when it enters the canyon from the east. The exposed rock, billions of years old, is actually due not to the river sinking below sea level, but rather from the Earth's crust rising in a region known as the Colorado Plateaus.

The origins of the Grand Canyon can be traced back about 75 million years, during the formation of the Rocky Mountains. After millions of years, the mountains' formation eventually resulted in the Colorado Plateaus, a large flat region of about 130,000 square miles that is higher in elevation than the surrounding regions.

When the Gulf of California finally opened up about 5 million years ago, the formerly landlocked river changed course, cut through the plateau and exposed the billion-year-old rocks of the Grand Canyon. Scientists and geologists are able to study the region's geologic history by examining the exposed sediments, formations and groups within the canyon; the newer formations are near the top, and the oldest ones are near the canyon floor, some of which are as old as two billion years.

EARLY INHABITANTS
The first known permanent settlers of the Grand Canyon area were the Ancestral Puebloans, or Anasazi. They first settled around 4,000 years ago. After droughts and harsh environmental factors drove them away, other Native Americans would eventually call the region home, including the Paiute and Navajo.

The first time Europeans saw the Grand Canyon was in 1540, when Spanish Explorer García López de Cárdenas and about a dozen others, led by members of the Hopi Native Americans, came across it as they looked for the Seven Cities of Gold. They had known about the canyon, but it was impassible, and the river at the bottom too hard to reach. They gave up on their quest, and as a result the Spanish lost interest in the canyon.

After that, there was only limited exploration of the Grand Canyon by Europeans, until 1848 when Mexico ceded the Grand Canyon and surrounding southwest over to the United States under the Treaty of Guadalupe Hidalgo.

GETTING TO THE GRAND CANYON

The Grand Canyon by its very nature forces a remote location – the environment is just too un-developable to accommodate any kind of urban landscape. So regardless of how you are arriving into northern Arizona, you will *probably* have to hit the open road a bit.

Also, since the canyon is so huge, your starting point may well determine where in the canyon you decide to visit. Those heading south to the canyon will likely visit the North Rim, whereas those heading north will likely visit the South Rim (much of the visitor comforts within the Grand Canyon National Park are on the South Rim).

FROM LAS VEGAS

Many tour groups and independent vacationers begin their trek to the Grand Canyon by first flying into MacCarran Airport in Las Vegas, the largest area airport for many hundreds of square miles. From here, they can either drive the 280+ miles through fascinating but barren Nevada and Arizona landscape, or choose a tour company that specializes in Grand Canyon expeditions. These tours can range from standard bus to lavish private airplane or helicopter. Bus packages take the entire day or longer for a full tour, while airplane/helicopter packages are often half-day affairs.

BY PLANE

Six miles from the entrance to Grand Canyon National Park on the South Rim is the Grand Canyon Airport (GCN). This small, regional airport is served by neighboring cities (including Las Vegas) and is used by tourists wishing to bypass ground transportation. Flying from Las Vegas to Grand Canyon takes a little over an hour.

BY CAR

At less than 90 miles away, the nearest major city to Grand Canyon National Park is Flagstaff. Visitors from Phoenix and Tucson generally make their way to Flagstaff before the final leg of their journey to the South Rim.

BY BUS TOUR

Many tours to the Grand Canyon National Park originate from Las Vegas as well as other surrounding points. Visitors may inquire about these tours by asking their hotel concierge. Grand Canyon bus tours are very popular and there are many competing companies; as a result, they are usually very well advertised and easy to book. Visitors should be aware that the bus ride is often 7-8 hours, with only about 3-4 hours total of canyon-viewing time. Most tours include a short "photo-stop" at the Hoover Dam and lunch.

BY AIR TOUR
Private tour companies offer several different kinds of transportation options, from the relatively inexpensive bus ride to the lavish private sightseeing airplane and helicopter tours. These tours are usually much more expensive than the bus tours, but cut down the travel time considerably.

GRAND CANYON RAILWAY
(233 N. Grand Canyon Blvd, Williams, Arizona ☎ *800.843.8724* ⌁ *grandcanyonrailway.com)* For those wishing to make all (or part) of their journey to the Grand Canyon from the nearby city of Williams, a slice of American railroad history is waiting. In service since 1901, the Grand Canyon Railway travels on a special limited route originating from Williams and traveling to the canyon 65 miles north. The trip takes less than three hours, and is a very special way to see the countryside on a private track more then a century old.

While the ride is more a unique journey than a practical one, the experience is worth it for railroad enthusiasts. Travelers can choose from five different classes of service which feature different styles of train cars, including a spectacular glass-domed car for optimal viewing. Overnight packages are also available, but the train has layover time to allow for day trips. ($$$$)

NAVIGATING THE GRAND CANYON

To help differentiate exactly where in the Grand Canyon visitors are traveling, the area's huge landscape has been divided into several sections.

SOUTH RIM
The National Park Service owns and operates much of the Grand Canyon vicinity. While most of the canyon is an uninhabited natural landscape, there are a few places with tourist comforts. It is here, in the South Rim, where much of the tourist centers are located. Hotels and attractions here are open year-round, and the canyon's hiking trails and other activities are well-maintained. Most visitors to the canyon visit the south rim.

NORTH RIM
Nearly 1,000 feet higher than the south rim at places, the north rim is a desolate and rustic paradise for those who want to be miles away from everything. Trails for hiking, backpacking, and overnight camping are available in this secluded expanse. In fact, even though the north rim is less than 18 miles at its widest from the south rim, to drive from one side to the other requires a 200+ mile drive all the way around the canyon!

GRAND CANYON VILLAGE
The major tourist center is on the south rim, in a place called Grand Canyon Village. This "village" is actually a small tourist hub located within the confines of the park. As the National Park Service is not involved in the hospitality industry, however, they have involved **Xanterra Parks & Resorts** (grandcanyonlodges.com) to handle much of the hotel and resort business for the canyon.

The area has hotels, restaurants, canyon exhibits, lots of great walking paths, and more to make the canyon experience as easy as possible. Plus, most major facilities are within easy walking distance along a spectacular canyon rim path. In other words, for those wishing to explore the canyon from the comfort of a hotel room, this village is the best place to be.

INNER CANYON

Sometimes considered the "backcountry", the Inner Canyon encompasses everything below the canyon rim. Many hiking trails line the canyon walls en route to the floor, and permits may be required to access certain sites. There are precious few necessities in the Inner Canyon; most of them are in the form of unmanned campgrounds. Hikers and backpackers traveling through the inner canyon should have planned their trails and routes carefully, be in top physical condition, and be well-prepared for the unforeseen. Food, supplies, and medical availability are all but nonexistent.

RIVER

On the canyon floor, the Colorado River and its smaller tributaries are popular with rafters for extreme trips through the 277-miles of the canyon's inner gorge. Rafting trips generally last for many days and require participants to be in good physical condition with adequate supplies. As it is a mile down at places from the rim, for practical purposes, access to the river for fair-weather vacationers in the Grand Canyon National Park is all but impossible.

VIEWING THE GRAND CANYON

While many people opt to drive to the Canyon and enjoy the many services provided by either the National Park Service or a private tour group, there are several ways to experience and learn about this amazing natural wonder other than simply looking over the rim.

FROM THE RIM

The perimeter of the Grand Canyon offers countless overlooks and vistas of the landscape. Some views are better than others, but it is far from necessary to drive all the way around the canyon to get the full perspective. As visitors approach from whatever direction, the many well-signed overlooks will give visitors many great opportunities to see the sight. Even though the rim of the canyon is not always even (it can vary by as much as 1,000 feet), the view is still very similar.

Visitors touring the south rim, especially within the Grand Canyon National Park, will notice that the overlooks are more modernized, better equipped to handle a wider range of visitors, and are overall safer. The north rim, on the other hand, is much more rustic, and oftentimes doesn't even have a railing. *Always be careful when approaching the brink of any gorge, and never go further than you feel comfortable!*

FROM THE AIR

Those that want some of the best possible canyon views oftentimes opt for a private tour company that utilizes a plane or helicopter to fly over and around the canyon. Expect to pay well over $200 per person for this type of excursion – the best (and oftentimes easiest) views come at the highest prices.

On the upside, these excursions may not require an entire day. If your home base is Las Vegas, the planes may simply depart from MacCarran Airport, loop around the canyon, and land at the starting point. Check with the individual tour company for more information.

FROM THE RIVER

A mile down at points from the rim, the Colorado River surges through the canyon floor. For the real robust traveler, a view from a raft on the canyon floor is the best. Temperatures at bottom of the canyon are frequently in the triple digits (Fahrenheit), even when it is cool up top. Many books and Internet resources are available for planning a water-based excursion through the canyon. Viewing the canyon from the river is very athletically challenging, but offers some of the most secluded environments and a unique perspective.

ACCOMMODATIONS

Grand Canyon Village offers a wide variety of upscale accommodations for vacationers wishing to experience the best of the Grand Canyon in comfort. These facilities are all located within the Grand Canyon National Park and provide some of the best vacation experiences. Some of them are only a few feet from the canyon's edge. These resorts are all beautiful and upscale, with a rustic feel but with all the comforts of home.

BOOKING A ROOM
The hotels are operated by **Xanterra Parks & Resorts** for the National Park Service. For reservations or information about any of them, call their general reservation line at 303.297.2757 or visit www.xanterra.com. Rooms are often booked many months to a year in advance, and securing a reservation for a Grand Canyon hotel requires advanced planning, particularly when traveling during the busy summer season.

CANYON RIM ACCOMMODATIONS

When staying in a Grand Canyon hotel, the best choice of room is, of course, one with a sweeping view of the canyon itself. This is possible by staying in one of the hotels located almost directly on the canyon's rim. These hotels are all located on the rim in the Grand Canyon National Park

EL TOVAR HOTEL

(☞ South Rim) The El Tovar Hotel is as much a piece of history as it is the major (and first) resort within the Grand Canyon Village. With an opening in 1905, El Tovar is a National Historic Landmark that has seen more than its share of celebrities, politicians, and other famous folk. It features a restaurant, a sundries shop, and other basic necessities both in-room and as part of the hotel. The lobby is a grand entrance, reminiscent of the bygone era of national park lodges.

The hotel has only 78 rooms, each rustic and small, so visitors should not expect grand oversized accommodations. Though it has been recently renovated, it still maintains an antiquated appeal. The best feature of El Tovar, of course, is its location – only a few short feet to the Canyon's rim.

KACHINA AND THUNDERBIRD LODGES

(☞ South Rim) Between the two historic hotels of Bright Angel and El Tovar rests the more contemporary Kachina and Thunderbird Lodge. With the feel of a smaller hotel and multiple rooms with canyon views, the rooms at these hotels are nice but the frills are limited. In fact, there is not even a front desk (guests use the neighboring El Tovar or Bright Angel to check-in). However, the location provides great canyon viewing and nearby restaurant access within short walking distance.

BRIGHT ANGEL LODGE

(☞ South Rim) Built around 1935, the Bright Angel Lodge is a National Historic Landmark. The lodge features about 140 rooms and separate cabins ranging from very affordable (some guest rooms share a community bathroom and do not have tele-

vision) to luxurious. Just off the canyon's rim, the hotel's separate cabins (called "rim cabins") are truly romantic and feature almost unbeatable views of the Grand Canyon.

OFF-RIM ACCOMMODATIONS

There are several accommodation options within the Grand Canyon National Park that are not located on the rim. Nonetheless, they offer a pristine natural environment less than a mile from one of nature's most awe-inspiring vistas.

MASWIK LODGE

(☞ *South Rim*) A short quarter-mile drive from the canyon's rim, the Maswik Lodge boasts more of a motel atmosphere. This budget-friendly hotel features an on-site cafeteria, a bar, and a gift and sundries shop. There are two sections of the hotel, north and south, with the north rooms featuring more upscale accommodations. The hotel also seasonally operates several on-site cabins, which are open and available during the summer time.

YAVAPAI LODGE

(☞ *South Rim*) About a mile from the rim rests the largest hotel within the Grand Canyon National Park. Built in 1962 and featuring 348 rooms within a picturesque forest setting, the Yavapai Lodge has recently undergone renovations to update many of its facilities. There is a cafeteria and a gift and sundries shops. Like some of the other hotels in the village, not all rooms have air conditioning.

OTHER ACCOMMODATIONS

Though the south rim is the major tourist center for Grand Canyon visitors, there are places to stay elsewhere within the Grand Canyon National Park. Following are some very unusual and unique accommodation options for visitors to the park.

PHANTOM RANCH
(☞ *Canyon Floor*) The Phantom Ranch allows for a truly unique overnight experience on one of the world's most impressive landscapes. Built in 1922, the ranch is the only hotel located on the canyon floor, right next to Bright Angel Creek off the Colorado River, about a mile down from the canyon's ridge. Accessible only by foot, by mule, or by water, the hotel is perfect for campers, hikers, and rafters. It features dormitory-style accommodations, separate cabins, running water, a separate shower building, and very limited amenities. All supplies are brought in by mule-train.

Getting to Phantom Ranch is half the fun. The National Park Service offers overnight mule trips specifically designed to take advantage of the ranch. Meals must be ordered in advance, as there is no food service on the canyon's floor. Accommodations are rustic, and the temperature climbs well into the hundreds (sometimes over 20 degrees Fahrenheit warmer than the rim).

GRAND CANYON LODGE
(☞ *North Rim*) The only hotel accommodation option within the north rim area of the Grand Canyon National Park, the Grand Canyon Lodge is a remote and rustic experience for those willing to make the trek through the vastly unpopulated north rim region. The hotel boasts over a hundred cabins and 40 motel-style rooms, a restaurant and bar, and a gift and sundries

shop. The accommodations here, both the motel and the cabins, capture the true log-cabin feel of wilderness living. The Grand Canyon Lodge is open seasonally, only during the warmer months.

RESTAURANTS

There is a small selection of on-property dining choices for those staying in and around the Grand Canyon Village. Restaurants are operated by **Xanterra Parks & Resorts** for the National Park Service. For reservations or information about any of them, call their general reservation line at 303.297.2757 or visit www.xanterra.com.

EL TOVAR DINING ROOM AND LOUNGE
(☞ *El Tovar Hotel*) The most upscale dining option is located in the El Tovar Hotel. Serving breakfast, lunch, and dinner, the dining room is casual and features a diverse menu from steak to seafood. There is also a bar and lounge serving light food and a full range of beverages. ($$$)

BRIGHT ANGEL RESTAURANT
(☞ *Bright Angel Lodge*) For a more family-oriented dining choice, the Bright Angel Restaurant serves a wide range of food all day long. There is also a nearby bar, and a "fountain" which serves lighter food and drinks. ($$)

MASWIK & CANYON CAFETERIAS
(☞ *Maswik & Yavapai Lodges*) Located in the two off-rim hotels, these self-service cafeterias offer a wide range of simple foods, sandwiches, salads and drinks, and more. ($/$$)

PHANTOM RANCH CANTEEN
(☞ *Phantom Ranch*) For those robust few who make it to the Phantom Ranch section of the canyon floor, the Phantom Ranch Canteen is available for bag lunches, lunch or dinner with a very limited menu. Reservations should be made for meals well in advance. ($$)

SELECT ATTRACTIONS

The Grand Canyon is full of activities for the outdoor enthusiast. This section covers a few of the most popular (and most user-friendly) attractions for leisure visitors. For additional information on trails, campgrounds, permits, and other backcountry information, contact the National Park Service.

There are many, many trails throughout the Grand Canyon; books may be filled with trail information and still not contain all of them. By far, the most popular trails are those that take hikers from the rim to the canyon floor. This section summarizes a few of the more famous of these trails.

Important: do not hike any trail without being prepared. This section provides only an overview and not hiking advice. Consult additional sources for hiking information.

BRIGHT ANGEL TRAIL
(☞ *Grand Canyon Village*) The easiest and most popular trail to the canyon floor in the Grand Canyon National Park, the Bright Angel Trail is literally just outside the on-rim hotels within the Grand Canyon Village. It is well-maintained, not too steep, and has several rest houses along the 9.8-mile journey from the south rim to the Phantom Ranch. The total roundtrip is 19.6 miles.

However, even though it is the easiest way to get to the canyon floor, it is by no means a walk in the park. Even for experienced hikers it may take 6-7 hours to get down to the floor and back again, and the altitude difference between the rim and the floor may mean a pleasant 70-degrees at the rim but a boiling 90+-degree trek at the bottom.

In fact, it is strongly recommended that hikers do not make the entire journey from rim to river or Phantom Ranch and back again in one day. Remember, how ever far you walk down the trail, you have to walk back up again, and it may be much steeper than you remember.

This is also the trail used by mule-tours, so visitors should be aware of the "gifts" left behind on the trail by the animals.

VISITORS CENTERS
Scattered throughout the Grand Canyon National Park are various visitors centers designed to acquaint travelers to the area as well as sell books and gift items. There are several of these centers, including the **Canyon View** and **Desert View** Information Centers on the south rim, and the seasonal **North Rim Visitors Center**. These centers may also provide maps and other useful backcountry information. Follow signs to the closest one.

KOLB STUDIO
(☞ *Grand Canyon Village ✆ grandcanyon.org/kolb)* Housed in a building which literally teeters on the edge of the canyon near the trailhead of Bright Angel Trail, the Kolb Studio is a look back on the history of Grand Canyon tourism. In 1903 the Kolb Brothers, Ellsworth and Emery, founded a photography studio and built their darkroom on the canyon's edge. Over the years, the new building has expanded with new rooms and exhibits.

Today, the studio is operated by the Grand Canyon Association and has undergone recent renovations. Visitors may tour the studio and see works of art documenting the history of the Grand Canyon, as well as some breathtaking canyon views.

TUSAYAN MUSEUM

(☞ South Rim) About 20 miles from the Grand Canyon Village lays the ruins of an old Pueblo Native American village. The nearby Tusayan Museum tells the history of the people and life around the Grand Canyon as it existed 800 years ago. Visitors follow a trail around the ruins on either a self-guided or ranger-guided tour.

Every year, tens of thousands of marriage licenses are issued in Las Vegas, making it the most popular marriage destination in the USA.

Recommendations

There is so much information about Las Vegas! While this book provides an overview of the attractions, resorts, and other general area information, visitors are strongly advised to check multiple sources, including books, websites, and even contact the companies directly. The following section provides some additional sources in various mediums, some of which provided factual information used to compile this book.

TRAVEL SCENARIOS

There are so many reasons to visit Las Vegas: stressed out from work, romantic excursion, vacation with the family, or just plain boredom. Part of Las Vegas' beauty, however, is the ability to not have anything planned and still have an enjoyable vacation. Show tickets and upscale dinner reservations must be planned in advance, but this can generally be done through the resort's main reservation system, and there are even occasionally seats available for day-of performances.

That being said, this section provides a brief overview for a few of the possible vacation scenarios when visiting this city of pleasure.

GAMBLING

(**When to go**: *Anytime*; **Duration**: *1 night*) Despite all the other attractions that have popped up along the strip in recent years, we must not forget that it all began with legalized casino gambling. Though Las Vegas doesn't make as much gambling revenue as Atlantic City, it is still the major draw and primary reason for people to pay the resort town a visit.

In Las Vegas, most dedicated casinos are the same or similar: they will all (or mostly) have slots and table games, loyalty programs and other gaming options. When visitors come to Las Vegas, they may choose to play at one resort or at several resorts. Many times, loyalty programs and complimentary offerings will keep players at one resort as opposed to "spreading the wealth".

More often then not, however, gambling in Las Vegas encompasses only part of the full vacation experience. Staying overnight is preferred, although daytrips from Los Angeles or other areas are common.

ROMANTIC VACATIONS

(**When to Go**: Spring *or* Fall; **Duration**: *2-3 nights)* Las Vegas has been cited by many to be the ultimate romantic destination, and many couples have chosen to spend their vacations or honeymoons there. The primary reasons for this, among other things, are the upscale resorts with so many luxurious room, dining, and entertainment options. That being said, a successful romantic vacation hinges on picking the right resort in which to stay.

Couples will likely fly into McCarran airport and be whisked away in a private limousine or shuttle service to their strip hotel destination. The most romantic resorts are the most upscale ones: Caesars Palace, Bellagio, Venetian, and Mandalay Bay are among the top choices. Couples will likely spend most of their time within one of these resorts, as quality food, entertainment, and accommodations are all under one roof.

Swimming pools, bars, and nightlife are also popular for romance. Again, fortunately, all the upscale strip resorts (and many off-strip resorts) have these facilities in spades, so once a resort choice is made, these decisions are much easier.

FAMILY FUN

(**When to Go**: *Spring or Summer*; **Duration**: *2 nights*) A trip to Las Vegas isn't just about grown-ups anymore. Although the heyday of Las Vegas as a family destination disappeared with the 1990s, there are still many things to divert the young (and young-at-heart) in your group.

First, where should a family stay? Many of the resorts, particularly the upscale South and Mid-Strip resort, cater to a more expensive, upscale adult crowd. Fancy restaurants and bars abound, which may not suit families. The most consistently family-friendly resort in Las Vegas is Circus Circus. This average-quality resort is jam-packed with child activities, from the circus performers to the midway arcades. MGM Grand, Monte Carlo, and Mandalay Bay may attract families as well, as well as those resorts with large pool areas.

When seeing a show, be warned that most shows in Las Vegas are *not* intended for children. Ask the resort's concierge about which shows are most suitable for your family.

YOUNG SINGLES AND FRIENDS

(**When to Go**: *Warmer months*; **Duration:** *1+ night*) When it comes to hot nightspots and cool pool parties, any young party-goer would be hard-pressed to find a better selection than Las Vegas. Nearly every resort (and especially those on or just off the strip) has at least one first-class bar and/or lounge. Plus, there is a recent trend for entire resorts to single out the hip, young, and rich.

The Palms caters almost exclusively to the hip young tourist, with bars and restaurants reflecting the ultimate in lavish contemporary style. On the other side of the strip, the Hard Rock Hotel offers a more rock/alternative ambience for the same young and hip crowd.

For the more inexpensive and down-home trek through Las Vegas, many friends prefer the old school bright lights of The Fremont Street Experience. Here, the Vegas locals mingle with the tourists to create an eclectic mix. The rooms, food, drinks, and table minimums are cheaper, and the bars and casino floors are rowdier.

ON THE CHEAP

(**When to Go**: *Winter*; **Duration**: *0-2 nights)* When traveling on a budget, the cheapest time to visit Las Vegas is undoubtedly winter. Desert weather gets surprisingly cool in December and January (average between about 40 and 60 degrees Fahrenheit). As a result, many of the outdoor establishments (such as swimming pools) close down seasonally, and bars and clubs have limited hours.

However, when the hotel occupancy rate drops, so do the prices at even the most upscale resorts! Plus, being the "indoor" city that Las Vegas is, much enjoyment can be had simply by rolling out of bed on a chilly winter's morning and moseying down to the resort's main areas.

THE "BEST"

Without too much editorializing, I have tried on this single page to note some of the best attractions in Las Vegas. This is of course an impossible task, because there is never a definitive "best" for anything – it all depends on your taste, your budget, and whatever other factor you wish to consider when making such a claim. That being said, here are some recommendations:

If you want a luxurious resort, try **Bellagio**, **Caesars Palace**, **Mandalay Bay** (including **THEhotel**), **Golden**

Nugget, **Paris Las Vegas**, **The Mirage**, **The Venetian**, **Wynn**, or **Treasure Island**.

If you want a great swimming area, check out the expansive pool areas at the **Flamingo**, **Mandalay Bay**, the **MGM Grand**, **Caesars Palace**, or **Bellagio**.

If you want to dine at a world-class restaurant, visit **3950 Restaurant** or **Aureole** in Mandalay Bay, **Le Cirque** or **Picasso** at Bellagio, or the **Eiffel Tower Restaurant** at Paris Las Vegas.

If you want to see a fabulous show, get tickets for any **Cirque du Soleil** production (particularly **KA** or **'O'**). For something different, see **Penn & Teller** or the Broadway-style **Mamma Mia!**

If you want to see showgirls, put the kids to sleep and head for **Zumanity**, **Folies Bergere**, or **Jubilee!**

If you want to see the strip's best free shows, don't miss the **Fountains of Bellagio** or the **Volcano** at The Mirage.

If you want a taste of Las Vegas nightlife, don your clubwear and head to **Tangerine** at Treasure Island, **Rain** or **ghostbar** at The Palms, or **Light** at Bellagio.

INTERNET RESOURCES

Websites can be excellent sources of up-to-date and current information. Online travel guides and travel agents can provide lots of third-party information. However, this section focuses on some of the "official" Las Vegas web sites and promotional sites that are specific to Las Vegas-related information and that are not mentioned elsewhere in this book.

LAS VEGAS CONVENTION AND VISITORS AUTHORITY

(🕐 lvcva.com) This web site is dedicated to helping business and travel professionals find information about various Las Vegas businesses.

VISIT LAS VEGAS

(🕐 visitlasvegas.com) The major arm of the Las Vegas Convention and Visitors Authority, Visit Las Vegas provides comprehensive information for tourists. Though it is principally promotional-driven, it bills itself as the "Official Las Vegas Tourism Web Site." The information is vast.

VEGAS.COM

(🕐 vegas.com) A travel agency of sorts dedicated exclusively to Las Vegas tourism, VEGAS.com provides a ton of information about all the resorts and area attractions (including hotel ratings), and visitors may even book hotel rooms online.

CHEAPO VEGAS

(🕐 cheapovegas.com) This is a great, no-nonsense travel site that doesn't talk down (or up) to its readers. It features descriptions and reviews of the major hotels and resorts and basic ratings.

CITY OF LAS VEGAS

(🕐 lasvegasnevada.gov) This is the official municipal City of Las Vegas website, featuring city services and information for locals and tourists. Government and local law are among the topics covered.

LAS VEGAS STRIP HISTORICAL SITE
(lvstriphistory.com) This is a very comprehensive website that goes into much detail about almost every aspect of Las Vegas' strip history. It tracks property and company ownership, old and new resorts, and even the prominent people involved in the strip's creation.

Index

3

3950 Restaurant, 211

A

Adelson, Sheldon, 122
Adventuredome, 141
Ah Sin, 98
AJ's Steakhouse, 182
Al Dente, 102
Aladdin, 90
Alex, 133, 212
Alizé, 178, 212
All-American Bar & Grille, 176
Alliante Golf Club, 242
America, 87
American Superstars, 203
amusement park, 141, 144, 146
Andiamo, 171
Andre's, 89
Andre's French Restaurant, 212
Angel Park Golf Club, 242
Antiquities Tour, 165
Antonio's Italian Ristorante, 176
Appian Way, 110
Aquaknox, 123
aquarium (Mirage), 119
Arc De Triomphe, 97
Area 51, 250
Area Attractions, 235
Arthur, Dirk. *See* Xtreme Magic Starring Dirk Arthur
Atomic Testing Museum, 236
Augustus Café, 109

Aureole, 212
Auto Collection, 115

B

Backstage Buffet, 218
Backstreet Arcade, 90
Bali Hai Golf Club, 243
Bally's Avenue Shoppes, 101
Bally's Las Vegas, 100
Bally's Steakhouse, 102
Bally's Steakhouse, 223
Bamboleo, 176
Barbary Coast, 105
Bars, 227
Bartolotta, 133
Bay City Diner, 163
Bay Side Buffet, 70, 217
Beach Club 25, 146
Bellagio, 93
Bellagio Botanical Gardens, 96
Benihana, 171
Bennett, William H., 142
Big Al's Oyster Bar, 179
Big Apple Bar, 87
Big Kitchen Buffet, 102
Big Shot, 146
Billy Bob's Steak House and Saloon, 186
bingo, 32, 136, 163, 169, 170, 184, 186, 187
Binion's Horseshoe, 157
Binion's Original Coffee Shop, 159
Binion's Ranch Steakhouse, 159

Binion's Gambling Hall, 157
Binion's Ranch Steakhouse, 223
Bishop. Joey, 35
Blackstone's Steakhouse, 89
Blue Agave, 178
Blue Man Group, 205
Bonanza Hotel, 100
Bond, James, 79
Bonsai, 92
Borg Invasion 4D, 172
Bouchon, 213
Bougainvillea Café, 181
Boulder City, 246
Boulder Station, 184
Boulevard Mall, 242
bowling, 54, 174, 179, 186, 187, 240
Boyd Gaming, 106, 155, 156, 165, 166, 173, 178, 185
Bradley Ogden, 109
Bridge Avenue Shopping, 166
Bright Angel Lodge, 262
Bright Angel Restaurant, 265
Bright Angel Trail, 266
Broadway Shows, 204
Broiler, 170, 184
Brooklyn Bridge, 86
Brookstone, 110
Buffet (Bellagio), 95, 217
Buffet (Golden Nugget), 160, 217
Buffet (Hilton), 172
Buffet (Monte Carlo), 89
Buffet (Sahara), 143
Buffet (Wynn), 133, 217
Buffet at TI, 128, 218
Buffets, 216
Burger Barn, 70
Burton, Lance. *See* Lance Burton, Master Magician
Buzio's Seafood Restaurant, 176

C

Cabana Bar, 173
Caesars Palace, 107
Café at Harrah's, 117
Café Bellagio, 95
Café Lago, 109
California Hotel, 166
Calypso's, 80
Canaletto, 123
Canter's Delicatessen, 128
Canyon Blaster, 141
Canyon Ranch Café, 124
Capital Grille, 224
Caravan Café, 143
Caribe Café, 119
Carluccio's Trivoli Gardens, 213
Carnaval Court, 117
Carnegie Delicatessen, 119
Carnival World Buffet, 176, 218
Carson Street Café, 160
Carter, Howard, 75
Casino Baraka, 248
Casino MonteLago, 248
Castle Walk, 77
Casual Dining, 55
Celebrity Shows, 196
Celine Dion
   A New Day, 207
Center Stage, 164
Chanel, 133
Chang's, 102
Cheesecake Factory, 220
Cheetah's, 231
Chicago Brewing Company, 157
Chin Chin Café, 87
China Express, 184
Chinese Kitchen Buffet, 154
Chinois, 213
Circus, 141

Circus Buffet, 141
Circus Circus, 139
Cirque Du Soleil, 85, 200
clothes, packing, 45
Club Armadillo, 187
Club Bingo, 142
Club Paradise, 231
Clubs, 227
Coast Casinos, 106, 173, 179
Cockeyed Clam, 114
Colorado River, 253
Colosseum, 110
Comedy Stop, 80
Commander's Palace, 213
Coney Island, 88
Corsa Cucina, 133
Cortez Room, 174
Courtyard Buffet, 145
Coyote Ugly, 87, 227
Craftsteak, 83
Cravings, 119, 217
Crazy Armadillo, 145
Crazy Girls, 197
Crazy Horse Too, 231
Cyber Speedway, 143
Cypress Street Market, 109

D

Dallas Events Center, 187
Dam Restaurant, 183
Dan Marino's Fine Food, 183
Daniel Boulud Brasserie, 133
Davis, Sammy Jr., 35
Dealertainer's Pit, 114
Déjà Vu Showgirls, 231
Delmonico Steakhouse, 123
Desert Inn, 132
Desert Passage, 92
Desert Pines Golf Club, 243

Dion, Celine, 110. *See* Celine
    Dion: A New Day
Dolphin Habitat, 120
Downtown Resort Buffets, 218
Dragon Noodle, 89
Drai, Victor, 106
Drai's, 106
Du Parc, 98

E

Eiffel Tower Experience, 99
Eiffel Tower Restaurant, 213
El Cortez, 152
El Tovar Dining Room, 265
El Tovar Hotel, 262
Elements, 92
Embers, 114
Emeril's, 83
Emeril's New Orleans Fish House, 214
Emperor's Buffet, 115
Empress Court, 109
Engelstad, Ralph, 113
ESPN Zone, 87, 220
Evening at La Cage, 197
Excalibur, 76
Executive Fitness, 138
Exotic Shows, 197
Extraterrestrial Highway, 250

F

Fabulous Flamingo, 111
Fall of Atlantis, 110
Fantasy Faire Midway, 77
Fantasy Market Buffet, 178, 218
Fashion Show Mall, 240
Fast Food, 55
Feast, The, 184

Ferris Wheel, 141
Festival Fountain, 110
Fiamma, 83
Fin, 119
Fine Dining, 55
Fiore Steakhouse, 176
Firelight Buffet, 186
Fireside, 114, 224
Fischbacher, Siegfried. *See* Siegfried & Roy
Fitzgerald's, 154
Fix, 95
Flamingo, 110
Flamingo Beach Club Café, 112
Flay, Bobby, 109, 215
Fleur de Lys, 70
Folies Bergere, 198
Food Court (Luxor), 74
Forum Shops, 109
Fountains of Bellagio, 95
Four Queens, 156
Four Seasons Hotel Las Vegas, 72
Francesco's, 128
Fremont Street Experience, 150
Frémont, John C., 26
Fremont, The, 155
French Market Buffet, 179, 219
Fresh Harvest, 186
Fusia, 74

G

Gallagher's Steakhouse, 87
Gallagher's Steakhouse, 224
Gallery of Fine Art, 96
GameWorks, 241
Gans, Danny, 203
Garden Grill, 141
Garden of the Dragon, 171
Garden of the Gods, 108

Garduño's, 178
Gaughan, Jackie, 153
Gaylord India Restaurant, 176
Ghirardelli Chocolate Company, 117
Ghostbar, 227
Gilley's, 228
Gold Coast, 173
Golden Gate Hotel, 162
Golden Nugget, 159
Golden Steer, 224
golf course, 132, 134
Golf Courses, 242
Gondola Adventures (Lake Las Vegas), 249
Gondola Rides, 125
Gonzalez y Gonzalez, 87
Gourmet Feast, 170
Gourmet Restaurants, 211
Grand Buffet, 219
Grand Café, 170
Grand Canal Shoppes, 124
Grand Canyon, 253
Grand Canyon Lodge, 264
Grand Canyon Railway, 257
Grand Canyon Village, 258
Grand Garden Arena, 85
Grand Lux Café, 124
Grand Pool, 84
Grand Spa, 84
Great Sphinx of Giza, 73
Greek Isles, 188
Groom Lake, 238, 250
Guadalajara, 170
Guadalajara Bar & Grille, 184
Guggenheim Hermitage Museum, 125
Guy Savoy, 109

H

Hamada of Japan, 112
Hamada's Asiana, 176
Hard Rock Café, 220
Hard Rock Hotel, 181
Harley-Davidson Café, 221
Harrah, William, 32
Harrah's Las Vegas, 115
Henderson, 247
Herbst Gaming, 180
Hill, Virginia, 111
Hilton (Las Vegas), 170
Hilton Steakhouse, 171, 224
Hilton Theater, 173
History of Las Vegas, 25
History of the Future, 172
Hollywood Theatre, 85
Hooter's Casino, 183
Hooters Restaurant, 183, 221
Hoover Dam, 245
Hoover Dam (history), 28
Horn, Roy. *See* Siegfried & Roy
Hotel Last Frontier, 135
Hotel Nevada, 162
House of Blues, 71, 221
House of Lords, 143
Hughes, Howard, 31, 34, 122, 132, 135
Hugo's Cellar, 157
Hugo's Cellar, 214

I

Il Fornaio, 87
IMAX, 75, 76, 141
Imperial Palace, 113
inclinator, 73
Insanity, 146
Ipanema Beach, 175

Isla Mexican, 128
Island Buffet, 80

J

Japonais, 119
Jasmine, 95
Joël Robuchon. *See* Joël Robuchon at the Mansion
Joël Robuchon at the Mansion, 83, 214
Jubilee!, 198

K

KÀ, 85, 200
Kady's Coffee Shop, 138
Katchina, 262
Kerkorian, Kirk, 33, 36, 81, 107, 111, 122, 171
Kid's Quest, 185, 187
King Tut Museum, 75
Klingon Encounter, 172
Kolb Studio, 267
Kristofer's Steak House, 138

L

L'Atelier de Joël Robuchon, 83
La Femme, 85, 199
La Rêve, 207
Lagasse, Emeril, 83, 123, 214
Lake Como, 93
Lake Las Vegas, 247
Lake Las Vegas Golf Courses, 243
Lake Las Vegas Marino, 249
Lake Mead, 244
Lake Mead National Recreation Area, 244
Lance Burton, 202

Lance Burton, Master Magician, 202
Las Vegas Art Museum, 238
Las Vegas Hilton. *See* Hilton (Las Vegas)
Las Vegas National Golf Club, 244
Las Vegas Natural History Museum, 236
Las Vegas Outlet Center, 241
Las Vegas Premium Outlets, 242
Las Vegas Resorts, 59
Las Vegas Review-Journal, 45
Las Vegas Ski & Snowboard Resort, 251
Las Vegas Weekly, 45
Lawford, Peter, 35
Le Boulevard, 99
Le Cirque, 95, 214
Le Provençal, 98
Le Village Buffet, 98, 219
Legends Deli, 80
Legends in Concert, 204
Les Artistes, 98
Liberace Museum, 235
Liberace, Wladziu, 37
Lied Discovery Children's Museum, 239
Light, 228
light (Luxor), 75
Lillie's Noodle House, 160
Limericks Steakhouse, 155
Lion Habitat, 84
Little Buddha, 178
Live Shows, 195
Local Publications, 45
Louis Vuitton, 133
LOVE, 200
Lucky Lookout Balcony, 155
Lucky's Café, 145

Lutèce, 123
Luxor, 72
Luxor Steakhouse, 74

M

M&M's World, 241
Madam Tussauds, 125
Magic of Rick Thomas, 202
Magic Shows, 201
Magnolia's Veranda, 157
Mah John Chinese Kitchen, 176
Main Street Station, 164
Maloof, 177
Mamma Mia!, 205
Mandalay Bay, 68
Mandalay Beach, 69
Mandalay Place, 74
Manhattan Express, 87
Mardi Gras, 175, 178
Margarita Grille, 172
Margarita's Cantina, 136
Margaritaville, 112, 222
Marina Hotel, 81
Market City Caffe, 89
Market Street Café, 167
Marriage, 53
Martin, Dean, 35
Maswik Lodge, 263
Medications, 46
medieval, 76
Merlin's Magic Motion Machine, 78
Mesa Grill, 109, 215
Mexitalia, 141
MGM Grand, 80
MGM Grand Adventures, 81
MGM Grand Buffet, 84
Michael's, 106
Michael's, 215

Midway (Circus Circus), 142
Mina, Michael, 95
Ming, 114
Ming's Table, 117
Mirage, 117
Mirage Resorts, 33, 34, 88, 93, 118, 126, 131, 132, 159
Mix, 70
Mizuno's, 80
Molly's Buffet, 155, 218
Mon Ami Gabi, 98
Monaco, 88
monorail, 71
Monte Carlo, 88
Monte Carlo Pub & Brewery, 228
MonteLago Village, 249
MonteLago Village Resort, 248
Monterey Room, 174
Montgolfier balloon, 97
motion theater, 76
Mount Charleston, 250
Mount Charleston Hotel, 251
Mount Charleston Lodge, 251
Mr. Lucky's 24/7, 182
Museums, 235
Mystère, 200

N

N9ne Steakhouse, 178
Naga, 145
NASCAR Café, 143, 222
Nearby Cities, 246
Neon Museum, 237
Neonopolis, 239
Neros, 109, 225
New Frontier, 135
New York – New York, 85
Night Clubs, 227
Nike, 70

Nine Fine Irishmen, 87
Nobhill, 83, 215
Nobu, 182
Noodles, 95
North Rim (Grand Canyon), 258

O

O, 201
Oasis Spa, 74
observation deck, 99, 144, 146
Okada, 133
Old Las Vegas Mormon Fort, 237
Olives, 95
Onda, 119
Orchard Coffee Shop, 136
Orleans, 178
Orleans Arena, 179
Ortanique, 98

P

Packing for your Trip, 45
Paco's, 143
Pair O' Dice, 135
Palace Station, 169
Palapa, 182
Palms, 176
Paradise Buffet, 156, 218
Paradise Garden Buffet, 113
Paris Las Vegas, 97
Park Avenue Poolside, 87
Pasta Palace, 170, 184
Pasta Pirate, 167
Pearl, 83
Penazzi Italian Ristorante, 117
Penn & Teller, 202
Penske Wynn Ferrari Maserati, 135
Phantom

The Las Vegas Spectacular, 205
Phantom Ranch, 264
Phantom Ranch Canteen, 266
Pharaoh's Pheast Buffet, 74
Phil's Deli, 136
Phil's Steakhouse, 136
Picasso, 95, 215
Piero's Italian Cuisine, 215
Pietro's, 80
Ping Pang Pong, 174
Pink Flamingo, 111
Pink Taco, 182
Pinot Brasserie, 123
Pizza Palace, 114, 184
Planet Hollywood, 110, 222
Planet Hollywood Resort & Casino, 91
PlayLV, 161, 163
Plaza Las Vegas, 163
Pool Café (Bellagio), 94
Ports O' Call Buffet, 174
Postrio, 123
Presley, Elvis, 36, 91, 171
Prime Rib Loft, 179, 225
Prime Steakhouse, 95
Primm Valley Resorts, 86
Puck, Wolfgang, 216
Pure, 229
Pyramid Café, 74
Pyramids Motel, 115

Q

Quark's Bar & Restaurant, 172

R

Raffles Café, 70
Railhead, 185
Rain, 229
rainfall, average, 45
Rainforest Café, 84, 159, 223
Range Steakhouse, 117
Rat Pack, 35
Rat Pack is Back, 204
Red 8, 133
Red Rock Canyon, 251
Redwood Bar & Grill, 167
Regale Italian Eatery, 77
Rehab, 182
Research, 23
Residences at MGM Grand, 82
Resorts
    Downtown Las Vegas, 149
    Mid-Strip, 105
    North Strip, 131
    Off-Strip, 169
    South Strip, 67
Restaurants, 211
Rio, 175
Ristorante Italiano, 138
Riviera, 137
Riviera Comedy Club, 138
Riviera Shopping Arcade, 139
rm, 70
Roberta's, 154
roller coaster, 65, 87, 88, 141, 144
Rosemary's Restaurant, 216
Round Table Buffet, 77
Roxy's Diner, 145
Royal Star, 123
Royal Treatment Spa, 78
Rumjungle, 70

S

Sahara, 142
Samba, 119
Sam's Town, 185

San Francisco Shrimp Bar & Deli, 163
Sands, 122
Sapphire, 232
Sarno, Jay, 107, 139
Savannah Steakhouse, 80
Seablue, 83
Second City, 207
Second Street Grill, 156
Sensi, 95
Shadow, 229
Shark Reef, 71
Sherwood Forest Café, 77
Shibuya, 83
Shintaro, 95
Shopping, 239
Showcase Mall, 241
Siegel, Benjamin "Bugsy", 30
Siegel, Bugsy, 111
Siegfried & Roy, 38
Siegfried & Roy's Secret Garden, 120
Sinatra, Frank, 35
Sir Galahad's, 77
Sirens of TI, 128
skiing, 250
Skylofts, 82
sky-painted ceiling, 98, 99, 125
Slingshot, 141
Social House, 127
Sound Trax, 170
South Rim (Grand Canyon), 258
Spa (Imperial Palace), 114
Spa at Bally's, 101
Spa at Caesars Palace, 108
Spa at Wynn, 134
Spa by Mandara, 98
Spa Mandalay, 70
Spa Moulay, 248
Spa Tropicana, 80

Spago, 216
Speed - The Ride, 144
Spice Market Buffet, 92
Splash, 199
St. Mark's Square, 124
STACK, 119
Stage Deli, 84
Star Trek
    The Experience, 172
Starwood Resorts, 91
Statue of Liberty, 86
Steak House (Circus Circus), 140, 225
Steak House (Treasure Island), 128
Steak House at Camelot, 77
Steakhouse46, 112, 225
Steakhouses, 223
Stratosphere, 144
Street of Dreams, 90
Strip Clubs, 231
Studio 54, 230
Studio Café, 84
Stupak, Bob, 145
Sundance Hotel, 154
SuperBook (Hilton), 171
SW Steakhouse, 133
swim-up blackjack, 79, 182

T

Tableau, 133
tallest building, 144
Tangerine, 230
Tao, 230
Taqueria Cañonita, 124
tennis, 90, 112, 173
Terrace Pointe Café, 133
Terrible's Buffet, 181
Terrible's, 180

Texas Station, 186
Theatre Ballroom, 161
Theatre for the Performing Arts, 93
Thebes, 73
THEHotel at Mandalay Bay, 69
Theme Restaurants, 220
Thomas, Rick. *See* Magic of Rick Thomas
Thunderbird, 262
Tintoretto Bakery, 124
Tips and Tipping, 56
Todai, 219
toiletries, packing, 46
Tony N' Tina's Wedding, 206
Tony Roma's, 156
Top of the World Restaurant, 146, 216
Tournament of Kings, 207
Tournament Players Club - "The Canyons", 244
Tower (Stratosphere), 145
Trattoria Del Lupo, 70
Travel Scenarios, 271
Treasure Island, 126
Treasures, 232
Tremezzo, 92
Triple 7 Restaurant, 165
Tropical Breeze, 113
Tropicana, 78
Tsunami Asian Grill, 123
Tumbleweed Motel, 115
Tusayan Museum, 268
Tuscany Italian Café, 80

U

Upper Deck, 161
Urban Outfitters, 70

V

Valentino, 123
Vegas Club, 161
Veldon, Simpson, 73
Venetian, 121
Venezia, 123
Ventuno, 112
Vic & Anthony's Steakhouse, 160
Victorian Room, 106
Village Food Court (Excalibur), 77
Village Seafood Buffet, 219
Viva Las Vegas, 208
volcano (Mirage), 119
Voodoo Lounge, 230

W

wave pool, 70, 90
Websites, 23
Weddings, 53
Westside Deli, 141
WET – The Spa at TI, 127
White Tiger Habitat, 121
Wildlife Habitat, 113
Williams, Claudine, 116
Willy and Jose's Cantina, 186
Winning Streaks, 117
Wolfgang Puck Bar & Grill, 84
World's Fare Buffet, 138
World's Greatest Magic Show, 202
Wynn Collection, 134
Wynn Esplanade, 133
Wynn Golf and Country Club, 134
Wynn Las Vegas, 131
Wynn, Steve, 34, 159

X

Xanterra Parks & Resorts, 258
Xtreme Magic Starring Dirk
    Arthur, 203

Y

Yanni's, 188

Yavapai Lodge, 263

Z

Zanzibar Café, 92
Zeffirino Ristorante, 123
Zoological-Botanical Park, 238
Zumanity, 201

About the Author

Dirk Vanderwilt is the executive editor and creator of the *Tourist Town Guides*™ series, and author of several of the series' guides. He lives in New York City.

NOTES:

NOTES:

NOTES:

NOTES:

NOTES:

TOURIST TOWN GUIDES™

Explore America's
Fun Places

Books in the *Tourist Town Guides*™ series are available at bookstores and online. You can also visit our website for additional, updated book and travel information. The address is:

http://www.touristtown.com

Atlantic City (3rd Edition)

Millions of people visit this vacation destination each year. But there is so much more to Atlantic City than just casinos.

Price: $14.95; ISBN: 978-0-9792043-0-2

Gatlinburg

Not just the "gateway to the Smokies" anymore, Gatlinburg is a favorite vacation destination in one of America's most beautiful regions.

Price: $14.95; ISBN: 978-0-9792043-2-6

Jackson Hole

The spirit of the American West is alive and well in Jackson Hole, and this independent guidebook will help give you the insight on the area's very best.

Price: $14.95; ISBN: 978-0-9792043-3-3

Key West

There is much to see and do Key West. From beaches to restaurants to nightlife, this book will help plan your Conch Republic vacation.

Price: $14.95; ISBN: 978-0-9792043-4-0

Las Vegas (2ⁿᵈ Edition)

The city has become synonymous with the American ideals of vacation and pleasure. But there is much more to Las Vegas than casinos!

Price: $14.95; ISBN: 978-0-9792043-5-7

Myrtle Beach

It is a city that has become the American answer to a tropical paradise. With this completely independent guide, get the insight on the best of Myrtle Beach.

Price: $14.95; ISBN: 978-0-9792043-6-4

Niagara Falls (2ⁿᵈ Edition)

There is so much more to Niagara than just the falls. Whether on your first or tenth visit, this guide will help you explore the many wonders that the area has to offer.

Price: $14.95; ISBN: 978-0-9792043-7-1

Wisconsin Dells (2ⁿᵈ Edition)

With waterparks, wax museums, and so much to offer visitors, Wisconsin Dells is indeed a classic American vacation destination.

Price: $13.95; ISBN: 978-0-9792043-9-5

TOURIST TOWN GUIDES™
www.touristtown.com

ORDER FORM #1
ON REVERSE SIDE

Tourist Town Guides™ is published by:

Channel Lake, Inc.
P.O. Box 1771
New York, NY 10156

TOURIST TOWN GUIDES™
ORDER FORM

Telephone: With your credit card handy, call toll-free 800.592.1566

Fax: Send this form toll-free to 866.794.5507

E-mail: Send the information on this form to orders@channellake.com

Postal mail: Send this form with payment to Channel Lake, Inc. P.O. Box 1771, New York, NY, 10156

Your Information: ( ) Do not add me to your mailing list

Name: _____

Address: _____

City: _____ State: _____ Zip: _____

Telephone: _____

E-mail: _____

Book Title(s) / ISBN(s) / Quantity / Price
(see previous pages or www.touristtown.com for this information)

_____

_____

_____

Total payment*: $_____

Payment Information: (Circle One)   Visa / Mastercard

Number: _____ Exp: _____

Or, make check payable to: **Channel Lake, Inc.**

*Add $3.00 per order for domestic shipping, regardless of the quantity ordered. International orders call or e-mail first! New York orders add 8% sales tax.

www.touristtown.com

**ORDER FORM #2
ON REVERSE SIDE**

(for additional orders)

Tourist Town Guides™ is published by:

Channel Lake, Inc.
P.O. Box 1771
New York, NY 10156

TOURIST TOWN GUIDES™
ORDER FORM

Telephone: With your credit card handy, call toll-free 800.592.1566

Fax: Send this form toll-free to 866.794.5507

E-mail: Send the information on this form to orders@channellake.com

Postal mail: Send this form with payment to Channel Lake, Inc. P.O. Box 1771, New York, NY, 10156

Your Information: ( ) Do not add me to your mailing list

Name: _____

Address: _____

City: _____ State: _____ Zip: _____

Telephone: _____

E-mail: _____

Book Title(s) / ISBN(s) / Quantity / Price
(see previous pages or www.touristtown.com for this information)

_____

_____

_____

Total payment*: $_____

Payment Information: (Circle One)   Visa / Mastercard

Number: _____ Exp: _____

Or, make check payable to: **Channel Lake, Inc.**

*Add $3.00 per order for domestic shipping, regardless of the quantity ordered. International orders call or e-mail first! New York orders add 8% sales tax.